CULTIVATING
CONSCIENCE

CULTIVATING CONSCIENCE

How Good Laws Make Good People

Lynn Stout

PRINCETON UNIVERSITY PRESS
PRINCETON AND OXFORD

Library of Congress Cataloging-in-Publication Data

Stout, Lynn A., 1957–
Cultivating conscience : how good laws make good people /
Lynn Stout.
p.   cm.
Includes bibliographical references and index.
ISBN 978-0-691-13995-1 (hardback : alk. paper) 1. Conscience.
2. Law and ethics. 3. Law—Moral and ethical aspects. I. Title.
BJ1471.S725 2011

2010021515

British Library Cataloging-in-Publication Data is available

This book has been composed in Scala
Printed on acid-free paper. ∞
Printed in the United States of America

1 3 5 7 9 10 8 6 4 2

CONTENTS

ACKNOWLEDGMENTS

This book took some time to conceive and to write. As I explored the idea of conscience and sorted through the scientific evidence on conscience and its relationship to law, I was aided immeasurably by the suggestions, questions, and insights of many people. These include my marvelous colleagues at UCLA and at Georgetown; participants at workshops at those schools, at the Institute for Advanced Studies, and at Chapman Law School, Claremont University, Harvard Law School, New York University, Stanford Law School, Vanderbilt Law School, and Washington University; various individuals affiliated with the Gruter Institute, the Alfred P. Sloan Foundation, and UCLA's Behavior, Evolution and Culture program; and the wondrous Treynor family. I am deeply grateful to all for their insights and encouragement, and apologize to any whom I have failed to mention.

Most particularly, however, my research was inspired and influenced by my conversations with especially pioneering and intellectually courageous economists who encouraged me to look beyond the *homo economicus* model, including George Akerlof, Margaret Blair, Harold Demsetz, Bill Dickens, Robert Frank, Herb Gintis, Mike Jensen, Douglass North, Isabel Sawhill, Paul Zak, Luigi Zingales, and the much-missed Jack Hirshleifer. This book is dedicated to them. It is also dedicated to the memory of my mother, Sally Cowan Stout—a woman who knew a thing or two about conscience.

Readers should note that much of the material in chapter 3 is drawn from an earlier work, a chapter that I wrote for the book *Moral Markets: The Critical Role of Values in the Economy* (ed. Paul J. Zak, Princeton University Press, 2008).

PART ONE

CHAPTER ONE

FRANCO'S CHOICE

We should expect the best and the worst from mankind, as
from the weather.

—*Marquis De Vauvenargues*

On a quiet August evening in 2002, Franco Gonzales stood
on the corner of Seventh Street and Grand Avenue in down-
town Los Angeles, waiting for the bus. Los Angeles is a city of
suburban commuters, and by nine p.m. the corner of Seventh
and Grand was deserted. Suddenly an armored truck drove by.
Its rear door swung open mysteriously, and a plastic bag fell
out to land at Gonzales' feet. Inside the bag was $203,000 in
cash.

Franco Gonzales took the money home. Gonzales, a plump,
boyish man in his early twenties who worked as a dishwasher
in a restaurant, spent the rest of the night agonizing over what
to do. He wanted to keep the money for himself and for his
mother, who lived in a farming village in Mexico. But Gonzales' mother had taught him that stealing was wrong. He worried that keeping the money would be dishonest. He also worried about what would happen if the police somehow learned
that Gonzales, who was working in the United States without
legal documentation, had acquired sudden wealth. Finally, it

does not seem implausible that Gonzales, raised a Catholic, worried about his immortal soul.

By the time the sun rose, Gonzales had made his decision. He called 911 to report his find and asked the police to return the money to its rightful owner.[1]

ENTER HOMO ECONOMICUS

When I first studied economics in the late 1970s, my instructors taught me that people generally do not behave like Franco Gonzales. Rather (my professors told me), most people act like members of the species *homo economicus;* they act selfishly and rationally. "Economic Man" does not worry about morality, ethics, or other people. He worries only about himself, calculatingly and opportunistically pursuing the course of action that brings him the greatest material advantage.

My professors and I both knew, of course, that *homo sapiens* does not always act like *homo economicus*. Franco Gonzales certainly did not. Although his decision to return the money might have been inspired by a number of subjective motives one could describe as "selfish" (e.g., a desire to avoid guilt or obsessive worry, or the hope of earning praise or eternal salvation), by returning the cash he had made himself poorer by $203,000. From an objective perspective, he had acted unselfishly. Nevertheless, my professors insisted, individuals like Franco Gonzales were the exceptions that proved the rule. Most people, most of the time, tried to maximize their own wealth. Self-sacrificing behavior was rare, unpredictable, and unworthy of serious study.

As an undergraduate student studying the exchange of goods and services in anonymous markets, the *homo economicus* approach struck me as a fairly plausible description of real behavior. These days, however, the assumption that people are fundamentally self-interested has spread well beyond economics. In political science, Ph.D. dissertations analyze politicians and bureaucrats as rational, self-interested actors. Public policy departments and business schools incorporate economic theory into their basic curricula and serve up the *homo economicus* account as standard fare. In the nation's law schools, students are routinely instructed in "law and economics," an approach that treats law as a kind of pricing system that requires people to pay damages for negligence or breach of contract in order to increase the "price" of bad behavior.

Today we see the results of this intellectual evolution. Over the past quarter-century, the precepts of economics have been drilled into the heads of millions of undergraduate and graduate students. A generation weaned on the idea of rational selfishness has graduated from our nation's universities and moved into leadership positions in the worlds of law, business, government, and higher education. They have brought with them an unquestioned belief in the power of material "incentives" that undergirds almost every policy discussion. Are people cheating on their taxes? Increase the penalty for tax fraud. Are CEOs taking dangerous risks with their firms? "Incentivize" them with deferred stock grants. Are America's children failing to learn their ABCs? Tie teachers' salaries to their students' test scores.

SIGNS OF CONSCIENCE

Largely missing from all this talk of "incentives" and "accountability" is any serious discussion of the possibility that we might encourage or discourage particular behaviors by appealing not to selfishness, but instead to the force of conscience. Many modern experts would snicker at the very idea.

Conscience is viewed as the province of religious leaders and populist politicians, not lawyers, businessmen, or regulators.

Yet before dismissing conscience, it is worth stopping to recognize that, for most of us, ethical and moral concerns are an omnipresent theme of our everyday lives. If you doubt this, simply consider your own train of thought on a typical day. Your interior monologue is likely to include scores, if not hundreds, of normative judgments. ("That driver is a jerk; it's thoughtless of my neighbor to leave her empty garbage cans out; that cashier was a nice guy; I really ought to call my Aunt Martha.") Our language similarly reveals our preoccupation with moral assessments. Just as the Inuit are said to have many nouns for snow, English has a multitude of words to describe unselfish, conscience-driven behavior, including:

virtuous	kind
fair	agreeable
honest	ethical
trustworthy	decent
upright	praiseworthy
faithful	altruistic
thoughtful	humane
loyal	charitable
selfless	principled
conscientious	cooperative
generous	considerate
caring	compassionate

Most tellingly, another simple English word often used to describe unselfish behavior is "good."

Where there is so much smoke, there are pretty high odds of finding fire. This book argues it is time to take the idea of conscience—meaning an internal force that inspires unself-

defined

conscience

ish, prosocial behavior—far more seriously. Although Franco Gonzales' story was unusual enough to be reported in the national press (a small fortune doesn't fall at someone's feet every day), the remarkable tale of the honest dishwasher is, in many ways, not all that remarkable. Civic life in the United States is filled with similar, if more modest, acts of courtesy, consideration, and forbearance. People return misplaced wallets and jewelry to lost-and-found departments. Pedestrians give directions to strangers. Cashiers correct customers who have mistakenly overpaid them. Beefy young men stand patiently in line behind frail senior citizens. Drivers wait for red lights to turn green, even when the police are nowhere in sight.

Unselfish, prosocial behavior is so deeply woven into the warp and woof of Western life that it often goes unnoticed. We rarely stop to think about how the strangers around us routinely behave as if our own comfort and welfare were, if not necessarily at the top of their "to-do" list, still worth consideration. We take for granted the innumerable small, unselfish acts that bind us together in civil society, just as we take for granted the gravitational force that keeps us from floating out into space.

But sometimes gravity produces results dramatic enough to make one ponder. When an apple fell on Newton's head, he stopped to think. When a young dishwasher goes out of his way to return $203,000 in cash to an anonymous owner, we also should stop to think.

THE PUZZLE OF PROSOCIAL BEHAVIOR

I first became interested in unselfish prosocial behavior through my research on corporations and corporate law.[2]

Many readers may find this odd: the business world is often described as a place where the selfish pursuit of material gain goes unchecked. After studying corporations for nearly two decades, however, I became convinced that the *homo economicus* model did a surprisingly poor job of predicting the behavior that I observed inside them. Far from pursuing their own interests in a cutthroat manner, people in corporations often cooperated and sacrificed for collective goals, much like bees in a beehive. Personal ambition was confined to channels that served the corporate collective. And while corporate managers and employees might, like bees, deal ruthlessly with outsiders, teamwork was usually the norm inside the firm. What's more, it was a norm that seemed to promote business success. Corporations characterized by a high degree of internal trust, honesty, and cooperation usually thrived. Those torn apart by infighting and opportunism often failed.

Once the phenomenon of unselfish cooperation captured my attention in the corporate environment, I began to notice cooperation in the outside world as well. My daily interactions with strangers in Los Angeles—hardly a city known for its morals or public spirit—were, if not entirely free of stress and conflict, still characterized by a notable degree of cooperation and mutual consideration. Yawning commuters waited patiently in line at the coffee shop for their morning lattes rather than trying to push or bribe their way to the front of the line. Visiting tourists tipped waiters in restaurants and hotels they would never visit again. Morning newspapers sat in driveways well into the evening without being stolen. People donated time, money, even blood.

My growing suspicion that the *homo economicus* model missed the essence of much of modern life spurred me to find out more. I began to research the social science and life science literature to see what I could learn about the causes and consequences of prosocial behavior. There was a surprisingly large amount to learn.

THE EMERGING SCIENCE OF UNSELFISH PROSOCIAL BEHAVIOR

In June 2005, the science journal *Nature* reported the results of a remarkable study.[3] Human subjects were divided into pairs and each pair was asked to play a "trust game." In the trust game, one member of each pair was designated the "investor" and given some money. The investor was then asked to make a choice: she could either keep all of the money for herself, or give some or all of it to her partner in the game, designated the "trustee." If the investor decided to share any portion of her money with the trustee, the shared amount was tripled by the researchers. The trustee then faced his own decision: he could either keep the tripled funds for himself, or return all or some portion to the investor. The subjects played the trust game anonymously, using written forms to record their decisions, and they were told they would play the game only once.

If two members of the species *homo economicus* were asked to play a trust game this way, the investor would never choose to share with the trustee, because any investor foolish enough to share would discover that the trustee would keep all the tripled money. The subjects in the *Nature* study didn't, however, behave like *homo economicus*. Typically, the investor shared between two-thirds and three-quarters of her funds, and the trustee typically repaid the investor's generosity by returning slightly more money than the investor had initially chosen to share.[4]

This finding, alone, was not novel. The trust game was designed many years ago by social scientists who wanted to study, under laboratory conditions, whether people always act selfishly. Virtually all trust game studies have concluded people do not. Investors frequently share, and trustees frequently return the favor. This finding has been replicated in countless carefully controlled experiments around the world.

But in the 2005 *Nature* study, the researchers did something more. They divided their test subjects into two groups. One group inhaled a nasal spray containing the hormone oxytocin before they played the trust game with each other. (Oxytocin is associated with mate bonding and maternal care in mammals; women experience a rush of oxytocin when breastfeeding.) The other group inhaled a placebo. When the behavior of the two groups was compared, the researchers found that while investors in both groups typically shared at least some of their funds with trustees, investors who had inhaled oxytocin *shared more.*

The *Nature* study illustrates a dramatic change in the way contemporary experts study human behavior. Anthropologists and psychologists are no longer content to develop their theories of human nature from introspection or case studies, in the style of a Sigmund Freud or Margaret Mead. They now put their ideas to the test through surveys, statistical analyses of large demographic databases, and carefully controlled experiments using human subjects. In the fields of medicine and biology, scientists study behavior and emotion—including prosocial behavior and emotion—the same way they study heart disease and cancer, using blood analyses, tissue samples, and brain imaging technology. Evolutionary ecologists and psychologists mathematically model the conditions under which organisms can evolve a capacity for unselfish cooperation. Field biologists test the models against the actual behavior of different species.

The result is a large and rapidly growing body of data on when, how, and why people (and sometimes other species) act unselfishly. From this data a revolutionary new science is emerging. The new science—the science of unselfish prosocial behavior—is a bit like meteorology. Like meteorologists who study weather, scientists who investigate prosociality are studying a complex phenomenon. Like meteorologists, they make imperfect predictions. Sometimes it rains when it was forecast to shine, and sometimes people ruthlessly pursue their own gain at others' expense when the evidence suggests they should act unselfishly. But just as meteorologists can make ballpark predictions about tomorrow's weather, we can forecast with rough accuracy when people are likely to make purely selfish choices, and when they are not. Indeed, we can do more. Meteorologists can predict the weather, but they usually can't change it. But by manipulating certain variables, social scientists can encourage—or discourage—unselfishness toward others in a laboratory setting.

This possibility should interest anyone who lives among, cares about, or deals with other human beings. But it should especially interest those who study and care about law, regulation, public policy, and business management. Each of these fields deals with the central problem of getting people to "conscientiously" follow rules—to work hard and honestly, to pay taxes instead of cheating, to keep commitments, to respect others' rights and property, and to refrain from violence, theft, and mayhem.

Contemporary experts often assume the best way to get people to follow rules is to use material incentives and disincentives, much like the circus trainer who relies on sugar cubes and a whip to make an animal perform a trick. Yet by assuming only incentives matter, they may be missing an essential ingredient in the recipe for changing human behavior. This essential ingredient is conscience.

A NOTE ON LANGUAGE

Conscience, unfortunately, is a vague and unscientific term. As a result, although I will use the word "conscience" in this book, I will also frequently employ the more exacting phrase "unselfish prosocial behavior." Only an academic could love such a label, but each word in this three-word phrase is important.

The two modifiers, "unselfish" and "prosocial," emphasize that we are indeed discussing behavior with both of two important characteristics. First, it does not materially benefit oneself (is not "selfish"). Second, it does benefit others, including especially the broader society (it is "prosocial," not "asocial" or "antisocial"). Both modifiers are important, because not all prosocial behavior is unselfish. A surgeon who removes a patient's infected appendix may be motivated only by a selfish desire to be paid, but she has acted prosocially by relieving her patient's suffering. Similarly, not all unselfish acts are prosocial. Suicide bombings, while unselfish, would be judged by most people as harmful to society.

The third word in our three-word phrase, "behavior," is even more important. This is because it highlights that we are indeed referring to behavior, and not to emotions. We are talking about *acts,* not *feelings.* This distinction is crucial, because in discussing the ideas in this book with friends and colleagues, I have found the conversation often begins with confusion and misunderstanding due to limits of the English language. The problem is not that English lacks words for unselfish prosociality—as noted earlier, it has many. The problem is that none of the words distinguish clearly between *behavior* and *emotion*. For example, if I describe Grandma Sally as "charitable," it is not clear whether I am describing Grandma Sally's actions (an actual gift of money) or her attitude (a sincere desire to give money, if only she had any).

This makes it easy to confuse the claim that people often act unselfishly to benefit others with a claim that people often experience unselfish *feelings*. The confusion can lead us to discount the incidence and importance of unselfish behavior, because while altruistic acts are common, it is easy to suspect altruistic feelings may be rare. One can imagine any number of subjectively "selfish" concerns that might have spurred Franco Gonzales to return the $203,000 that fell at his feet. Perhaps he wanted to avoid the pang of guilt; perhaps he wanted to experience the warm glow of feeling virtuous; perhaps he simply wanted to avoid the fires of Hell.

Alternatively, Gonzales' decision may have been prompted by a peculiar type of mental error. Objectively, it was extremely unlikely anyone could have traced the lost $203,000 to Gonzales if he used a modicum of care and foresight in storing and spending it. Nevertheless, Gonzales may have worried, irrationally, that discovery and punishment were somehow inevitable. H. L. Mencken described conscience as this type of irrational fear when he defined it as "the inner voice that tells us someone is watching."

Emotions like pride, guilt, and irrational worry feel subjectively "selfish." But the *behavior* they inspire is not. However egoistic her motive, the person who sacrifices time or wealth to help or to avoid hurting someone else has acted, objectively, unselfishly. Franco Gonzales made a sacrifice when he decided to return the cash to its anonymous rightful owner. One does not need to believe in unselfish emotions to believe in, and value, this sort of unselfish behavior.

Indeed, from the perspective of an employer trying to prevent employee theft, a government agency trying to encourage taxpayers not to cheat, or an environmental activist trying to convince citizens to recycle their garbage, motivation is beside the point. It doesn't really matter whether selfish feelings prompt people not to steal, cheat, or litter. What matters is they *don't* steal, cheat, or litter—even when they would be materially better off if they did.

As a result, this book will describe an act as unselfishly prosocial whenever it requires the actor to sacrifice time, money, or some other valuable resource to help, or to avoid harming, others. This conception of unselfishness clearly encompasses acts of "active" altruism, as when an individual donates money to charity, or rushes into a burning building to rescue someone from the flames. But it also includes an often-overlooked form of unselfishness we might dub "passive" altruism. Passive altruism, which perhaps most closely resembles what laymen call "ethics," occurs when someone refrains from breaking rules or taking advantage of others even though it would be personally profitable to do so. Common examples of passive altruism include the taxpayer who declines to cheat on her tax return; the shopper who refrains from stealing small items when the cashier's back is turned; and the driver who obeys the speed limit when the police are nowhere in sight. Although such passively prosocial behaviors are less eye-catching than someone risking her life to save a stranger, they are essential to economic growth and civilized life.

Thus I will use the phrase "unselfish prosocial behavior" to capture both active and passive forms of altruistic action. I will also sometimes employ another term from social science, "other-regarding behavior," to describe actions that evidence concern for someone or something beyond one's own material interests. Finally, for variety's sake, I will also sometimes use commonplace terms like "cooperation," "altruism," "conscience," and even "morality." Each of these words carries baggage. For example, "cooperation" implies deliberation and intent. Yet many forms of cooperative behavior seem unconscious and automatic. (A bank robber in Ohio was recently arrested after he waited patiently in line, wearing a ski mask, to rob the teller.) [5] "Altruism" also causes confusion, because as just noted, we tend to associate it mostly with affirmative acts of generosity, even though passive altruism may be more common and important. Finally, many people associate the idea of "morality" primarily with a belief in a particular religious text or with cultural proscriptions on dress and behavior, especially sexual behavior. Indeed, "morality" is sometimes pressed into service to justify actions most people consider strikingly harmful to others, like stoning adulterers. This book uses the word "morality" in an ecumenical sense, to refer to acts that reflect concern for the rights and welfare of those around us. Used this way, the word "morality" embodies notions of honesty and consideration, of "doing the right thing" rather than simply pursuing one's own material interests.

WHY STUDY CONSCIENCE?

A principal theme of this book is that conscience—that is, unselfish prosocial behavior—is a very real, very common, very powerful, and very important phenomenon. We are a far nicer species than we often assume we are. It is easy enough to doubt this when reading newspaper stories of mass rape in Darfur, piracy in the Gulf of Aden, or looting in New Orleans in the wake of Hurricane Katrina. But why are such stories reported in the newspapers? They are reported because they are news, and they are news because they are rare. Rape, piracy, and looting are the exceptions, not the norm, in human interaction.

That thought should comfort us. Many people find the ideas of rampant crime, political corruption, war, famine, and genocide highly distressing. (The fact that we find such thoughts distressing is itself evidence of our altruistic inclinations—why should we be concerned if terrible things are happening to others, as long as they are not happening to us?) It can be depressing to believe people are capable of selfishness and evil. In contrast, we can find solace in the idea of conscience. People are indeed capable of doing evil—but they are also capable of, and surprisingly often inclined toward, doing good.

But in addition to offering spiritual consolation in troubled times, the idea that most people have a conscience is of tremendous practical importance. The emerging scientific evidence has begun to shed light on exactly why, and when, people act in a prosocial fashion. We are beginning to understand the sorts of circumstances that encourage people to "follow their conscience," and the sorts of circumstances that instead encourage asocial or antisocial action. This means we do not always need to rely on crude material rewards and punishments to encourage prosocial behavior. We can enlist as well the power of conscience: the cheapest and most effective police force one could hope for.

That possibility should be of obvious interest to anyone who studies, makes, or enforces the law. Law, after all, is mostly about promoting unselfish prosocial behavior: persuading people to pay taxes they would rather not pay, to perform contracts they would prefer to break, and to obey traffic rules they would rather ignore. As a result, law and conscience are deeply intertwined. Although many experts view law only as a system of material incentives and disincentives, the scientific evidence teaches that the relationship between law and behavior is more complex. Law can reward and punish, but it can do more as well. If we can gain a better understanding of the ways in which law can activate—or disengage—the force of conscience, we can not only understand the law better, we can use it more effectively.

But the phenomenon of conscience isn't important only to legal experts. Just as conscience helps explain why people follow legal rules, it helps explain why people follow other types of rules as well, such as employers' rules for employees, parents' rules for children, and schools' and universities' rules for students. It may also help explain why people adhere to difficult-to-enforce ethical rules and to the sorts of cultural rules ("social norms") that make communal life bearable, like the rule that one should wait one's turn instead of pushing ahead in a line, and put litter into trashcans instead of dropping it in the public street.

The phenomenon of conscience accordingly should interest anyone who studies or cares about the human condition, whether from an academic perspective (sociologists, psychologists, political scientists, management specialists) or from a more practical stance (teachers, parents, corrections officers, religious leaders, civic organizers, business executives). Twenty-first-century Americans still enjoy a remarkably cooperative, law-abiding culture. Even in large cities, most people obey the law, keep their promises, pay their taxes, and act courteously toward strangers, without ever stopping to think how unselfish their behavior may be. Lawbreaking, corruption, violence, and deception are the exceptions rather than the rule.

But many believe our cooperative, ethical culture is under siege, and our collective conscience is on the decline.[6] The news is full of anecdotal evidence: seemingly endless financial scandals at major banks and corporations; widespread claims of political corruption; high-profile incidents of falsified research and academic plagiarism in our nation's most prestigious universities. In his best-selling study *Bowling Alone: The Collapse and Revival of American Community*, sociologist Robert Putnam presents hard data to document this sense of social malaise.[7] Putnam demonstrates how recent decades have seen dramatic declines in the rates at which Americans participate in politics, in community activities, and in charitable and philanthropic endeavors. Even more alarming, Putnam reports, Americans perceive each other as less honest and less trustworthy. Economically stressed, alienated from our communities, and jaded by the spectacle of scandals in our corporations, universities, and city halls, we are losing our collective moral compass. Increasingly, we are acting more like selfish consumers, and less like conscientious citizens.

That prospect should worry us deeply. Humanity is a long way from conquering the physical world: our species may yet be extinguished by a wayward comet. But most of the pressing policy problems we face today, including terrorism, crime, financial scandals, disease pandemics, and environmental degradation, can be traced to human behavior. As the cartoon character Pogo famously observed, we have met the enemy, and he is us.

How can we best address these problems? Today's experts often automatically assume that the best way to change human behavior is to harness the force of greed by using material incentives to reward good actions and to punish bad ones. This approach reflects a long tradition in economic theory of accepting, even celebrating, selfishness. Since at least the days of Adam Smith, economists have preached that self-interest is noble and greed is good.

Yet emerging evidence suggests that cultural habits of unselfish prosocial behavior—a phenomenon related to what political scientists sometimes call "social capital"—are powerful engines for social stability and economic growth.[8] Trust, honesty, and cooperation turn out to be statistically associated not only with personal happiness, but with economic prosperity as well. A healthy, productive society cannot rely solely on carrots and sticks. It must also cultivate conscience, and tap into the human potential to unselfishly help others and, perhaps more important, to ethically refrain from harming them. This is especially true in societies characterized by large and diverse populations, free migration, complex production, and anonymous exchange—in other words, in societies like our own.

A number of social institutions, including schools, churches and community organizations, may play a part in encouraging and supporting unselfish prosocial behavior. But law in particular may play a critical role. This book explores how.

ON THE SCOPE AND STRUCTURE OF THIS BOOK

Although this book focuses on the relationship between conscience and law, I have tried to create a guide to the workings of conscience that can be used by laypersons and experts from other fields as well, such as business management; public administration; nonprofit organizations; education; and urban planning and development. The writing style is geared toward nonexperts, and the chapters are structured to allow readers from a variety of backgrounds to pick and choose the chapters and the ideas they find most interesting or useful.

Part One (chapters 1, 2, and 3) introduces readers to the idea of conscience and explores how and why it is overlooked in so many contemporary law and policy discussions. This first chapter has explored the basic idea of unselfish prosocial behavior ("conscience"). Chapter 2 investigates why and how conscience has dropped out of sight in most contemporary legal and policy discussions, tracing conscience's mysterious disappearance to the increasing influence of economic thinking and a growing emphasis on material "incentives" as the best and possibly only way to mold human behavior. Chapter 3 then explores a second and still more curious reason why we have lost sight of conscience: for a variety of reasons, including our psychological biases, the structure of our language and our society, and the way we select and train experts in law, economics, and business, we tend not to "see" conscience, even when it happens under our very noses.

Part Two (chapters 4 through 6) seeks to put the idea of conscience to work by surveying the enormous body of scientific evidence generated in recent decades on how and why people engage in unselfish prosocial behavior. For readers skeptical of whether conscience really exists, chapter 4 introduces the research technique known as "experimental gaming," and shows how hundreds of carefully designed and carefully controlled experimental games run by researchers around the globe have consistently proven that unselfish prosocial behavior is a real, common, and powerful phenomenon. Chapter 5, perhaps the key chapter in this book, then employs the evidence to develop a rough working model of conscience. In particular, chapter 5 argues that unselfish prosocial behavior follows certain patterns: the vast majority of people are willing to sacrifice to follow ethical rules and help others, but they are only willing to do this when the social conditions are right. The result is a "Jekyll/Hyde syndrome" that causes most people to shift predictably between selfish and unselfish modes of behavior in response to certain social cues. Chapter 5 uses this insight to develop a three-factor model in which conscience is triggered primarily by three particularly powerful social cues: instructions from authority; beliefs about others' unselfishness; and perceived benefits to others. Each of these three factors, chapter 5 shows, maps onto a fundamental and well-established trait of human nature (obedience, conformity, and empathy). Chapter 6 closes by exploring how the idea of the Jekyll/Hyde syndrome and the three-factor model are supported not only by the experimental gaming evidence, but by developmental psychology and evolutionary theory as well.

Part Three of the book (chapters 7 through 9) is designed to appeal to a legal audience, and could perhaps be skipped by readers with other interests. In particular, chapters 7 through 9 apply the lessons of the three-factor model to our understanding of tort law (which discourages negligent accidents); contract law (which enforces contractual promises); and criminal law (which deters theft, fraud, violence, and mayhem). As readers with a legal background may recognize, the fields of tort, contract, and criminal law exemplify the three basic types of legal rules employed by modern societies (liability rules, property rules, and "inalienability" rules).[9] Thus, by showing that the three-factor model has useful applications in tort, contract, and criminal law, I demonstrate more broadly that the model offers insights into virtually all other areas of law as well. I also offer examples of how, by paying attention to conscience and especially the three-factor model, we can not only understand the law better—we can use it more effectively.

The Conclusion returns to the broader question of why contemporary legal and policy experts should be eager to do the extra work needed to incorporate the idea of conscience into their analysis. The answer is simple: we can't afford not to. Growing empirical evidence indicates that cultural habits of unselfish prosocial behavior are essential to both economic growth and psychological well-being. Evidence is also accumulating that unselfish prosocial behavior is on the decline in the United States. Just as environmental scientists have become concerned about many sources of scientific data that point to the possibility of global warming, some social scientists have become concerned about the possibility of "conscience cooling." If Americans are indeed becoming collectively more selfish, unethical, and asocial—concerned only with their own material welfare, and not with the fates of their communities, nation, or future generations—the shift threatens both our happiness and our prosperity. It's time to cultivate conscience. Law can play an important role in that process.

CHAPTER TWO

HOLMES' FOLLY

I often doubt whether it would not be a gain if every word of
moral significance could be banished from the law altogether.
—*Oliver Wendell Holmes, Jr.*

If we want to see how the idea of conscience has dropped out
of modern legal thinking, perhaps the best place to start is in
Boston, on January 8, 1897. It was a bleak day in the city on
the Charles River. The skies were overcast and snow was on
the way. The unpleasant weather did not stop more than five
hundred lawyers, judges, professors, and students from turning out to crowd into Isaac Rich Hall at Boston University.
The occasion was the Hall's dedication as the new home of the
Boston University School of Law, and the dedication speaker
was Massachusetts Supreme Court Justice Oliver Wendell
Holmes, Jr.[1]

THE CYNIC ON THE CHARLES

Holmes is a larger-than-life figure in American law. Even
before his 1902 appointment to the U.S. Supreme Court,
where he served for nearly thirty years, Holmes distinguished

himself as Chief Justice of the Massachusetts Supreme Court, as a professor at Harvard Law School, and as author of the celebrated 1881 study *The Common Law*. Holmes was distinguished in other ways as well. He was tall and straight-backed, with a lush handlebar mustache. He had fought in the Civil War and been wounded three times in battle. He was Class Poet of his 1861 graduating class at Harvard College.[2]

Of all Holmes' accomplishments, none has proven more enduring than the speech he delivered that dreary day in Boston. Holmes' speech was subsequently published in the Harvard Law Review under the title *The Path of the Law*, and it has become one of the most influential essays in the legal canon.[3] This is because *The Path of the Law* provides an early and cogent statement of an idea that has come to occupy the heart of modern jurisprudence: the idea that law promotes social order by using punishments and rewards to change the "cost" of behavior.

Holmes' overarching theme in *The Path of the Law* was the folly of connecting law with morality. "Nothing but confusion of thought," Holmes argued, could result.[4] In advancing this theme Holmes described what has come to be known as the "bad man" theory of law:

> If you want to know the law . . . you must look at it as a bad man, who cares only for the material consequences which such knowledge allows him to predict, and not as a good one, who finds his reasons for conduct . . . in the vaguer sanctions of conscience. . . .
>
> Take again . . . the notion of legal duty, to which I have already referred. We fill the word with all the content which we draw from morals. But what does it mean to a

bad man? Mainly, and in the first place, a prophecy that if he does certain things he will be subjected to disagreeable consequences by way of imprisonment or compulsory payment of money.[5]

Holmes' bad man does not view law as a system of moral commands. He sees law only as an instrument of possible punishment. From the bad man's perspective, "[t]he duty to keep a contract at common law means a prediction that you must pay damages if you do not keep it,—and nothing else."[6] Similarly, the bad man does not distinguish between a tax on lawful behavior and a fine for committing an illegal criminal act. "But from his point of view, what is the difference between being fined and being taxed a certain sum for doing a certain thing?"[7]

Holmes' bad man is not romantically bad, in the fashion of a Jesse James or Clyde Barrow. He is not particularly rebellious. To the contrary, he will follow rules quite reliably if this allows him to avoid "disagreeable consequences." Nor is he cruel or sadistic. The bad man does not feel malice toward others, he merely feels *indifference*. He does not care about anyone, or anything, beyond his own material circumstances. Holmes' bad man lacks the irritating, inconvenient, nagging little internal voice we call "conscience."

Holmes was not so cynical as to believe all men were in fact bad men. His experience in battle had affected him deeply, and on other occasions he would speak with passion on military duty and self-sacrifice.[8] But Holmes made it clear in *The Path of the Law* that he believed it important to analyze law from the bad man's viewpoint. "You can see very plainly that a bad man has as much reason as a good one for wishing to avoid an encounter with the public force, and therefore you can see the practical importance of the distinction between morality and law."[9] Morality was a good thing, but apart from and irrelevant to the law.

HOLMES THE ECONOMIST

At the time Holmes advanced his bad man thesis, his views were regarded as somewhat shocking. Law and morality had been viewed as deeply intertwined for centuries, and conscience was taken seriously as a constraint on behavior. Consider the ancient Latin aphorism that the University of Pennsylvania, founded in 1740, employed as its motto: *Leges Sine Moribus Vanae* (Laws Without Morals Are Useless).

Today, however, Holmes' bad man thesis has become the dominant approach for thinking about how law influences behavior. To understand why, we must put the law aside for the moment and consider another discipline: economics.

Holmes delivered *The Path of the Law* in an era when economics and law were viewed as very distinct fields, with different goals, subjects, and methodologies. Economics dealt with the production and distribution of material goods; law dealt with rights and principles. Economists studied voluntary exchange in anonymous markets; legal scholars focused their attention on state-enforced duties. Economists sought to create wealth; legal scholars sought to promote justice.

Holmes was one of the first great thinkers to merge the two fields, and to apply the tools of economics to understanding the legal system. As many scholars have since pointed out, Holmes' bad man is a nineteenth-century legal scholar's depiction of *homo economicus*. Like Holmes, economists typically begin any analysis by assuming people are driven by self-interest. Thomas Hobbes adopted this approach as early as 1651, when he argued in *Leviathan* that men seek "principally their owne conservation, and sometimes their delectation [enjoyment] only."[10] Adam Smith famously claimed in *The Wealth of Nations* that the butcher, brewer, and baker each works to put dinner on our table, not from benevolence but from "self-love" and "a regard to his own interest."[11] John Stuart Mill viewed "political economy" as concerned with man "solely as a being who desires to possess wealth."[12] Nineteenth-century theorist Francis Edgeworth put the point even more bluntly: "The first principle of Economics is that every agent is actuated only by self-interest."[13]

As any student who takes an introductory class in economics soon learns, this approach offers enormous insights into the relationship between price and production, the connection between supply and demand, the causes of shortage and surplus, and a variety of other weighty matters. Yet does self-interest also explain how we deal with our families, friends, colleagues, and neighbors? The tools of economics may work well in the marketplace, but are they good at explaining behavior in the voting booth, on the highway, or at a wedding?

HOMO ECONOMICUS JUMPS THE FENCE

Economists spent little time worrying about such matters in Holmes' day. The question of whether Economic Man behaved as selfishly on the public street as he did on the floor of the stock exchange simply wasn't on the table. The great economic thinkers of the nineteenth and early twentieth centuries—Francis Edgeworth, Vilfredo Pareto, David Ricardo, Alfred Marshall—were content to focus their attention on buyers and sellers exchanging goods and services in an impersonal marketplace.

All this changed in the 1960s. Economics became ambitious, even (scholars from other disciplines grumbled) imperialistic. Led by Gary Becker of the University of Chicago—who has applied economic analysis to divorce, childbearing, drug addiction, lotteries, education, and racial discrimination, among other topics—economists began to use the tools of rational choice to analyze not only markets, but also households, firms, politics, and the legal system. *Homo economicus* jumped the fence and set out to claim new territory.[14]

Some scholars from other disciplines—anthropologists, sociologists, psychologists—griped about the economists' incursions into what they viewed as their own backyards. More than one found occasion to disparage the *homo economicus* model as a simple-minded caricature of human nature. But others outside economics found the idea of people as rational maximizers of their own self-interest quite appealing. Political scientists, criminologists, business school professors, and policy analysts embraced the tools of rational choice. Meanwhile, Gary Becker was awarded the 1992 Nobel Prize in Economics for "extend[ing] the domain of microeconomic analysis to a wide range of human behaviour and interaction."

THE RISE OF "LAW AND ECONOMICS"

Nowhere was the sudden enthusiasm for economics more obvious than in the nation's law schools. The foundations of the "law and economics" school were laid during the 1960s and 1970s by a gifted cohort of economists and legal scholars that included Ronald Coase, Guido Calabresi, Harold Demsetz, George Priest, and Richard Posner. (Coase went on to win a Nobel Prize; Calabresi became the Dean of the

Yale Law School; and Posner, after establishing his reputa-
tion as a leader in the law and economics movement at the
University of Chicago Law School, became Chief Judge of the
U.S. Court of Appeals for the Seventh Circuit.) Following in
Holmes' footsteps, they argued that law was best understood
as a system of material incentives.[15]

The law and economics movement proved a stunning triumph in its reach and influence. In a study of intellectual
change in legal academia, Steven Teles concluded that "law
and economics is the most successful intellectual movement
in the law of the past thirty years, having rapidly moved from
insurgency to hegemony."[16] "Today," Teles writes, "law and
economics is dominant in private law and plays an important
role in much of the rest of legal education. The law schools of
Harvard, Yale, Chicago, and Stanford boast over a dozen law
and economics practitioners each, organized into well-funded
research centers."[17] Another way to gain a sense of the movement's influence is to consider the sheer volume that has
been written on the subject. Law review articles employing
the law and economics approach number in the uncountable
thousands. Hundreds of full-length books have been published, including dozens that incorporate the phrase "law and
economics" in their titles.

The professors who wrote these books and articles have
had decades to teach their students the value of applying economic reasoning to law. Many of these students are now successful lawyers, business leaders, politicians, regulators, and
judges. The result is a generation of legal experts instructed
in the ways of *homo economicus*. (For the occasional judge
who missed out on economics training, one enterprising law
and economics scholar, Henry Manne, for more than two

decades hosted a renowned "Economics Institute for Federal Judges" which offered two- and three-week "crash courses" in law and economics at suitably luxurious resort locations. By 1990, Manne's Institute had hosted 40 percent of the federal judiciary, including Ruth Bader Ginsberg and Clarence Thomas.)[18]

"LAW AS (ONLY) INCENTIVE"

Chapters 7, 8, and 9 will examine how, despite the dominance of the law and economics movement in academia, law itself often seems to rely, at least implicitly, on the possibility of conscience. Nevertheless, the law and economics movement has transformed the way contemporary experts look at law. To understand how, let us take a moment to consider what, exactly, the movement stands for. The precepts of law and economics are neatly captured in the opening paragraphs of Posner's influential and oft-cited treatise on the subject, now in its sixth edition:

> This book is written in the conviction that economics is a powerful tool for analyzing a vast range of legal questions . . . Many lawyers still think that economics is the study of inflation, business cycles, and other mysterious macroeconomic phenomena remote from the day-to-day concerns of the legal system. Actually the domain of economics is much broader. As conceived in this book, economics is the science of rational choice in a world—our world—in which resources are limited in relation to human wants. The task of economics, so defined, is to explore the implications of assuming that man is a rational maximizer of his ends in life, his satisfactions—what we shall call his

"self-interest." . . . The concept of man as a rational maximizer of his own self-interest implies that people respond to incentives.[19]

This idea of "law as incentive" deserves a closer look. As Posner notes, the central tenet of the law and economics school is that "people respond to incentives." Economist Steven Landburg has similarly written, "Most of economics can be summarized in four words: 'People respond to incentives.'"[20]

Even a moment's thought quickly reveals that the notion that people respond to incentives is neither novel nor controversial. (Although, as we shall see in chapter 8, they sometimes respond in odd ways.) Taken alone, the claim that "people respond to incentives" borders on the banal. Of course most people react to punishments and rewards. If they didn't, no one would bother to use them. If all law and economics stood for was "people respond to incentives," it would be neither interesting nor influential.

This is not, however, all that law and economics stands for. Law and economics scholars do more than simply assume that punishments and rewards matter. Typically, they adopt Oliver Wendell Holmes' view that material incentives are the *only* things that matter—or, at least, the only things worth discussing. In *The Path of the Law*, Holmes made this point quite explicitly. Recall his opening gambit that "[i]f you want to know the law . . . you must look at it as a bad man, who cares only for the material consequences."[21]

Few contemporary law and economics experts are as forthright on this point as Holmes was. Nevertheless, most follow his lead by focusing on the incentive effects of law with a laserlike intensity that precludes examining other ways the law might influence behavior. One can hear the echo of Holmes' voice in Posner's suggestion that "[p]unishment is, at least from the criminal's standpoint . . . the price society charges for a criminal offense."[22] (Posner, a great fan of Holmes, keeps a portrait of the mustachioed jurist on his office wall.)[23]

But let us stop for a moment to think about what it means to assume *homo economicus* cares only about material incentives. If this is true, Economic Man is a being without a conscience. He will happily lie, cheat, steal, renege on his promises, even murder, whenever doing so advances his material interests. To quote economists Paul Milgrom and John Roberts, this view posits that people are "fundamentally amoral, ignoring rules, breaking agreements, and employing guile, manipulation, and deception if they see personal gain in doing so."[24]

The resulting portrait of human nature is anything but flattering. Indeed, as we shall see in the next chapter, it implies we are psychopaths. This puts experts who rely on the assumption of rational selfishness in something of an uncomfortable position. Unless they can find some way around the obvious implications of the *homo economicus* model, they are forced to argue that rational people would never care about truth, justice, the American Way, or saving the whales. And what does advancing such an argument suggest about one's *own* character?

To deal with this awkward implication, experts typically offer three types of arguments in defense of *homo economicus*. Let us consider each briefly in turn.

SMOOTHING SHARP EDGES

Perhaps the most common response experts offer when confronted with the suggestion one might not want *homo economicus* as a son-in-law is to argue that economic theory does not necessarily assume people are selfish. After all, most discussions of Economic Man describe him as a "rational maximizer" not of money or wealth per se, but of his own utility. The exact meaning of "utility" (a word akin to happiness or satisfaction) is the subject of lively debate. Nevertheless, the concept is broad enough to capture a range of desires above and beyond the accumulation of material wealth.

This allows fans of *homo economicus* to default to an interesting strategy. They try to round Economic Man's sharp edges by observing there is nothing in economic theory intrinsically inconsistent with ethical or kind behavior. All we have to do (they explain) is assume that *homo economicus* gets "utility" from behaving ethically and from helping others. This makes apparently unselfish behavior—giving to charity, volunteering at the Y, obeying the law when no one is looking—consistent with self-interest "broadly defined." (At this point, the economist dusts her hands, sighs with relief, and says "Now that problem's taken care of!")

The strategy is both crafty and common.[25] Unfortunately, as famed economist Harold Demsetz has pointed out, it reduces the idea of people as rational maximizers to a tautology.[26] Any and all types of philanthropic, destructive, or downright bizarre behaviors—from murder, to suicide, to donating blood, to speaking in tongues while handling snakes—becomes by definition "self-interested." This circularity raises problems beyond a lack of intellectual rigor. Most worrisome, it erodes the value of economics as a predictive tool.

The point is important enough to be worth exploring through an example. Consider one of the most basic rules of economics, the Law of Demand. The Law of Demand predicts that as the price of a good falls, consumer demand for the good increases. Conversely, when price rises, demand falls.

When gas is cheap, Americans of every stripe drive to the store to pick up quarts of milk in gas-guzzling SUVs. When gas becomes expensive, dinosaurian SUVs are "out" and gas-sipping hybrids are "in."

What happens if we assume people can get utility not only from increasing their own wealth, but from increasing others' wealth? In brief, the usual predictions of the Law of Demand can be turned on their heads. Suppose, for example, we assume altruistic consumers care more about making Exxon shareholders wealthy than about preserving their own wealth. If Exxon raises the price it charges for gas, consumers might buy *more* gas from Exxon, because a higher price means more money for Exxon's stockholders.

For economics to retain its predictive power, we must assume people get utility primarily from improving their own material circumstances. To quote Demsetz again, we must assume we are "an acquisitive species" that prefers more wealth for ourselves to less.[27] Without this assumption, we cannot even predict whether raising the price of gas decreases demand, or increases it. Theorists look less cold-blooded when they suggest *homo economicus* can get utility from acting altruistically. Such concessions, however, seriously erode the utility of the *homo economicus* model. A sheathed knife is less menacing, but also far less useful.

THE LAW AND NORMS SCHOOL

In addition to suggesting that Economic Man can have a "taste" for ethics and altruism, some law and economics scholars in recent years have sought to paint a more nuanced portrait of *homo economicus* by arguing that even selfish individuals might behave themselves if they fear not only the wrath of the law, but also the wrath of their neighbors. This idea underlies the expanding literature on "law and norms."

The idea of norms first captured the attention of the legal academy through the work of legal scholar Robert Ellickson. In the early 1980s Ellickson visited Shasta County, a rural area of California north of San Francisco, to see how farmers and ranchers settled disputes over trespassing cattle. What he found surprised him. Although Shasta County had laws to settle disputes over trespassing cattle, the farmers and ranchers often didn't know the laws, and even when they did, *they almost never paid attention to them.* Instead, Ellickson found, "rural residents in Shasta County were frequently applying informal norms of neighborliness to resolve disputes even when they knew their norms were inconsistent with the law."[28]

Ellickson described this pattern of cooperation in his famed study *Order Without Law: How Neighbors Settle Disputes* (1991), in which he argued that social order often seems driven by informal social conventions he dubbed "norms." Examples include the norm of keeping one's word; Shasta County's norm of neighborliness; and (especially important for our purposes) the norm of obeying rules even when violations would not be detected or punished. In describing how norms contribute to social order, Ellickson gave serious consideration to the possibility that people might follow social norms not only out of concern for their reputations or fear of retaliation, but because *they thought they ought to.* As Ellickson put it, the realities of social order "demand that rational-actor analysts pay attention to the force of conscience."[29]

In the nearly two decades since its publication, *Order Without Law* has become something of a legal classic, providing the foundation for a variation on the law and economics school of legal thought—the "law and norms" school—that explores how the informal social conventions Ellickson described interact with formal law to influence human behavior.[30] Oddly, though, most of the law and norms scholars who have followed in Ellickson's footsteps have declined to accept his invitation to consider how conscience might influence behavior. Instead, they emphasize how people follow social norms out of selfish fear of retaliation ("If I'm not nice to my neighbor, she won't be nice to me"), selfish desire to avoid loss of reputation ("If I'm not nice to my neighbor, other people won't want to do business with me"), or selfish desire to avoid the social slings and arrows called "third-party social sanctions" ("If I'm not nice to my neighbor, other neighbors may give me dirty looks and stop inviting me to parties"). Although norms scholars sometimes acknowledge that people may "internalize" social norms in a way that causes them to follow the norms without regard to self-interest,[31] most hew rather closely to the *homo economicus* approach. As legal scholar Larry Mitchell puts it, "the new norms jurisprudes seem unanimous in accepting the basic economic premise that people act exclusively (or pretty much so) to maximize self-interest."[32]

This emphasis on self-interest has limited the ability of norms-based models to explain much human behavior. (Why do many people obey norms even when others aren't around to observe them? Why don't the elderly and terminally ill run amok?) The curious persistence of the *homo economicus* account in the norms literature has been forthrightly explained by Eric Posner, a son of Richard Posner who is himself a prominent legal scholar. The younger Posner observes that "people appear to obey norms both in order to avoid being sanctioned by others ('shame') and in order to avoid being sanctioned by their own conscience ('guilt')." Nevertheless, he goes on to note,

> assumptions about guilt are not sufficiently rigorous to enable predictions about which norms are internalized and which are not. Whether a theory of social norms should incorporate a psychological theory of internalization (thus losing rigour) or can safely ignore this phenomenon (thus losing realism) remains to be seen. [33]

Eric Posner's musings illustrate how, while many contemporary legal scholars embrace Ellickson's idea of norms, they do not know quite what to do with his suggestion that conscience plays an important role in why people follow them. Most end up simply ignoring conscience as something eccentric, poorly understood, and impossible to predict. This choice reflects the third argument generally used to defend the assumption of rational selfishness: the *homo economicus* model may not be perfect, but it's the best model of human behavior we've got.

"IT TAKES A MODEL TO BEAT A MODEL"

Although the law and economics school dominates the contemporary legal landscape, it does have competition. Especially during the 1970s and early 1980s, law and economics vied with an alternative school of jurisprudence called the "law and society" school. Law and society scholars approach law from a very different perspective than law and economics scholars, using methods drawn not from economic theory but from "softer" social sciences like history, anthropology, and sociology. Rather than trying to predict human behavior by assuming selfish rationality and applying the deductive method, they prefer an inductive approach, making detailed observations of actual human behavior in the field. Indeed, many law and society scholars cannot really be said to be interested in "predicting" human behavior at all. They are interested in observation, focusing their efforts on developing detailed anecdotal accounts of particular practices followed by particular individuals in particular settings.

This approach has opened the law and society movement to the criticism that, while it has done of good job of pointing out the weaknesses in the *homo economicus* approach, it has failed to develop a viable alternative.[34] The closest thing to a prevailing model of human behavior to emerge so far from the law and society school is the so-called *homo sociologicus* model of human nature as a "blank slate" upon which different societies and different cultures can imprint different values and goals.[35] Where the *homo economicus* account predicts that individuals fall out of their mothers' wombs fully equipped with a hardwired personal objective ("maximize personal wealth"), *homo sociologicus* is thought to draw all his beliefs, preferences, and desires from the society around him. He can be taught to cooperate or compete; to embrace people from other cultures or reject them; to adhere to rigid gender roles or to switch easily between baking cookies and fixing toilets; taught to be nice or taught to be nasty.

In his best-selling book *The Blank Slate* psychologist Steven Pinker provides a compelling account of how, just as the *homo economicus* model dominates discussions in economics, policy, law, and business, the *homo sociologicus* model wields influence among intellectuals in sociology, anthropology, psychology, and the humanities.[36] Although law and society scholars rarely embrace the *homo sociologicus* model explicitly, they tend to adopt a similar approach, treating human behavior as something that is both exceptionally flexible and chiefly determined by history and circumstance.

This means the typical law and society scholar often can do little to predict how people will behave other than observing "people will do whatever their culture tells them to do." This approach provides little guidance for policymakers seeking practical solutions to practical problems. Nor does it permit tenure-seeking academics to reduce the interaction between law and behavior to impressively elegant algebraic equations. The result is an air of indeterminacy that has limited the law and society school's influence by making it look mushy and ad hoc. In contrast, law and economics—with its emphasis on mathematics and hard predictions—seems precise and scientific.

Scientists like to say "it takes a model to beat a model." Few lawyers, judges, or policymakers—and perhaps even few law and economics enthusiasts—would argue the *homo economicus* model is completely accurate. But *homo economicus* has at least one appealing characteristic: he is utterly predictable. He can always be counted upon to serve his own material interests. No matter what the problem, better incentives will fix it. As a result, by the close of the twentieth century most experts in law, policy, and business were willing to hold their noses and employ rational choice as the best available approach.

CONCLUSION: HOLMES' TRIUMPH

When Oliver Wendell Holmes delivered *The Path of the Law* over a century ago, many in his audience found the idea that law had nothing to do with conscience somewhat shocking. Today, Holmes' "bad man" thesis is routinely embraced by academics, lawyers, policymakers, regulators, and judges. The argument Holmes advanced explicitly in *The Path of the Law*—that law changes behavior only by imposing material consequences—is often accepted implicitly as a truth that does not require further examination. Many experts automatically think of law as an incentive system designed to encourage some behaviors by rewarding them and to discourage others by punishing them. They also tend, like Holmes, to dismiss the phenomenon of conscience as something that can safely be disregarded.

Chapters 7, 8, and 9 explore in greater detail how this has led many contemporary legal experts to focus almost obsessively on the incentive effects of law, and to ignore more subtle ways in which legal rules influence behavior. Legal experts are hardly alone, however, in their fascination with the power of incentives. Just as economic thinking has seeped into our nation's law schools, it has seeped into the thinking of political scientists, public policy analysts, and business and management experts. The belief that material rewards and punishments are the best and possibly only way to change human behavior dominates public policy and many private institutions as well. Whether the problem is crime, corporate scandals, employee shirking, bank failures, political corruption, school reform, or increasing the supply of human kidneys available for organ transplants, discussion usually begins and often ends with drumbeat calls for "accountability" and "better incentives."

The result is a collective obsession with material punishments and rewards even in situations where the approach seems bizarre and possibly counterproductive. Consider, for example, our nation's response to widespread angst over the state of American public schools. In 2001, the U.S. Congress passed the No Child Left Behind Act to promote "accountability" in public education.[37] No Child Left Behind (NCLB) puts schools whose students fail to make adequate progress at risk of losing federal funding, in order (the theory goes) to "incentivize" underperforming schools to make greater efforts.[38] A similar emphasis on appeals to self-interest is being applied at the level of individual teachers, as districts have developed "performance-based" pay schemes to reward teachers whose students perform better on standardized tests.[39] Florida, for example, has adopted a "merit pay" system that ties a portion of teachers' pay to their students' performance.[40]

To a professional educator, the idea that money is the best and perhaps only way to motivate teachers borders on the irrational. (If money were our primary concern, most of us wouldn't be teachers.) Not surprisingly, there is little evidence such measures improve education. Although average math and reading scores have risen in many states following NCLB's passage,[41] critics argue this is due primarily to teachers "teaching to the test" and school systems gaming the system by pushing low-performing students out of their classrooms.[42] At the individual level, "increased use of teacher merit pay in American education is occurring with virtually no evidence on its potential effectiveness . . . there is no U.S. evidence of a positive correlation between individual incentive systems for teachers and student achievement."[43] Experts nevertheless continue to press for greater teacher and school "accountability" on the theory that "to improve outcomes, the state must replicate market incentives."[44] Meanwhile, the state of Georgia, where educators in some schools receive a $2,000 bonus for better scores on student achievement tests, has had to order an investigation into what appears to be widespread teacher tampering with student answer sheets.[45]

A similar single-minded focus on material incentives has for many years characterized the debate over executive compensation—with, many experts now believe, disastrous results. For most of the twentieth century, even the most dedicated American CEOs were compensated with relatively modest salaries and the occasional corporate jet. In 1976, however, economist Michael Jensen and business school dean William Meckling published an influential article arguing that corporate managers are "agents" motivated only by self-interest, not concern for their companies.[46] By the early 1990s, Jensen's and Meckling's "agency cost" approach had been embraced by a generation of corporate scholars and compensation experts who argued that company executives and directors would only work hard and do a good job if their pay was somehow tied to corporate performance.[47] This pay-for-performance ideology was expressly adopted by the U.S. Congress in 1993, when it amended the federal tax code to limit corporate deductions for executive salaries that were not tied to an explicit performance formula.[48]

The 1993 tax changes are generally credited with the subsequent widespread adoption of stock option and other performance-based pay schemes at most large U.S. corporations.[49] Options and performance-based pay have since been cited as leading causes of the skyrocketing compensation increases executives have enjoyed since 1993; as the primary motivation behind accounting frauds at firms like Worldcom and Enron; and as the reason many banks and corporations like insurance giant AIG took on excessive risks in the quest for short-term profits, leading to the fall 2008 credit crisis and the near-collapse of the American economy.[50] The quest to "incentivize" executives seems to have left Corporate America in a rather deep hole. Nevertheless, many would-be reformers want to keep digging, and argue the way to rescue American companies is not to de-emphasize material rewards for executives but instead to invent better ones.[51] This knee-jerk response seems even odder when one stops to consider that many of the individuals who are calling loudest for better monetary incentives for executives are tenured academics or government bureaucrats whose own relatively modest pay is not tied to much of anything.

These examples illustrate how the relentless emphasis on material incentives that first characterized neoclassical economics, and then the law and economics movement, has now spilled over into everyday discussions of public policy. Indeed, it can be seen in the *New York Times* bestseller lists. Economists who once wrote dry and technical treatises now publish splashy paperbacks for the general public. The most obvious example may be Steven Levitt and Stephen Dubner's bestseller *Freakonomics: A Rogue Economist Explores the Hidden Side of Everything* (2005).[52] But *Freakonomics* has plenty of competition, including Steven Landsburg's *The Armchair Economist: Economics and Everyday Life* (1995);[53] Tim Harford's *The Undercover Economist: Exposing Why the Rich Are Rich, the Poor Are Poor, and Why You Can Never Buy a Decent Used Car* (2005);[54] David Friedman's *Hidden Order: The Economics of Everyday Life* (1996);[55] and Tyler Cowan's aptly titled *Discover Your Inner Economist: Use Incentives to Fall in Love, Survive Your Next Meeting, and Motivate Your Dentist* (2007).[56]

How did Economic Man earn this place of privilege? As noted earlier, the idea of rational selfishness has achieved widespread acceptance in part through economists' clever ability to concede the possibility of altruism without actually attributing any importance to it; in part through norms theories that seem to explain apparently unselfish behavior as a product of selfish fear of loss of reputation; and in part because of the appealing scientific patina of rational choice when compared to the mushiness of the *homo sociologicus* model. Yet there may be still another, less well-recognized but far more important, phenomenon behind the rise of *homo economicus*.

This phenomenon came to my attention when I encountered it repeatedly while discussing the ideas in this book with friends and colleagues. In brief—and despite overwhelming scientific evidence—contemporary Americans in general, and experts trained in law or in economics in particular, tend *not to notice unselfish prosocial behavior*. We are curiously blind to our own goodness. This collective blindness, to which I turn next, may explain as much as anything can why so many people believe that selfish behavior is common and unselfish behavior rare—when exactly the opposite may be true.

CHAPTER THREE

BLIND TO GOODNESS:
WHY WE DON'T SEE CONSCIENCE

We are not ready to suspect any person of being defective in
selfishness.

—*Adam Smith*

Many people probably find the notion that people sometimes act as if they care about more than themselves—that is,
sometimes act as if they have a conscience—rather obvious.
Yet it has become standard operating procedure for experts
in a wide range of fields, including law, business, and public policy, to assume that the best way to predict and channel
human behavior is to treat people as rational maximizers
who relentlessly pursue their own material interests. This is
puzzling, because *homo economicus* is—not to put too fine a
point on it—a psychopath.

HOMO ECONOMICUS AS PSYCHOPATH

Antisocial Personality Disorder (APD) is the formal psychiatric
label for psychopathy. The hallmarks of APD are extreme selfishness and lack of consideration for others, along with tendencies "to lie, cheat, take advantage, [and] exploit."[1] According

to the American Psychiatric Association *DSM-IV*, an individual can be diagnosed as suffering from APD if he or she shows three of the following seven characteristics:

1. failure to conform to social norms with respect to lawful behaviors as indicated by repeatedly performing acts that are grounds for arrest;
2. deceitfulness, as indicated by repeated lying, use of aliases, or conning others for personal profit or pleasure;
3. impulsivity or failure to plan ahead;
4. irritability and aggressiveness, as indicated by repeated physical fights or assaults;
5. reckless disregard for safety of self or others;
6. consistent irresponsibility, as indicated by repeated failure to sustain steady work or honor financial obligations;
7. lack of remorse, as indicated by being indifferent to or rationalizing having hurt, mistreated, or stolen from another.[2]

Let us see how our friend *homo economicus* stacks up against the list. Obviously *homo economicus* lacks remorse (item 7); why would he feel badly just because he hurt or misled another, as long as he advanced his own material welfare? Next consider items 5 and 6, "irresponsibility" and "reckless disregard for safety of . . . others." *Homo economicus* feels responsible for, and cares about, no one but himself. What about "deceitfulness" (item 2)? *Homo economicus* has no compunction lying any time it serves his interests. "Failure to conform to social norms with respect to lawful behaviors" (item 1)? Any time he thinks he won't be caught.

Although Economic Man is neither impulsive nor cranky—items 3 and 4—he shows each of the other five characteristics on the APD list. (Only three are needed for an APD diagnosis.) Unburdened by guilt, pity, or remorse, he plots his course through life unconcerned with the wake he leaves behind, caring neither about the injuries he inflicts on others nor the blessings he bestows. Indifferent to others' welfare or the commands of the law, he will lie, cheat, steal, neglect duties, break promises, even murder, when a cold calculation of the likely consequences leads him to conclude he will be better off.

THE RARENESS OF PSYCHOPATHY

Such individuals do exist. Consider Helen Golay and Olga Rutterschmidt, two Los Angeles septegenarians recently arrested on charges of murder. Golay and Rutterschmidt had long and sordid histories that included allegations of petty theft, credit card pyramid schemes, and fraudulent lawsuits. As they aged they became bolder, and began befriending homeless men in order to take out insurance policies on their lives. According to the police, Golay and Rutterschmidt arranged for the "accidental" deaths of at least two homeless men whom they had insured for a total of $2.8 million. (One of the victims died under the wheels of a 1999 Mercury Sable the two women purchased using false names; the Sable was found in an alley with the victim's DNA on the undercarriage.) At the time of their arrest, Golay and Rutterschmidt were trying to purchase insurance policies on the lives of several additional homeless men whom they had met at a church in their neighborhood.[3]

Luckily, very few people act like this. The American Psychiatric Association estimates that only 1–3 percent of the U.S.

population suffers from APD,[4] and many of these individuals are safely locked away in prison, as Golay and Rutterschmidt are today. The rareness of psychopathy is obvious not only from mental health statistics but from casual observation. My home town of Los Angeles has a population of 3.8 million souls crammed into 465 square miles, averaging roughly 8,000 people per square mile.[5] Yet Los Angeles—hardly a city known for virtue—makes do with 9,700 police officers, only a third of whom are likely to be on duty at any particular time.[6] This means Los Angeles maintains civil order with only one active police officer for every 1,173 residents and fewer than seven officers per urban square mile.

If everyone in Los Angeles behaved like Helen Golay and Olga Rutterschmidt, the result would look like a shark tank at feeding time. Instead, daily life in LA more closely resembles a choreographed water ballet. Across LA—in the urban canyons of the city center, in middle-class suburbs, in busy shopping malls, even in troubled neighborhoods like Watts and Compton—the vast majority of people try not to litter, attempt to stop at red lights, rely on others to prepare their food, and pay for their coffee and donuts at the convenience store instead of stealing them when the cashier isn't looking. Murders are unusual enough to be reported in the newspapers.

This reality poses a challenge to the claim that rational selfishness provides a good description of human behavior outside anonymous markets. Nevertheless, authorities in many fields—including not only economics but also business, political science, policy, and especially law—continue to apply the *homo economicus* model. Why?

Chapter 2 explored some of the more obvious reasons why rational choice has flourished. This chapter argues that there may be another, largely unrecognized but possibly even more important reason why so many experts embrace the idea of rational selfishness. This second reason is an odd distortion in our perceptions of the world and of other people. Rational selfishness seems a more accurate description of human behavior than it actually is because *most people tend not to notice common forms of unselfish behavior.*

BLIND TO GOODNESS

This tendency can be seen through a simple thought experiment. Imagine you are enjoying your morning coffee in a diner when you gaze out the window and notice an unshaven, raggedly dressed man lying passed out on the sidewalk. Beside the man sits a sign that reads "Homeless Veteran, Please Help." Next to the sign is a paper cup that holds a few dollar bills and some loose change. As your coffee cools, you watch person after person walk by the unconscious homeless man. No one offers him assistance, and no one puts any money in the cup. What thoughts run through your mind?

You may speculate that the homeless man is an alcoholic or mentally ill. You may shake your head at a society that allows its citizens to fall into such a state. You may think to yourself, "People are so unkind and selfish—just like *homo economicus.*" Here is one thought that almost certainly will *not* cross your mind: "How remarkably unselfish people are! Person after person is walking by *without stealing any of the money in the cup.*"

Yet you are witnessing repeated acts of passive altruism as you watch the pedestrians pass by without stealing from the homeless man's cup. The money is there for the taking. The homeless man is unaware and unable to defend his property. The police are nowhere in sight. Anyone who walks by without taking money is committing an unselfish act—sacrificing an opportunity to make himself or herself better off, in material terms, at another's expense.

A skeptic might argue the passersby don't take the money not out of altruism, but because they selfishly fear that if they did, a witness might call attention to the theft. This simply moves the problem back a step. Why would a witness bother to raise the alarm? Trying to stop the homeless man from being robbed is itself an altruistic act. *Homo economicus* would elect not to get involved.

Civilized life depends in large part on this sort of endemic, but invisible, altruism. Newspapers are left in driveways when no one's about; frail people use ATM machines without hiring armed guards; stores stock their shelves with valuable goods watched over by only a few salesclerks. Each of these common situations requires that the vast majority of people refrain from relentlessly taking advantage of every possible opportunity to make themselves better off at others' expense. In the dry language of social science, they require most people, most of the time, to act to some extent in an unselfish prosocial fashion. Nevertheless, we almost never take conscious note of the countless acts of passive altruism we observe each day. We may *observe* unselfishness, but we don't *see* it.

There is one place, however, where unselfish behavior becomes more "seeable": in the experimental laboratory. In one of the great ironies of social science, this discovery was made by a group of mathematicians and economists who had no interest in conscience whatsoever.

UNSELFISH PROSOCIALITY IN THE LAB

On Main Street in Santa Monica, California, only a few blocks from the public beach and municipal pier with its colorful carousel, sits the steel-and-glass structure that is the current headquarters for the enigmatic think tank known as the RAND Corporation. RAND (the military acronym for "research and development") was founded with Pentagon backing during the height of the Cold War. Its original purpose was to bring together some of the finest minds in the world and to encourage them, in the words of RAND scientist Herman Kahn, to "think the unthinkable."[7]

Across America, schoolchildren were being drilled to save themselves from a hailstorm of Soviet missiles by cowering under their desks. At RAND, mathematicians, economists, and political scientists were preparing for holocaust by trying to figure out how to win it. Thermonuclear war is not a nice business. To study the subject, the RAND scientists began by assuming that both the Soviet Union and the United States each cared only about the fate of its own people. In essence, they applied the *homo economicus* model of purely selfish behavior at the level of the nation-state.

Given this starting point, the RAND scientists naturally gravitated toward game theory, a branch of economics that analyzes how rational and selfish actors would behave in "games" in which each seeks to maximize his individual winnings. The RAND researchers were particularly interested in one of the most famous problems in game theory: the so-called Prisoner's Dilemma.

THE COLD WAR AS PRISONER'S DILEMMA

The prisoner's dilemma game is named after a story in which two burglary suspects are arrested trespassing in an empty home. The two suspects are placed in separate prison cells where they cannot communicate with each other. Each is then told that if neither confesses, both will be charged with trespass and sentenced to one year in jail. Each prisoner is also

given an offer: if he chooses to confess and implicate his partner in burglary, the informer will go free, while the noncon-
fessing prisoner will be convicted of burglary and sentenced
to fifteen years. But—here comes the catch—both prisoners
are also told that if each informs on the other, both will be
convicted of burglary and sentenced to ten years in jail.

	You squeal	You don't squeal
Your partner squeals	**10**, 10	**15**, 0
Your partner doesn't squeal	**0**, 15	**1**, 1

Figure 1: Payoffs in a Prisoner's Dilemma. The first number, **in bold**,
shows the sentence that you will receive, and the second number shows
the sentence your partner will receive, depending on whether either or
both of you cooperates by remaining silent or defects by "squealing."

Figure 1 illustrates the "dilemma" each prisoner faces. No
matter what his fellow prisoner chooses to do, he will be better off squealing. Yet if both prisoners selfishly "defect" and
squeal, they will be individually and collectively worse off (ten
years in prison each) than if both unselfishly "cooperate" by
remaining silent (one year in prison each).

The prisoner's dilemma applied directly to the Cold War
arms race. Collecting nuclear weapons is not like collecting
Beanie Babies. Nukes are expensive and dangerous to acquire

and to maintain. Both the United States and the Soviet Union would have been better off if they could stop accumulating deadly weapons and spend their time and resources on civilian projects—education, vaccinations, building highways— instead. At the same time, stockpiling weapons remained the individually best or "dominant" game strategy, because the nation that stopped stockpiling might fall so far behind in the arms race as to invite attack from its better-armed rival.

PROSOCIALITY PREVAILS

Game theory gives a clear prediction for what rational and purely selfish players would do in a prisoner's dilemma like the arms race: they would always defect. Nevertheless, the RAND scientists thought it might be interesting to see what happened when real people played the game in real life. In 1950 they arranged for two colleagues, RAND mathematician John Williams and UCLA economist Armen Alchian, to play a series of prisoner's dilemma games with each other.

The result was the first recorded instance of a finding that would be subsequently replicated in hundreds of experiments. *Real people playing prisoner's dilemmas often cooperate.* Alchien, the economist, choose to cooperate 68 percent of the time. Williams, the mathematician, cooperated in 78 percent of the trials.[8]

John Nash was a brilliant but mentally unstable mathematician at RAND who would later win the Nobel Prize in economics for his work on game theory. (Nash's life eventually became the subject of the best-selling biography *A Beautiful Mind*, subsequently made into an Oscar-winning film in which the ectomorphic Nash was played by brawny Australian heartthrob Russell Crowe.) Nash puzzled over Williams' and

Alchian's choices. He sent around a note in which he mused, "One would have thought them more rational."[9]

As it turned out, however, the RAND outcome was anything but unusual. To the contrary, *prosocial behavior has proven ubiquitous* in the lab. Hundreds of studies demonstrate that subjects playing anonymous prisoner's dilemma games with strangers choose cooperation over defection about 50 percent of the time.[10]

Later we explore this result and the world of experimental gaming in greater detail. Before we delve deeper into the scientific evidence, however, this chapter explores the question of why, despite what we shall see is overwhelming evidence of prosociality, so many intelligent and sophisticated observers continue to assume people act mostly selfishly. As it turns out, a surprising number of factors conspire to make it difficult for us to recognize altruistic behavior in everyday life, *even when it happens under our noses.* Taken alone, any one of these factors might lead someone to overlook the reality of widespread unselfishness. Working together, they blind even the most sophisticated observers to our collective enthusiasm for behaving like "good" rather than "bad" men and women.

REASON ONE: CONFUSING ALTRUISTIC ACTIONS WITH ALTRUISTIC FEELINGS

One important reason why people overlook the reality of unselfish behavior has been already been mentioned in chapter 1: ambiguities in the English language that make it easy to confuse the claim that people often *act* unselfishly with the claim that they have unselfish *feelings.* When we do nice things for others, introspection often makes us aware of the subjectively "selfish" emotions that underlie our apparent generosity. For example, one person might decline to steal from the homeless veteran's cup because he wants to avoid the painful pangs of guilt; another might have a yen for the warm glow that goes with feeling good about herself; still another might refrain from the theft out of fear of some afterlife purgatory. Because such emotions and irrational fears "feel" selfish, it is easy to jump to the conclusion that purely altruistic emotions are rare or nonexistent.

Purely altruistic emotions may indeed be rare or nonexistent. (While I remain an optimist on this point, chapter 6 discusses how evolution might favor the development of internal reward systems to promote prosocial behavior.) Whether truly altruistic emotions exist, however, is irrelevant to the question of whether altruistic behavior exists. When we sacrifice our material welfare to help someone else, our act is objectively unselfish. The passerby who declines to steal from the unconscious homeless man when she could safely do so has passed up a chance to make herself materially better off.

One does not need to study or believe in altruistic emotions to study or believe in this sort of altruistic action. To the regulator or policymaker, it doesn't matter if "selfish" feelings prompt people to keep promises, follow rules, and help others. What matters is that they *do* keep promises, follow rules, and help others—even when they have little or no external incentive to do so. We don't need to fully understand the workings of conscience to study, and value, how it affects behavior.

REASON TWO: THE MISUNDERSTOOD NATURE OF "MORALITY"

A second problem with language that helps explain why many experts overlook the role of conscience has to do with the fact that conscience is often associated with morality, and, at least among intellectuals, morality has acquired something of a bad reputation. This is not because intellectuals are an especially unprincipled lot. (I suspect most compare favorably to political consultants or used car salesmen.) Nevertheless, many members of the intelligentsia tend to view the idea of moral constraints with suspicion because they have come to think of "morality" in terms of culturally idiosyncratic rules about dress, diet, and sexual deportment.

Diet, dress, and deportment rules vary from place to place and from time to time. Most modern societies find eating human flesh abhorrent. But Hindus also reject beef, and many Buddhists shun meat entirely. Some cultures view nakedness as evil, others find masturbation wicked, still others treat swearing as a sin. Despite (indeed, perhaps because of) the fact that such rules vary widely among cultures, their proponents often speak of them in moral terms—a practice that conveniently relieves the speaker from the burden of having to explain or justify the rules. The idea of morality as a result is so often and so easily misused that it is easy to suspect it has no content. Consider one feminist writer's reaction to the notion of regulating sexual mores: "I do love the idea that the Law has nothing better to do than referee the naked Hokey Pokey: 'No, no—you put *that* in. No! No! Not in *there*! Yes, we know it happens to *fit* in there, but that's not where it belongs.'"[11]

Such cynical reactions obscure an essential truth. Universal "moral" rules do exist, and these rules have two interesting things in common. First, they are shared in some form by every orderly society. In his book *Human Universals*, anthropologist Donald Brown describes hundreds of "universals" of human behavior and thought that have been identified by ethnographers in every culture. Moral universals include proscriptions against murder and rape; restrictions on some forms of violence; concepts of property and inheritance; the ideas of fairness and of taking turns; admiration for generosity; and a distinction between actions under self-control and those not under self-control.[12]

This does not mean, of course, that every member of every culture always complies with universal moral rules. But violations are condemned, except when the victim either is deemed deserving of punishment due to some transgression, or is not viewed as a member of the relevant community whose interests deserve consideration. (This last observation explains why some of the most enduring and acrimonious moral debates we see today, including debates over abortion, animal rights, and the fate of Palestinians living in Gaza, center on who exactly qualifies as a member of the relevant "community.")

Second, universal moral rules generally have to do with helping, or at least not harming, other people in one's "ingroup." As Charles Darwin wrote after being exposed to a variety of cultures during his voyage on the H.M.S. *Beagle*, "To do good unto others—to do unto others as ye would they should do unto you—is the foundation-stone of morality."[13] Similarly, in *The Origins of Virtue*, Matt Ridley argues that around the globe, murder, theft, rape, and fraud are viewed as "crimes of great importance" because they involve one person placing his or her own comfort and interests above the interests of another person—in Ridley's words, "because they are selfish or spiteful acts that are committed for the benefit of the actor and the detriment of the victim."[14]

The fact that idiosyncratic rules about diet, dress, and sexual deportment are often described in terms of "morality" or "values" should not tempt us into becoming moral relativists, nor into dismissing the importance of moral constraints on behavior. At its most basic level, conscience demands we sometimes take account of others' interests, and not only our own selfish desires, in making our decisions. In the words of Romantic poet Percy Bysshe Shelley—an avowed atheist whose personal life reflected a certain disdain for the sexual deportment rules of his day—"the great secret of morals is love."[15] At this level morality is both an important concept, and a widely shared one.

REASON THREE: THE BANALITY OF GOODNESS

Once we understand that it is a mistake to define morality in terms of disputes over gay marriage or Janet Jackson's "wardrobe malfunction" at the 2004 Super Bowl, it becomes easier to perceive a third factor that often keeps people from recognizing the importance of conscience. This third factor, ironically, is the sheer ordinariness of much conscience-driven behavior.

Many unselfish acts fail to capture our notice because they are (as the phrase "common decency" suggests) so commonplace. No paper would run the story, "Man Doesn't Steal, Even When No One's Looking!" Human beings overlook such common expressions of conscience because they perceive their environment with what psychologists term "selective attention." The world is simply too busy and too complicated a place for us to monitor everything going on around us. Instead, we filter out most stimuli, taking conscious note only of the limited objects and events that capture our attention. A classic example is the famous "cocktail party" effect. If you are at a noisy party chatting with a friend, you are unlikely to take conscious note of any of the many murmuring conversations around you—until someone across the room speaks your name.

An important category of events that capture attention are *unusual* events. This is why extreme instances of unselfish behavior, as when Franco Gonzales returned $203,000 in untraceable lost cash to an anonymous owner, attract notice. No one is surprised, however, when one person standing in a checkout line points out to another that she has mistakenly dropped a $5 bill.

Unselfishness is especially likely to go unnoticed when it takes the form of ethical restraint (passive altruism). Active altruism—sacrificing money, time, or other valuable resources to help others—is relatively rare, and attracts attention. In contrast, passive altruism (declining to take advantage of another's vulnerability) is so omnipresent, we literally don't see it. Our nation was shocked to see hundreds of looters running wild in the streets of New Orleans during the lawless aftermath of Hurricane Katrina. Few people stopped to marvel at the fact that tens of thousands of New Orleans residents were *not* looting.

Writing on the war crimes trial of Otto Adolf Eichmann, philosopher Hannah Arendt famously described the bureaucrat who engineered the Nazi death camps as exemplifying "the banality of evil." Goodness, too, is often banal; too ordinary and mundane to be of interest. Conscience, like gravity, is a force so deeply intertwined with our daily lives that we take it for granted.

REASON FOUR: SMALL SACRIFICES GO UNNOTICED

A related explanation for why many common forms of pro-sociality fail to capture our attention is that, while almost any unselfish act involves some degree of self-sacrifice, the sacrifice involved can be quite modest. Consider again the unselfishness of the passerby who refrains from helping herself to the money in the homeless man's cup. The passerby could make herself materially better off by taking the money. However, unless the cup contains a lot of cash, she will not make herself much better off, and her opportunity for gain is offset by the risk the homeless man might awake and object.

Many other common forms of prosocial behavior similarly involve only marginal self-sacrifice. It does not take too much skin off my nose to give directions to a lost stranger, or to wait in line rather than shoving to the front, or to pay for my coffee at the Seven-Eleven rather than sneaking it out when the cashier's back is turned. As a result, most of the time I do not consciously recognize my behavior to be self-sacrificing. Small acts of kindness and consideration go unnoticed and unremarked, even by the kind and considerate themselves.

Nevertheless, small acts of kindness and consideration carry big social consequences, for at least two reasons. First, an unselfish act that requires only a modest sacrifice on my part may provide much larger benefits to someone else. When I stop to give directions to a lost stranger, I lose a few seconds of my time, but I may save the stranger hours of bewildered wandering. Similarly, when the passerby refrains from stealing from the homeless man, she is unselfishly giving up the opportunity to pocket a few more dollars for herself. The homeless man, on the other hand, gets to keep not only his money but also his peace of mind, and can feel free to panhandle on the public street without taking extraordinary measures (acquiring a large safe, a handgun, or a pit bull) to protect his person and property.

Second, even small acts of unselfishness, when summed up over many people and many interactions, produce large aggregate social gains. Because we can rely on most of our fellow citizens to behave themselves most of the time, we can go about our daily lives safe in the belief that promises usually will be kept, our personal property usually will be left unstolen and unmolested, and our own persons usually will be safe from kidnapping, mayhem, and murder. Just as thin and fragile reeds can be woven together to make a basket that is strong enough to carry a heavy load, when many small acts of restraint and consideration on the part of many individuals are woven together, they form a peaceful and prosperous society.

REASON FIVE: THE PECULIAR SALIENCE OF CHEATING

In addition to being likely to overlook routine and modest forms of unselfish behavior simply because they are routine and modest, people may tend to overlook considerate, law-abiding behavior for yet another reason: they are too busy paying attention to rudeness and cheating.

The power of cheating to capture our attention has been demonstrated by evolutionary psychologist Leda Cosmides using the following experiment.[16] Suppose a researcher shows you four cards laid face down on a table, as shown in figure 2. The backs of the cards are marked D, F, 3, and 7. The researcher tells you that each card has a number on one side and a letter on the other. She also tells you a rule: if a card is marked "D" on one side, the other side should be marked with a "3." She then asks you to identify which of the four cards you would need to turn over in order to determine if the cards all follow this rule. What would you answer?

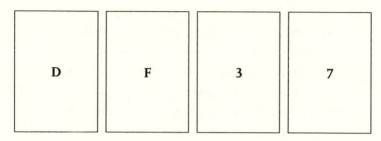

Figure 2

Most people's eyes promptly glaze over when they are asked to solve this problem, and fewer than 25 percent answer it correctly. (You would need to turn over the cards marked D and 7, to see if the other sides were marked with a 3 or a D, respectively.)

So let us consider a different problem. Suppose four people are drinking in a bar, as shown in figure 3. One person is drinking beer; one person is drinking cola; one person looks forty years old; and one person looks fourteen. The bar owner tells you that no one should be drinking an alcoholic drink unless they are at least twenty-one years old. Which of the four people would you need to check to make sure the rule is being followed?

A large majority of test subjects quickly figure out that they would need to check the person drinking the beer (to see if she is 21 or older) and the person who looks fourteen (to see if he is drinking alcohol). This is curious, because the first problem and the second are *logically identical* versions of something called the "Wason selection task." Why does the second version seem so much easier to solve?

Cosmides asked experimental subjects to take on several different versions of the Wason task in order to find out why some versions seemed easier to solve than others. She found

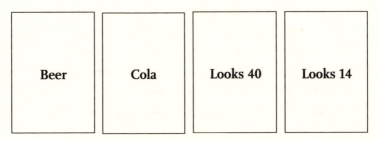

Figure 3

that people performed best on the Wason task when the solution involved *detecting cheating*. Cosmides and her anthropologist husband John Tooby went on to argue that human beings, as highly social animals, have evolved an ability to quickly spot instances when others aren't "following the rules." They hypothesized that the human brain has evolved a specialized "cheater-detection module" that makes even unsophisticated individuals skilled at solving logic puzzles that involve cheating.[17]

Cosmides' and Tooby's modular thesis is controversial. Their results may demonstrate not that the brain has evolved specialized systems to detect cheating, so much as that cheating sparks our interest and motivates us to apply greater brainpower to a particular logic problem than we are willing to apply when it is presented in a more abstract and less engaging form. Whatever the reason for Cosmides' results, however, they demonstrate that humans have a special talent for spotting selfish misbehavior.

This "nose for cheating" leads us to fixate our attention on the relatively rare instances where people behave badly. (This fixation is both evidenced and reinforced by the headlines of any newspaper.) Our fascination with cheating may also have the indirect effect of distracting us from, and making us relatively insensitive to, the many instances where people behave well. This leads us to assume unrealistically that other people are not as "nice" as we are—not as honest, responsible, considerate, or law-abiding. The result, once again, is a tendency to view the *homo economicus* account as a more accurate and universal description of human nature than it really is.

REASON SIX: NAIVE REALISM

Yet another psychological phenomenon that can lead us to overestimate others' selfishness is a habit of thinking that psychologists dub "naive realism."[18] In lay terms, naive realism means that we tend to assume that our own perceptions accurately reflect objective reality, so that other rational people must share our perceptions and see the world as we do. One consequence of this belief is a tendency to assume that when others behave in a way that seems inconsistent with our views, their apparent disagreement is driven not by a different perception of the world but by bias—especially the bias that flows from self-interest.

Suppose, for example, you are driving down the highway and suddenly realize you need to merge into the right-hand lane to take the next exit ramp off the highway. To you, it appears that there is a gap in the traffic in the right-hand lane that leaves you just enough room to merge in front of a blue Toyota. When you turn on your right turn signal, however, the Toyota speeds up and closes the gap, making it impossible for you to merge into the right-hand lane. What is your reaction? You may jump to the conclusion the Toyota's driver shared your perception that there was room to merge safely, but sped up out of a selfish desire not to let another car get in front. You are likely to discount the alternative possibility that the Toyota driver was not motivated by selfishness, but sincerely believed the gap was too small to allow a safe merger.

Naive realism tempts us to believe other people are more self-serving than they actually are. By extension, it also makes the *homo economicus* account seem a more compelling portrait of human nature than it truly is.

REASON SEVEN: THE CORRELATION BETWEEN EXTERNAL AND INTERNAL SANCTIONS

The previous sections have explored a number of reasons why people are psychologically predisposed not to "see" common forms of unselfish behavior. This tendency is reinforced by yet another factor: most societies are structured to reward actions that help others, and to punish actions that harm others.

This reality is especially obvious to anyone who studies or works in the law. As we will see in Part Three, a variety of legal rules create material incentives for prosocial behavior. Tort law, for instance, discourages us from negligently injuring others in part through the threat of liability. Contract law encourages us to keep our promises lest we be forced to pay damages for breach. The result is a strong correlation between internal sanctions (conscience) and external sanctions (legal punishments). This correlation makes it easy to jump to the conclusion that it is law, not conscience, that keeps most people from injuring others and from breaking promises.

Nor, as law and norms scholars like to point out, is law the only external force that encourages good behavior. Although a person who lies, cheats, or steals may suffer at the hands of the law, he might also suffer at the hands of his colleagues and neighbors. The fact that many of the considerate acts we observe (waiting one's turn, donating blood) involve people who know each other or share the same workplace or neighborhood raises the possibility that apparently unselfish behavior is often motivated simply by selfish fear of retaliation or concern for reputation.

The common correlation between internal sanctions (conscience) and external sanctions (legal and social sanctions) makes it difficult to convince a cynic that the incidence of unselfish behavior we see in daily life is greater than can be explained by legal and social incentives alone. Suppose, for example, that I walk down the street past several husky individuals, and none of them mugs me. I have performed this experiment in many places and on many occasions, with great success. I suspect the principal reason I have escaped being mugged is that the vast majority of people prefer, unselfishly, not to hurt or frighten me just to get the contents of my wallet. Yet I cannot exclude the possibility that the only reason I have not been mugged is that potential muggers fear being arrested and jailed. Nor can I prove that they are not, instead, deterred by the fear that I might defend myself and harm *them*, or the concern that their mugging might be observed by someone who knows them who would carry news of their misbehavior back to their community, harming their reputation.

The end result, political scientist Jane Mansbridge has written, is that "We seriously underestimate the frequency of altruism when, having designed our lives to make self-interest and altruism coincide, we interpret such coincidences as demonstrating the pervasiveness of self-interest rather than altruism."[19] In the process, we overestimate the accuracy of the *homo economicus* model.

REASON EIGHT: DARWINIAN DOUBTS ABOUT ALTRUISTS' SURVIVAL

So far, the factors we have considered—the conflation of altruistic action (which is common) with altruistic emotion (which may be rare); general distrust of the idea of morality; the human tendencies to overlook small and common incidents of unselfish behavior and to fixate on selfishness; the correlation between internal and external sanctions—work to blind expert and lay person alike to conscience. There is still another factor, however, that discourages academics in particular from taking the idea of conscience seriously. This factor is evolutionary biology.

It is easy to for someone with a passing acquaintance with Darwin's theory of natural selection to jump to the conclusion that unselfish behavior is likely to be rare because altruistic individuals must, of necessity, lose out to egoists in the Darwinian struggle for "survival of the fittest." The evolutionary argument against altruism is straightforward. Even if some people are capable of unselfish behavior, it is obviously true that many also are capable of selfishly pursuing their own welfare at others' expense. In a world where altruists and egoists interact (the argument goes), the latter enjoy a distinct advantage. Consider two primitive hunters–an altruist and an egoist. When the altruist snares a rabbit, he shares the meat; when the egoist snares a rabbit, he keeps it for himself. It is easy to see which of the two will get thin in hard times. Similarly, when the altruist sees the egoist threatened by a leopard, he rushes to the egoist's defense. When the egoist sees the altruist threatened by a leopard, he takes advantage of the big cat's distraction and flees. This sort of thinking has lead many authorities to conclude that pop singer Billy Joel got it right when he sang "Only the Good Die Young."

Yet the claim that Darwinian pressures should quickly snuff out altruists runs into a significant problem: the empirical evidence doesn't support it. Perhaps altruism among strangers shouldn't be common, but it *is* common. This pattern is evidenced not only by everyday life but by hundreds of formal experiments.

As a result, evolutionary theorists in recent years have revisited the old notion that altruism should be seen only among blood relatives (the so-called selfish gene hypothesis popularized by Richard Dawkins).[20] Although altruism is common in families, altruism outside the family is common as well. Chapter 6 explores a number of modern theories that support the evolution of altruism, including theories based on reciprocity, partner selection, sexual selection, group-level evolution, and gene-culture evolution. For present purposes, the bottom line is: despite Darwinian pressures, evolution need not stamp out altruism.

REASON NINE: WHO STUDIES HOMO ECONOMICUS?

Finally, let us consider one last factor that helps explain why so many experts assume people are mostly selfish, despite the evidence of conscience all around them. This last factor is the nature and training of the experts themselves.

Considerable evidence suggests that beliefs about others' selfishness or unselfishness can be influenced by formal training, especially formal training in economics. For example, students who take courses in economics describe others as more selfish than students who have not taken economic courses do.[21] This finding likely reflects, at least in part, the results of direct instruction: economic theory teaches students to assume people are selfish "rational maximizers."

There is a second source of biased perceptions, however, that may be at least as important as overt indoctrination. This is the fact that students and researchers in certain fields, including both economics and law, devote the lion's share of their time and attention to studying situations where people in fact behave selfishly. Conventional economics, for example, analyzes anonymous markets, an arena where self-interested behavior is both common and socially acceptable. Studying law may produce a similar prejudice. The legal system is typically brought into play only when cooperation breaks down and individuals become embroiled in conflicts requiring outside resolution. This makes it easy for law students who spend hours studying case law—the documentary debris of crimes, horrible accidents, difficult divorces, and bitter contract disputes—to conclude selfish behavior is the rule.

Experts who specialize in law or in economics, and others who receive economic or legal training (a category that includes not only economists and lawyers but also politicians, businessmen, and indeed most college graduates) may come, as a result of that training, to perceive people as more selfish than they really are. The phenomenon is similar to that of the police officer who, after years of dealing mostly with criminals, cynically comes to expect the worst from her fellow citizens.

Nor is it inconceivable that many individuals who choose to specialize in economics, business, and possibly law tend to perceive others as relatively selfish because they are more inclined toward self-interest themselves. (One can see how someone who is relatively selfish might find the *homo eco-*

nomicus model especially persuasive.) Although this possibility has received little formal study, studies have found that students who specialize in business are more selfish in their attitudes and dealings with others than students pursuing other studies, and also cheat more than their peers.[22] Similarly, in a *New Yorker* magazine profile of influential law and economics guru Judge Richard Posner, Posner described his own character as "exactly the same personality as my cat . . . cold, furtive, callous, snobbish, selfish, and playful, but with a streak of cruelty."[23] Leave out the playfulness and the cruelty, and we have a wonderful description of *homo economicus.*

Such observations are not intended to suggest that any person who embraces the *homo economicus* model is herself a psychopath, or even that one might not want to invite her to parties. (As the co-author of a casebook on law and economics, I particularly want to discourage readers from leaping to such conclusions.)[24] The point is that individuals who are relatively self-regarding themselves might tend to assume others are selfish as well. This, combined with the biased perceptions that result from formal training in economics or other fields where selfish behavior is the norm, might easily persuade experts in certain fields—including law, business, and economics—to overestimate the accuracy of the *homo economicus* model.

CONCLUSION: VISIBLE SELFISHNESS, INVISIBLE ALTRUISM

Self-interest exists. So does conscience. Nevertheless, we focus on the first, and rarely notice the second. A surprising variety of factors work together to encourage people in general, and experts trained in economics, business, and law in particular, to overlook the role conscience plays in directing human behavior. Some of these factors reflect the limits of the English language; some spring from psychological quirks and biases; some arise from the way healthy societies structure external incentives; some stem from the tastes and training of those who study law, economics, and policy. All conspire to make us greatly overestimate the incidence of selfish behavior, and seriously underestimate the incidence of unselfishness.

The result is that experts in a wide range of disciplines assume that the *homo economicus* model paints a more accurate and more universal portrait of human nature than it really does. Of course, only an extremist would argue that people always act selfishly. Yet our collective tendency to overlook unselfish acts makes it easy to assume conscience is such a weak force it can be safely assumed away.

But what if conscience is neither rare nor weak? What if, like the "dark matter" many astrophysicists now believe makes up most of the mass in the universe, conscience is all around us, and we simply have difficulty seeing it? If conscience is both ubiquitous and powerful, and if we can find some way to use it to change human behavior, it may offer enormous leverage in the quest for a better, more just, and more productive society.

To that possibility we now turn.

PART TWO

CHAPTER FOUR

GAMES PEOPLE PLAY: UNSELFISH PROSOCIAL BEHAVIOR IN EXPERIMENTAL GAMING

> You can discover more about a person in an hour of play
> than in a year of conversation.
>
> —*Plato*

It can be hard to convince a skeptic that conscience exists. (And, as we have just seen, we are psychologically predisposed to be skeptics.) The problem is made particularly difficult by the fact that healthy societies tend to reward prosocial behavior and to punish antisocial behavior. As a result, it is nearly impossible to absolutely disprove the claim that external incentives alone explain the apparently unselfish acts we observe in daily life. Perhaps the traveler who left a tip in a restaurant in a strange city planned to return some day, and hoped to ensure good service. Perhaps the pedestrian who gave directions to a lost stranger feared that if he refused, the stranger might describe him and his rudeness to a common acquaintance. Unselfish behavior often seems the product of conscience, but in day-to-day living, a host of other external influences, including legal sanctions and fear of retaliation and loss of reputation, cannot be definitively excluded.

This makes it difficult to determine from casual observation that conscience exists, and even more difficult to figure out how conscience works. As a scientist would put it, routine acts of conscience take place in "uncontrolled" conditions. To build a better understanding of conscience, we need to study behavior in a setting where researchers can eliminate the sorts of external rewards and punishments that muddy the waters in everyday life. That setting is the experimental laboratory.

ENTER BEHAVIORAL ECONOMICS

Chapter 3 told the story of the first accidental experimental tests of prosocial behavior, the prisoner's dilemma experiments conducted at RAND in the 1950s. Although they did not know it at the time, the RAND researchers had invented a new social science methodology that would soon become a standard technique of psychologists, political scientists, neuroscientists, anthropologists, and even economists. This book will refer to that technique as "experimental gaming," although it has acquired a variety of other labels including "experimental psychology," "experimental economics," and "behavioral economics." Whatever the label, the basic approach is the same. Rather than assuming people behave in a rational and selfish manner, researchers put human subjects in highly controlled conditions to see how they *really* behave.

Until recently, theoretical economists tended to view experimental gaming results as more suitable for cocktail party conversation than serious research. This state of affairs has changed. In recent years "behavioral economics" has acquired respectability even among the economic elite. In finance, for example, the idea that stock market prices are influenced by investor irrationality has gained such acceptance that the prestigious *Journal of Finance* regularly publishes papers on the topic.[1] In 2002, the Nobel Prize in Economics was shared by behavioral economist Vernon Smith and a psychologist, Daniel Kahneman of Princeton University.

Kahneman and his frequent collaborator, Amos Tversky, are viewed as founding fathers of behavioral economics, pioneers who devoted their careers to devising ingenious experiments to test how real people make decisions in an uncertain world. For example, they identified and labeled the "availability effect," the human tendency to overestimate the likelihood of any event that is observed in person or in the media.[2] The availability effect explains why many people worry about dying in a plane crash more than dying in a car crash, even though dying in a car crash is statistically far more likely. Airline disasters receive extensive media coverage, while car accidents often go unreported. Similarly, the availability effect explains why people overestimate the incidence of murders, child abductions, terrorist attacks, and other antisocial behaviors that attract media attention.

In recent years a number of prominent legal scholars, including many from the law and economics school, have embraced behavioral economics and published articles suggesting that the law should take account of Kahneman and Tversky's availability effect, as well as "framing" effects, "anchoring" effects, "endowment" effects, and a host of other common errors in human thinking revealed through behavioral experiments.[3] So far, however, there has been a curious imbalance in the way behavioral law and economics scholars use the lessons of experimental gaming. Following Kahneman and Tversky's lead, they show more interest in challenging the first prong of the rational selfishness assumption (rationality) than the second (selfishness).[4]

The result is an extensive and growing literature on the legal implications of what might be termed the psychology of stupidity. Law journal articles argue, for example, that courts should not enforce lengthy "form" contracts when buyers' "bounded rationality" keeps them from worrying about what might go wrong;[5] that products liability law should reflect consumers' tendency to systematically underestimate certain risks;[6] that criminals suffer from "hyperbolic discounting" that keeps them from fully appreciating the costs of future punishment;[7] and that "endowment effects" can cause people to become irrationally attached to objects, making monetary damages a better legal remedy than injunctions that reassign rights to specific property.[8] Behavioral law and economics has also been used to critique both jury decision-making[9] and judicial decision-making.[10] (One cannot help but ask: if neither judges nor juries can make rational decisions, who can?)

Yet experimental gaming offers more hopeful lessons about human nature as well. Beginning with the very first experiments at RAND, gaming has demonstrated that human behavior often violates not only the rationality part of the *homo economicus* model but the selfishness part as well. (Although John Nash described Alchian's and Williams' cooperative behavior in the RAND experiments as not "rational," it is more accurately described as not selfish.) Where irrationality tends to cause costly mistakes, unselfishness is a personality quirk that can make people collectively *better* off. This was seen in the RAND experiments themselves. Mutual unselfish cooperation produced better payoffs for Alchian and Williams than mutual selfish defection would have.

THE ADVANTAGES OF STUDYING PROSOCIAL
BEHAVIOR IN THE LAB

It would seem, then, that just as we can learn about our follies and foibles by studying how people make decisions in a laboratory environment, we can learn something about more positive aspects of human nature, like prosociality. Indeed, experimental gaming offers important advantages in this regard. First and foremost, in the experimental environment, researchers can eliminate the situational complexities that make prosocial behavior less "visible" in everyday life. This is important because, while few people resist the notion that humans are often irrational, many are skeptical of the claim that we are also often unselfish. In experimental gaming, however, researchers can "prove" prosocial behavior by virtually eliminating any chance that what seems like unselfishness might actually be motivated by some rational hope of extrinsic reward.

It should be noted that the original RAND experiments did not do an especially good job of this. Williams and Alchian were asked to play the prisoner's dilemma game with each other repeatedly. When people interact repeatedly, and know they are going to interact repeatedly, there is always a chance that cooperation reflects nothing more than selfish fear of retaliation, because defecting in early rounds may provoke "tit-for-tat" in later rounds of the game.[11]

In the decades since the RAND experiments, however, scientists have become far more sophisticated in their approach to studying unselfish behavior. Today, experimenters routinely work hard to eliminate retaliation and reputation effects. Sometimes, for example, they instruct subjects they will play the game only once, making retaliation impossible. They also run games involving large groups of players rather than matched pairs, which reduces reputational concerns by making it difficult to identify selfish "defectors." Many contemporary experiments are also run under conditions of strict anonymity, with the subjects playing in individual cubicles via computer or worksheet, their identities and their choice of strategy screened from both their fellow players and the researchers. Finally, it has become common practice to debrief subjects after testing to make sure they understood the rules of the game and the material consequences of choosing one strategy over another.

This ability to control the circumstances under which subjects play experimental games allows researchers to exclude extrinsic rewards for unselfish behavior. (Perhaps some subjects still irrationally hope for rewards, but if so their hope is groundless, and their objective behavior remains unselfish.) Experimental gaming thus is very useful for overcoming the common misperception that unselfish behavior is something rare and fleeting. By strictly controlling incentives, researchers can demonstrate to the satisfaction of all but the most rabid fans of *homo economicus* that unselfish prosocial behavior is a real and common phenomenon.

A second important advantage of studying unselfishness in the lab is that, by controlling the parameters under which subjects play experimental games, researchers also can overcome the notion that conscience is too random and quirky a phenomenon to incorporate into rigorous analysis. Experimental gaming permits researchers to run a particular game several different times, each time changing one aspect of the game while holding other parameters constant. This allows them to identify specific variables that promote, or inhibit, unselfish prosocial behavior. This particular advantage of experimental economics will prove especially important in the next chapter, which explores some of the more important factors that determine whether subjects choose "unselfish" cooperation or "selfish" defection in experimental games.

Yet a third advantage of using experimental game evidence is that there is, quite simply, an awful lot of evidence to use. Scientists have not only gotten far more sophisticated in designing experimental games, they have also run many, many more of them. In the half-century since Williams and Alchian first played prisoner's dilemmas at RAND, researchers have published the results of hundreds of experiments designed to test what human subjects do in a laboratory environment where self-interest, as measured by external rewards, conflicts with the interests of others. The results are remarkably robust. While individual subjects may differ in their proclivity to cooperate or defect, at the group level, researchers running similar games make strikingly similar findings. Unselfish behavior turns out to be anything but haphazard and quirky. To the contrary, it seems common and predictable.

SOME DISADVANTAGES

There are, of course, some disadvantages to experimental gaming. Most studies, for example, employ undergraduate and graduate students at American universities as subjects. For reasons of convenience and cost, impoverished students make ideal guinea pigs. Yet it is reasonable to question whether the patterns of behavior observed among American students represent human nature more generally.

A number of experiments, however, have tested how people play games in other regions of the world, including Israel,

China, Japan, Korea, and the former Yugoslavia.[12] One of the best recent examples was produced by a consortium of social scientists who, backed by a MacArthur Foundation grant, arranged for several common types of experimental games to be played by members of fifteen different non-Western hunting, herding, and farming cultures scattered around the globe.[13] The consortium found that no matter what sorts of subjects played the games—Machiguenga subsistence farmers in the Peruvian rainforest, Orma cattle herders in Kenya, Torguud nomads in Mongolia, Lamalara whale-hunters in Indonesia—human behavior simply didn't hew to the rational selfishness model. People of all ages, genders, and backgrounds routinely behaved in an unselfish prosocial fashion. As the MacArthur consortium put it, "there is no society in which experimental behavior is consistent with the canonical model from economic textbooks."[14]

Another criticism that might be leveled against experimental gaming is that the amounts of money subjects play for is often rather small. This raises the question of whether people would behave the same way in games with larger stakes. (Unselfishness may be common when it's cheap, but what about when unselfishness becomes costly?) In fact, most experimental games do involve relatively low stakes, for the simple reason that it is difficult to convince nonprofit foundations and universities to pay for more expensive experiments. However, a few studies have been done with much larger stakes, without much change in behavior.[15] In the MacArthur-funded study, for example, researchers were able to offer their subjects stakes that approximated two days' wages in the local currency. This did not change the results from those observed in games played by Western subjects for relatively smaller amounts.[16]

Another disadvantage of relying on the experimental gaming evidence is that, while it offers us a large body of data on *when* people choose cooperation or, selfishly, defection, it gives us far less insight into *why*. This limitation, however, is not a reason to ignore what we have learned about the "when." Some day we may fully understand the internal psychological mechanisms that underlie what we call "conscience," including emotions like love, honor, piety, and irrational fear of detection and punishment. Until that day arrives, experimental gaming still gives us a remarkable degree of traction by treating the average person as a black box whose inner workings are invisible. We don't know with certainty what goes on inside the box. In the lab, however, scientists can control the environmental factors that go into the box, and then observe the behavior that comes out. Comparing the two allows them to identify when most people choose to act in an unselfish fashion, and when most don't.

This approach has a behaviorist flavor, as it focuses on people's objective *actions* rather than their subjective *motivations*. (This is why economists who use experimental gaming often refer to their enterprise as "behavioral economics.") Yet despite its limitations, the strategy permits us to identify several interesting, and potentially important, patterns in unselfish behavior.

The remainder of this chapter introduces readers to three fundamental lessons about unselfish behavior that can be learned from experimental gaming. These lessons are gleaned from a trio of widely employed experimental games called *social dilemma* games, *ultimatum* games, and *dictator* games. These three games teach first, that unselfish behavior between strangers is quite common; second, that unselfishness can take the form not only of a willingness to sacrifice to help another (altruism) but also a willingness to sacrifice to harm another (spite); and third, that people recognize that other people often act altruistically and spitefully, and modify their own behavior in anticipation. Chapters 5 and 6 will use these findings as the framework for building a model of unselfish prosocial behavior. First let us turn to the findings themselves.

SOCIAL DILEMMA GAMES AND ALTRUISM

As its name suggests, the Social Dilemma is closely related to the Prisoner's Dilemma. However, where the archetypal prisoner's dilemma game is played by two people, social dilemma games can be played by more, and sometimes quite a few more, players.

Consider a common type of social dilemma called the "contribution game." A group of players is assembled, and each member given an initial stake of money. For example, a researcher might bring in four players and give each $20. The players are then told that they can choose between keeping their $20 for themselves and going home, or contributing some or all of their $20 to a common pool. The players also are told that any money contributed to the pool will be multiplied by some factor greater than one but smaller than the number of players in the game. For example, in a game with four players, the players might be told that contributions to the common pool will be tripled. Finally, the players are told that after the researchers triple the money in the pool, the money will be redistributed back to the players in equal shares—including an equal share to any player who chose *not* to contribute.

As in a prisoner's dilemma, the group achieves the best average result ($60 each) if all four players cooperate by contributing $20 to the common pool. As in a prisoner's dilemma, however, the best or "dominant" strategy for a selfish player in a social dilemma is always to defect. Using the example above, a rational and selfish player in our contribution game would keep her initial $20 while hoping to receive a share of anything the other three players were foolish enough to contribute to the pool. Suppose, for example, the other three each contribute their $20 to the pool. The three unselfish contributors end up with $45 each (one-fourth of the common pool, which the researchers have tripled from $60 to $180). The selfish non-contributor gets $65 (her original $20, plus another $45 from the common pool).

A rational and selfish person accordingly would not cooperate in social dilemma games. In the contribution game just described, for example, four selfish players would end up just keeping their initial $20 stakes. Yet in hundreds of actual social dilemma experiments, researchers have reported that a large portion of players cooperate. In a meta-analysis of more than 100 social dilemma experiments, sociologist David Sally found "cooperation rates" averaged about 50 percent.[17] Similarly, in a survey of single-play contribution games, psychologist Robyn Dawes and economist Richard Thaler reported average contributions of 40–60 percent.[18]

To appreciate the significance of this finding, recall that the *homo economicus* model predicts a *zero* probability that subjects would contribute *anything* in a properly structured one-shot social dilemma. Yet, unlike *homo economicus*, *homo sapiens* turns out to have a propensity for sharing in social dilemmas. This result, which has endured over a half-century of repeated testing with a wide variety of subjects, tells us something interesting and important: unselfish prosocial behavior is endemic. Subjects who cooperate in a one-shot social dilemma are choosing to maximize the group's payoff, rather than simply maximizing their own. There are several lay terms available to describe this type of other-regarding behavior, including *kindness, consideration, generosity,* and, more generally, *altruism.*

ULTIMATUM GAMES AND SPITE

Altruism is not the only type of unselfish behavior people exhibit in experimental games, however. This can be seen from the results of a second type of game that has been the subject of extensive study, the Ultimatum Game.

A typical ultimatum game involves two players. The first player, called the "proposer," is given a sum of money (again, assume $20). The proposer is told that she can decide to give any portion of the $20 that she chooses—all of it, none of it, or some amount in between—to the second player. The second player, called the "responder," is then presented with a choice of his own to make. He can accept the proposer's offer, in which case the $20 is divided between the two players exactly as the proposer suggested. The responder can also choose to reject the proposer's offer—in which case both players get nothing.

It is clear what *homo economicus* would do in an ultimatum game. The proposer would offer the minimum amount of money possible short of offering nothing (say, one penny). The responder would accept this token amount. This is because a rational and purely selfish responder would view a penny as better than nothing, and be willing to accept this amount. Knowing this, no rational and selfish proposer would offer more.

Studies consistently find that real people don't play ultimatum games this way. When real people play ultimatum games, the proposer usually offers the responder a substantial portion of her stake, most frequently half.[19] And if the proposer does *not* offer to share a substantial portion of the stakes, the responder usually responds by rejecting the offer. As one recent survey concluded, "[i]n a large number of human studies . . . in different countries, the majority of proposers offer 40% to 50% of the total sum, and about half of all responders reject offers below 30%."[20]

Revenge may be sweet, but in an ultimatum game, the responder who wants to taste it must pay a price. A responder who rejects any positive offer loses an opportunity to make himself at least slightly better off, in material terms, than he was before. Why would anyone choose to do this?

When experimenters quiz responders in ultimatum games about their motives for rejecting an offer, responders usually reply quite bluntly that they wanted to punish the proposer for making an "unfair" offer.[21] Moreover, experimenters have found that responders are much less likely to reject a low offer in an ultimatum game if they are told the offer was generated by a computer than by another person. They are also much less likely to reject a low offer when asked to play a variation on the game in which they are told that if they reject the offer, they get nothing, but the proposer still keeps the share she proposed for herself. In other words, responders accept even very low offers when they believe that rejecting the low offer won't punish the selfish, penny-pinching proposer.[22]

Such findings demonstrate that responders reject low offers in ultimatum games because they care about the *propos-*

ers' payoffs as well as about their own. If the altruistic cooperation seen in social dilemma games shows us the bright side
of our human capacity to care about what happens to others,
ultimatum games give a glimpse of a darker side. Responders who reject offers they perceive as too low are displaying a
willingness to make a material sacrifice not to help another,
but to *harm* her. Synonyms for this sort of behavior include
malevolence, antipathy, vengefulness, and *spite.*

Contemporary Western culture does not celebrate vengefulness; Sweeney Todd does not make much of a hero. Nevertheless, as the ultimatum game makes clear, spite is a basic
element of human nature. If this reality is not particularly
pretty, it still may be very useful. As will be explored in greater
detail later on, a little spite can go a long way toward encouraging prosociality by punishing selfish and asocial behaviors.
Thus, certain forms of spite, as well as altruism, may fall into
the category "unselfish prosocial behavior."[23]

DICTATOR GAMES AND SECOND-ORDER EFFECTS

Ultimatum games reveal how unselfish behavior can take the
form of a willingness to sacrifice one's own material rewards
to hurt others, as well as a willingness to sacrifice to help them.
But ultimatum games teach us something else as well. To see
what this "something else" might be, we need to compare the
results typically observed in ultimatum games with those typically observed in a similar but slightly different experimental
game called the *Dictator Game.*

Like an ultimatum game, a dictator game involves two players. As in an ultimatum game, one of the two is given a sum
of money and instructed to choose a rule for distributing this

money between the two players. A dictator game differs from an ultimatum game, however, in that the second player is not given any chance to respond to the first player's division of the loot. The second player receives whatever the dictator is willing to share with him, no more and no less. This is why the first player is the "dictator."

Strikingly, the majority of subjects asked to play the role of the dictator in an anonymous one-shot dictator game choose to share at least some portion of their initial stakes with the second player. For example, the MacArthur-funded researchers mentioned earlier reported that in the three cultures tested, dictators on average offered to donate 31 percent, 20 percent, and 32 percent of their stakes.[24] Dictator games thus confirm the same sort of altruistic sharing with strangers commonly observed in social dilemma games.

But the amounts that dictators share in dictator games are *smaller* than the amounts that proposers offer in ultimatum games. For example, the MacArthur researchers reported that while their dictators were generous enough to share, dictators' donations averaged only 70 percent, 60 percent, and 86 percent of the amounts that subjects in the same three cultures offered when playing ultimatum games.[25] Dictators share, but they do not share *as much* as proposers in ultimatum games do.

This is an important finding. It suggests that proposers in ultimatum games have an additional motive, beyond altruism, for sharing. That additional motive is the fear that the responder will react to a low offer by spitefully rejecting it.[26] Proposers in ultimatum games appear to *anticipate* that treating a responder too shabbily will prompt the responder to punish them by rejecting their offer. This suggests not only that people behave both altruistically and spitefully, but that *people know that other people behave both altruistically and spitefully—and plan accordingly.*

Our human capacity to act unselfishly thus changes behavior on at least two levels. At the first and most obvious level, many people indulge in altruism and spite. Put simply, sometimes people act differently than they would if they were concerned solely with maximizing their own material gains. At the second level, experimental games demonstrate that people know that many people indulge in altruism and spite. This knowledge can prompt even purely selfish individuals to alter their own conduct in anticipation of others' unselfish actions.

Such second-order influences may be quite important. Suppose, for example, a purely selfish economist signs a contract to sell $1,000 in economics textbooks to a prosocial Mother Theresa for use in Bangladeshi classrooms. Because of the small size of the sale and the difficulties of suing someone in a foreign country, if either party to the contract were to renege on the deal after the other had performed (that is, if the economist refused to ship the books after Mother Theresa had paid for them, or if Mother Theresa refused to pay after the economist shipped the books), it would not be economically rational for the disappointed party to enforce the contract by filing a lawsuit. As a result, whichever party performs first is vulnerable to the risk the other will behave selfishly, and refuse to perform his or her part of the bargain.

If Mother Theresa and the economist each expect the other to behave like *homo economicus,* each will refuse to perform first. No sale will occur. But if a purely selfish economist believes that Mother Theresa is (unlike himself) prosocial, second-order effects might prompt him to ship the books to

Bangladesh even before he receives a check. This is because the economist knows an altruistic Theresa will honor her commitment. We might call this sort of selfish reliance on another's unselfishness "rational trust in altruism."

A similar happy result may obtain when other-regarding Mother Theresa pays for the books before the economist ships them—*if* the economist believes that Mother Theresa is capable not only of altruism, but also spite. Even a selfish economist will refrain from exploiting Mother Theresa's vulnerability if he foresees that Mother Theresa will spitefully punish him by bringing a lawsuit, despite the fact that suing costs her more than she can hope to recover in damages. The economist's second-order behavior might be called "rational fear of vengeance."

Either way, one party's knowledge of the other's altruistic and vengeful tendencies promotes a trade that ultimately benefits both parties. This illustrates how, if people not only behave in a prosocial fashion but know that *other* people behave in a prosocial fashion, the forces of altruism and spite have far-reaching and mutually reinforcing "snowball" effects. Second-order effects allow societies to weave together many small and seemingly marginal acts of altruism and spite to create strong communities and markets.

CONCLUSION: LESSONS FROM THE LAB

Most modern legal and policy discussions begin, implicitly or explicitly, with the assumption that people are selfish actors whose behavior is best influenced through material incentives. Although in some contexts this assumption may be realistic (e.g., anonymous market transactions), a half-century of experimental gaming research demonstrates that in many other contexts, people simply refuse to behave like the "rational maximizers" economic theory says they should be.

Social dilemma games, ultimatum games, and dictator games offer us three basic lessons about human behavior. The first and foremost is that unselfish prosocial behavior is quite common. Researchers have run social dilemma games, dictator games, and ultimatum games countless times under a wide variety of conditions. Over and over, they have found that their subjects routinely act as if they care not only about their own material payoffs, but about others' payoffs as well. This finding is no longer open to reasonable dispute.

Second, unselfish behavior in games seems to take at least two important forms. People sometimes sacrifice their own payoffs to increase others' (altruism). They also, however, sometimes sacrifice to hurt others (spite). This book will focus the lion's share of its attention on the phenomenon of altruism, which certainly is the more admired quality. Nevertheless, spite can play an important role in fostering prosocial behavior. This possibility will be explored in greater detail in chapter 6, which examines how spite may have contributed to the evolution of human prosociality, as well as in chapters 8 and 9, which touch on the role spite plays in contract and criminal law.

Third, experimental gaming teaches us not only that people routinely indulge in unselfish behavior, but also that people know that *other* people routinely indulge in unselfish behavior. Our capacity to act unselfishly accordingly has first-level and second-level effects. At the first level, some people act unselfishly. At the second level, knowing that some people act unselfishly influences the behavior of even the purely selfish.

Second-order effects allow a large number of small, marginally unselfish behaviors to support and reinforce prosociality.

Taken together, these basic three lessons from experimental gaming reveal how the *homo economicus* assumption of purely selfish behavior may be dangerously misleading. At the same time, apart from their cautionary value, the three lessons are not quite as useful as one might hope them to be. A defender of rational choice might reasonably argue that it's not enough to know people sometimes look out for others, and sometimes don't. We want to know which, when.[27]

To appreciate the nature of the problem, let us return to the 50 percent cooperation rate typically observed in social dilemma experiments. This finding demonstrates that people often behave unselfishly. But it also demonstrates that *people often behave selfishly*. After all, if people never acted selfishly, we would observe cooperation rates of 100 percent.

Again, it takes a model to beat a model. If we are to use the data from experimental games to develop a model of human behavior that is superior to the *homo economicus* approach, in the sense that the new model permits better predictions about what people actually do, we need to know more than "unselfishness happens." We need to know *when* people are likely to act unselfishly, and when they are likely to act selfishly. What explains why some people cooperate when others don't, or why the same person cooperates at one time and not at another? What determines when we want to help others, when we want to hurt them, and when, like Rhett Butler, we don't give a damn? To this puzzle we now turn.

CHAPTER FIVE

THE JEKYLL/HYDE SYNDROME: A THREE-FACTOR SOCIAL MODEL OF UNSELFISH PROSOCIAL BEHAVIOR

There was a little girl and she had a little curl
   right in the middle of her forehead.
When she was good she was very, very good
   but when she was bad she was horrid.

—*The Annotated Mother Goose*

Experimental gaming proves we are a much nicer species than we often give ourselves credit for being. Whether or not most people really care about following the rules or helping others (are psychologically prosocial), they often *act as if they care* (are behaviorally prosocial). A half-century of research, including hundreds of experimental studies, demonstrates this beyond reasonable dispute.

Nevertheless, proving that people often sacrifice their material interests to benefit others is not, by itself, terribly useful. At least, it is not useful if unselfish behavior is random and mercurial. Professionals who work in law and law enforcement—judges, regulators, police officers—have practical goals. They want people to pay taxes, obey traffic rules, and refrain from murder, theft, and mayhem. Similarly, employers want employees to work hard and honestly, teachers want students to do their best, and parents want children to behave. The idea of conscience is not very helpful to accomplishing these goals unless we have some understanding of when conscience comes into play.

This chapter seeks to promote such an understanding by offering a simple model of when people engage in unselfish prosocial behavior—that is, when they follow conscience rather than self-interest. It relies on empirical findings that have been consistently reported by psychologists, sociologists, anthropologists, economists, and biologists. Using those findings, it offers a simple model for predicting when most people act will selfishly, and when most won't.

Although crude, the resulting portrait of human nature is considerably more nuanced than the one-dimensional cartoon of man as a cold calculator relentlessly pursuing "incentives." It is also a portrait that in many ways resembles Robert Louis Stevenson's nineteenth-century novella, *The Strange Case of Dr. Jekyll and Mr. Hyde*.[1]

THE JEKYLL/HYDE SYNDROME

Stevenson penned his tale at the end of the nineteenth century, around the same time Oliver Wendell Holmes proposed his "bad man" theory of the law. Stevenson's hero, however, is the antithesis of Holmes' bad man. Where the bad man is indifferent to others, Dr. Jekyll is prosocial: responsible, law-abiding, and concerned about others' welfare. That is, he is responsible, law-abiding, and concerned about others' welfare until he concocts and consumes the potion that transforms him into his asocial alter ego, Mr. Hyde.

Mr. Hyde cares about nothing and no one other than himself. (When readers first meet Hyde, he is trampling over a small child for the simple reason that she obstructs his path.) Hyde's "every act and thought centred on self."[2] He lies, steals, and eventually murders, simply because it suits him. In sum, Hyde acts like Holmes' bad man—like *homo economicus.*

Stevenson's story is an obvious metaphor for an obvious duality in human behavior. (As Dr. Jekyll muses in the novella's closing pages, "I thus drew steadily nearer to that truth . . . that man is not truly one, but truly two.")[3] Sometimes—for example, when buying a car or picking an investment portfolio—we pursue our own material interests without regard for others' welfare. Other times—while donating blood or attending a wedding reception—we act as if we care about how our actions affect others. This capacity to shift between our purely selfish and our prosocial "personalities" (between our Jekyll and Hyde selves, if you will) is present in almost everyone other than a psychopath. Indeed, it is so deeply ingrained in human nature that it shows up in functional brain imaging: researchers report that people use different neural pathways when they make selfish and unselfish decisions.[4]

This duality also leads us, in real life, to act rather as Stevenson's protagonist did in fiction. Most people would stop to help a small child in obvious danger, and very few would behave so Hydishly as to trample a child simply because she stood in the way. Yet most people also do little or nothing to aid the millions of imperiled children living in Afghanistan, Guatemala, Sudan, and other troubled regions of the world. What explains such apparent hypocrisy? Why do we sometimes show concern for others, and other times show indifference?

In Stevenson's tale, Dr. Jekyll's personality change is triggered by a potion. For the rest of us, the trigger seems to be something social psychologists call social context.

THE ELIXIR OF UNSELFISHNESS

To a rational choice theorist, the phrase "social context" may seem alien and even meaningless. This is because social scientists use the phrase to describe a subject's perceptions of *other people*, including such matters as beliefs about what others want; perceptions of what others need; and expectations about how others are behaving or would behave. Yet *homo economicus* is indifferent to what other people do, think, or want, unless their actions happen to change his material payoffs. As an economist might put it, *homo economicus'* preferences are fixed or "exogenous." No matter what others do, he always prefers more wealth to less.

Yet the empirical evidence demonstrates that human preferences—at least, our preferences as we reveal them through our behavior—are "endogenous," meaning they shift from place to place and time to time depending on circumstances. This flexibility jumps out at anyone who reviews the data from experimental games.

From a purely economic perspective, social dilemma, ultimatum, and dictator games are highly standardized experiments. They present the subjects who play them with economic incentives that are clear and fixed, predetermined by the nature of the game itself. *Homo economicus* would always play a social dilemma, ultimatum, or dictator game the same way, regardless of social setting, always choosing the strategy that maximizes his personal returns.

One of the most consistent findings to emerge from experimental gaming, however, is that human behavior is in fact extremely sensitive to a variety of *noneconomic* variables. To gain a sense of just how sensitive, recall the 40–60 percent cooperation rates typically reported in social dilemma experiments.

Although this basic result has been obtained in a remarkably large number of experiments run in a variety of cultures, in some experiments researchers have been able to produce cooperation rates both far higher, and far lower, by manipulating the noneconomic conditions under which the subjects are playing. For example, in his pioneering survey of more than one hundred social dilemma studies, David Sally found that researchers had produced cooperation rates ranging from a low of 5 percent (nearly universal selfishness) to more than 97 percent (nearly universal prosociality).[5] To appreciate this striking result, recall that economic incentives in a social dilemma are structured so that rational and selfish players should *never* cooperate.

Similarly, researchers have been able to manipulate the social context of some dictator games to the point where 100 percent of the "dictators" chose to unselfishly share their stakes.[6] Meanwhile, in other games, only 8–12 percent of dictators chose to share.[7] Again, a rational and selfish dictator would never share at all.

When the right social variables are mixed together, social context becomes a powerful elixir for triggering the Dr. Jekyll and Mr. Hyde aspects of our personalities. But what, exactly, are its ingredients? Why do people of all ages, genders, and backgrounds tend to act unselfishly in some situations, and selfishly in others? If we simply say "social context matters" without identifying which elements of social context matter most and how, we are implicitly embracing the *homo sociologus* model of humans as infinitely malleable creatures whose behavior is determined by an undefined "culture."

A THREE-FACTOR APPROACH TO SOCIAL CONTEXT

There is no need to step into this quagmire. Although the scientific evidence demonstrates beyond reasonable challenge that human behavior is far more flexible than the *homo economicus* model admits, this flexibility is not unlimited. People shift between selfish and unselfish behavior, but their shifts follow discernable patterns. Around the world and through the decades, certain variables have proven especially important in encouraging unselfish behavior in experimental games.

This insight can be employed to develop a relatively simple model of prosocial behavior that does not try to address every element of social context that might possibly matter, but focuses instead on the few select variables that matter most for the problem at hand. This chapter offers such a model, a "three-factor model" designed to be of particular utility to judges, regulators, and legislators seeking to use law to shape human behavior. The model can be summarized as follows:

> *Unselfish prosocial behavior toward strangers, including unselfish compliance with legal and ethical rules, is triggered by social context, including especially:*
>
> *(1) instructions from authority;*
> *(2) beliefs about others' prosocial behavior; and*
> *(3) the magnitude of the benefits to others.*
>
> *Prosocial behavior declines, however, as the personal cost of acting prosocially increases.*

WHY THESE THREE SOCIAL VARIABLES?

Before examining how each of the three social variables listed above promotes "conscience"—and before exploring the role personal cost plays in undermining conscience—it is important to address the question, why these three? Why not look at other social factors, like gender, race, religion, or early toilet training? Surely many different experiences and influences work together to determine when an individual will ruthlessly pursue her own interests, and when she will show concern for others.

Surely, many experiences and influences do. Yet there is good reason to focus our attention on the three social variables of instructions from authority, beliefs about others' behavior, and benefits to others.

First, these three variables are especially easy for lawmakers and policymakers to manipulate; that is, they offer especially good levers for shifting human behavior on a large scale. For example, there is little policymakers can do to influence the sorts of demographic factors, like age or gender, that have been weakly correlated with prosocial behavior in some experiments. As we will see in the next chapter, prosocial behavior increases with age, and while neither sex can be said to be reliably "nicer" than the other, some studies find slight differences in the way men and women behave in experimental games.[8] But unless we are willing to resort to wholesale murder or forced contraception, we cannot make our population older or younger, or change its gender ratio. Similarly, religious affiliation may be a factor in promoting prosociality, as organized religions often instruct their members to act "morally." The effect may vary by religion, however (one survey has found that Protestant Christians outscore Catholics on altruism.)[9] In any case, the Establishment Clause of the U.S. Constitution forbids lawmakers from using religion to influence behavior.

It is also generally impractical for lawmakers to promote unselfishness by manipulating a fourth important social variable that—like authority, conformity, and magnitude of benefits to others—has proven strongly correlated with prosocial behavior. This fourth social variable is something researchers call "social distance."[10] For example, cooperation rates in social dilemmas increase when players are allowed to see each other or to speak with each other, even though this does not change the economic incentives the players face in the game.[11] Similarly, dictators in dictator games become more generous when told the family names of their fellow players and potential beneficiaries.[12] We will see in the next chapter how this finding is supported by evolutionary theory, which predicts prosocial behavior should be more likely when dealing with individuals one perceives to be members of one's "in-group." But apart from occasional reminders of our common civic affiliations and duties, there is little lawmakers and regulators can do to force manufacturers and consumers, or drivers and pedestrians, to spend time with and strike up conversations with each other.

In contrast, the social variables of instructions from authority, perceptions of others' behavior, and beliefs about benefits to others, offer lawmakers some traction. Part Three explores a number of ways we can use the law to send authoritative signals about what behavior is expected and appropriate; to influence beliefs about what others are doing or would do; and to provide information about how behavior benefits others.

A second reason to focus on these three variables, however, is that the empirical literature indicates they are especially robust. A half-century of experimental gaming has consistently shown they are linked with unselfish behavior in the laboratory environment. This robustness is apparent in an impressionistic sense to anyone who takes the time to review a significant number of studies. It has been demonstrated more formally in meta-analyses that survey the results of numerous individual experiments by different researchers. David Sally's survey, for example, found that formal instructions to cooperate, evidence of others' cooperation, and increasing the benefits of cooperation to other players all played statistically important roles in determining cooperation rates in social dilemmas.[13] Other meta-analyses have reached similar conclusions.[14]

Finally, a third reason for emphasizing these three elements of social context is that each of the three variables maps onto one of three universal and well-studied traits of human nature. These three basic psychological traits are: *obedience* to authority; *conformity* to the behavior of those around us; and *empathy* for others. Obedience, conformity, and empathy have been extensively documented in the social and life sciences. Their importance to explaining behavior has been demonstrated not only in innumerable experimental games but also in countless case studies, surveys, and field experiments. Rational choice, with its obsessive focus on material payoffs, ignores all three as influences on human behavior. Nevertheless, overwhelming evidence demonstrates that obedience, conformity, and empathy play large roles in determining what people do—including, as we shall see, when they act in an unselfish prosocial fashion.

OBEDIENCE AND INSTRUCTIONS FROM AUTHORITY

In 1961, in a basement laboratory at Yale University, psychologist Stanley Milgram undertook the most notorious series of experiments ever conducted in human psychology.[15] Milgram recruited forty men from a wide range of backgrounds to participate in what they were told would be a test of how punishment improves learning. The recruits, who were each paid $4.50 for participating, were informed they were going to teach other subjects how to answer a series of word problems. The "teachers" would then quiz the "learners" on what they remembered from the lesson. If a learner gave a wrong answer, the teacher was to punish the learner for his mistake by administering electric shocks of increasing voltage, marked "Slight," "Strong," "Very Strong," "Intense," and "Danger: Severe," up to a maximum of 450 volts (marked simply "XXX").

Unbeknownst to the teachers, the learners were really actors collaborating with the experimenters. During the test itself, the teachers/subjects and learners/actors were placed in separate rooms where they could communicate with, but not see, each other. The learners/actors then pretended to make a series of mistakes. If the teacher/subject administered the punishing "shock" as instructed, the learner/actor pretended to be in pain, responding to the supposed shocks with escalating sounds of distress: first moans, then screams, then banging on the wall, culminating with an aptly named dead silence.

Before he began his experiment, Milgram quizzed several colleagues about what they thought the test subjects would do. All predicted the vast majority of subjects would refuse to administer the maximum 450-volt level "shock." In the experiment itself, however, twenty-seven out of forty subjects followed the experimenters' instructions and continued to administer shocks all the way up to the final, 450-volt level. None steadfastly refused before the 300-volt level, although several questioned the experiment along the way, and some offered to return their $4.50.

Milgram's experiments triggered a host of similar experiments, as well as a Milgram biography,[16] a rock song ("We Do What We're Told: Milgram's 37," on Peter Gabriel's 1986 album *So*) and a 1975 television docudrama starring John Travolta and William Shatner (*The 10th Level*). The experiments also helped inspire widespread adoption of ethical guidelines for tests on human subjects that would prevent Milgram from running his experiments at most American universities today.

Yet, as disturbing as Milgram's results may be, his findings have stood the test of time. People do indeed tend to do what authority tells them to do. A subsequent meta-analysis of Milgram-like experiments performed both inside and outside of the United States found that, without regard to time or place, between 61 and 66 percent of human subjects obey the commands of a researcher to the point of administering a potentially fatal voltage to another person.[17]

Obedience to authority is routinely discussed in basic psychology and social psychology textbooks.[18] Perhaps, given the nature of Milgram's experiments, it is only natural the discussions tend to focus on how obedience to authority leads people to do dreadful things to others. It is easy to see how slavish compliance has contributed to human misery, not only in Milgram's experiments but also in China's Cultural Revolution, at the My Lai massacre, and in the "killing fields" of the Khmer Rouge. Milgram himself was inspired by the desire to understand how millions of otherwise-decent Germans could have turned a blind eye to the attempted extermination of Europe's Jews in the Holocaust.

But this tendency to focus on the dark side of obedience to authority distracts us from recognizing that obedience can have a bright side as well. Although people can be instructed to harm others, they can also be instructed to refrain from harm, and even to help. The positive side of obedience is easy to observe in experimental gaming results. One of the most consistent findings in the literature is that subjects cooperate when an experimenter instructs them to cooperate. In Sally's meta-analysis, for example, formal instructions to cooperate were found to raise average cooperation rates in social dilemma trials by 34–40 percent compared to games where no instructions were given, depending on the exact regression formula employed.[19]

This willingness to obey instructions in social dilemmas is far more puzzling, from a rational choice perspective, than the obedience seen in Milgram's experiment. After all, Milgram's subjects were *paid* to follow instructions. In contrast, in a social dilemma experiment, obeying an experimenter's request to cooperate means the subject earns less than if he defects.

Nevertheless, people change their behavior in social dilemmas in response to mere hints about what the experimenter desires. In one social dilemma experiment, for example, subjects were told the name of the game was the "Community Game." These subjects exhibited a 60 percent cooperation rate. Meanwhile, a group of similar subjects were told they were playing the "Wall Street Game." These subjects showed a cooperation rate of only 30 percent.[20] Similarly, in dictator games, dictators share more when instructed to "divide" their initial stakes than when experimenters use the "language of exchange."[21]

Experimental gaming demonstrates that, just as authority can encourage us to harm others, it can encourage us to help them. Of course, while obedience to authority is a powerful force, it is not absolute. All of Milgram's subjects administered some shocks, but a significant minority refused to go all the way up to the 450-volt level. Similarly, even when asked to cooperate, some subjects in a social dilemma may selfishly defect. Nevertheless, as any teacher, minister, or military commander knows, obedience to authority plays an extremely important role in determining behavior, including prosocial behavior.

CONFORMITY AND EXPECTATIONS FOR OTHERS' BEHAVIOR

There's a saying that if you give people the freedom to do whatever they want, they will use it to imitate each other. This truth is apparent to anyone who watches teenagers at a shopping mall. It has also been demonstrated, time after time, in experimental psychology.

One of the earliest and most entertaining experiments on conformity was run in the 1960s at Columbia University by psychologists Bibb Latané and John Darley.[22] They invited students to come in for an "interview," showed the students into a waiting room, and gave them a lengthy questionnaire to fill out. Then, while the students were dutifully filling out their questionnaires, they blew a stream of thick white smoke into the room through a small vent. Through a one-way mirror, the experimenters watched their human guinea pigs as the room filled with smoke. In experiments where the subject was left alone in the room, the solo subjects acted quite rationally: they sniffed the smoke, inspected the vent it flowed from, and then 75 percent left the room (typically, within two minutes) to report the situation. In other cases, however, the test subject was asked to share the waiting room with two other "interviewees" who were actually actors collaborating with the experimenters. When the smoke began to fill the room, the actors did nothing more than cough, wave the smoke away, and doggedly continue to fill out the questionnaires. What did the test subjects do? Exactly as the actors did—in nine out of ten cases, the subject stayed in the room and failed to report the smoke.

Like obedience to authority, conformity is a fundamental aspect of human nature that shows up consistently in experimental gaming. Experimenters have repeatedly found that when players believe *other* players are likely to adopt unselfish strategies in games, they become far more likely to play unselfishly themselves.[23] Conversely, subjects led to believe others will play selfishly become more likely to play selfishly. Researchers have found, for example, that subjects who exchange promises to cooperate before playing a social dilemma game are much more likely to cooperate in the game itself,[24] even though the promises are not enforceable and, in anonymous experiments involving three or more players, subjects can't even tell who violated the promise. Nevertheless, promising does signal an intent to act cooperatively, which seems to trigger conforming cooperative behavior.

A similar phenomenon is observed in trust games. For example, consider a typical trust game in which one player (the investor) is given a sum of money and told that any amount he chooses to give the second player (the trustee) will be tripled. The trustee is then asked to decide whether she wants to return any of the tripled funds to the investor. The very fact that the trustee typically chooses to reciprocate the investor's generosity by returning some of the tripled funds itself suggests mimicry of the investor's prosocial sharing.[25] But researchers have further found that investors in a trust game share more when a trustee expressly promises in advance to repay, even though (again) the promise is unenforceable.[26]

Other evidence of conforming prosociality can be found in studies where subjects are asked to play several rounds of a particular game. In repeat game experiments, players who cooperate in initial rounds usually continue to cooperate in later rounds—but only if their fellow players also cooperated.[27] This is true even in the final round of a repeat game, when there is no longer any risk of retaliation. In fact, the effect of others' behavior is so strong that in one experiment where subjects were asked to simultaneously play a set number of rounds of a social dilemma game with two different groups, the subjects cooperated more with the groups whose fellow members cooperated, and less with the groups whose members tended to defect.[28]

Finally, in a few experiments, researchers have increased cooperative behavior in games by providing their subjects with information suggesting that *other* subjects in *other* games chose cooperation. For example, in a dictator game experiment, dictators shared more when given information indicating that other test subjects chose to share in other dictator games.[29]

Experimental games thus demonstrate that, in choosing between selfish and unselfish strategies, people tend to do what they think others will do. What explains this herd behavior? In Latané and Darley's experiment, the test subjects may have copied the actors who ignored the smoke pouring into the room because they inferred the actors somehow knew the smoke wasn't a threat. But this argument can't explain herd behavior in experimental games, where no inferences are needed to understand what's going on: it's perfectly obvious that defecting offers a higher personal return than cooperation.[30]

REPUTATION AND RECIPROCITY CAN'T EXPLAIN ALL CONFORMITY

Nor can conformity in experimental games be explained by two other, related arguments often offered to explain apparently altruistic behavior. These two arguments are reputation, and reciprocity (retaliation). Scholars who employ rational choice love to cite reputation and reciprocity as explanations for apparently altruistic behavior. After all, if I am only helping you to build a good reputation with others, or in exchange for your helping me, apparent self-sacrifice becomes a form of "enlightened" self-interest.

Reputation and reciprocity can indeed create selfish motives for seemingly unselfish cooperation in experiments where players who know each other interact, or in games where players interact repeatedly.[31] But we see conforming cooperation in games even where reputational harm and reciprocal cooperation or defection are impossible. For example, the hope of reciprocity cannot explain cooperation in the final round of an anonymous repeated prisoner's dilemma, because in the final round retaliation becomes impossible. By backwards induction, reciprocity cannot explain cooperation in any repeated prisoner's dilemma in which the players know the total number of rounds to be played. Knowing your fellow player will defect in the final round, you defect in the penultimate round; knowing this, your partner defects in the round prior to the penultimate round, and so forth back to the very first round.[32]

Even more obviously, neither reputation nor reciprocity can explain cooperation in anonymous, multi-player, one-shot social dilemma games where it is impossible even to identify which players are cooperating and which are cheating, much less to punish players who choose defection.[33] To fully understand this point, recall the basic conformity finding that subjects asked to play a single, anonymous round of a social dilemma are more likely to defect if they believe their fellow players will defect, and more likely to cooperate if they believe their fellows will cooperate. This basic finding directly contradicts the claim that prosocial conformity in social dilemmas can be explained by either selfish reputational concerns, or the selfish hope of reciprocal exchange. After all, in a one-shot, anonymous social dilemma, a belief other players intend to cooperate *increases* the anticipated material rewards from defecting.

Experimental gaming thus demonstrates that people conform to others' unselfish behavior *even when they cannot rationally expect either reputational benefits or direct reciprocity from the unselfish people they're imitating.* Economists who study cooperative behavior sometimes describe this willingness to imitate others' unselfishness as "strong reciprocity."[34] Sociologist Robert Putnam calls it "generalized reciprocity."[35] Yet "strong reciprocity" and "generalized reciprocity" are, in a sense, oxymorons. Aping the courtesy and generosity of people with whom we never expect to deal ourselves is not, and cannot be, a reciprocal transaction. This book accordingly will use the word "conformity" to describe such herd behavior.

As in the case of obedience to authority, it is easy to paint conformity in a negative light. ("If all your friends jumped off a bridge, would you jump too?") But we should not forget conformity has a bright side as well. We want people to conform to the law and to ethical rules. Indeed, this is much of what we try to capture when we speak of conscience.

EMPATHY AND BENEFITS TO OTHERS

Finally, let us turn to the last social factor in our three-factor model: the magnitude of the benefits to others from one's own unselfish actions. Although this on first inspection seems an economic variable (after all, we are talking about material rewards), it is really a social variable because we are talking about material rewards to *others*. *Homo economicus* should have no interest in helping anyone else, for a penny or a pound. Real people, however, seem inclined to rise to an occasion. The same person who refuses to stop to give directions to a lost stranger might willingly interrupt his daily routine to throw a life preserver to a drowning man.

Many readers likely find the idea that people sacrifice more for others when they expect their sacrifice to provide greater benefits intuitively quite plausible. Nevertheless, this pattern turns out to be somewhat difficult to observe in the gaming literature, due to tight research budgets. Given the limited money floating around in the academic world, most experimental games involve relatively small stakes. As a result, there is little formal evidence available about what happens when subjects are put in the position to provide large benefits to others.[36]

The limited data available indicate, however, that experimental subjects are indeed more likely to act unselfishly when they believe others benefit more from their unselfishness. For example, by raising the amount by which they multiply contributions to the common pool in a social dilemma game, researchers can raise the level of the benefit to the group from an individual's cooperative donation while holding the personal cost of donating constant. Such treatments indicate that the incidence of cooperation in social dilemmas does indeed rise with an increase in the magnitude of the benefits that flow to others from cooperating.[37] A similar finding has been reported in dictator games, where researchers have found that dictators share more when told researchers will multiply the amount the dictator shares with her partner. Some dictators become so enthused by the possibility of social gain that their partners end up with more than they do.[38] Such results come as close to evidence of true altruism—in particular, the desire to promote group welfare—as anything we have yet seen in experimental gaming.

As noted earlier, subjects cooperate more in experimental games when instructed to cooperate, and also cooperate more when they believe others will cooperate. Yet neither obedience nor conformity are innately altruistic behaviors. (Milgram's experiments showed how obedience can be used to induce people to harm others, and conformity doesn't necessarily either help or harm.) When experimental subjects behave as if they care about the size of the benefits they provide others, however, they are acting as if they do indeed pay attention to, and care about, others' welfare. Social scientists associate such altruistic behavior with a third fundamental trait of human psychology: *empathy*.

Like imitation and obedience to authority, empathy is well-documented in the life and social sciences. We can even "see" empathy using modern brain imaging technology. In a 2005 article in *Science*, a team of neuroscientists reported the results of an experiment in which they used functional magnetic resonance imaging (fMRI) to observe activity in the brains of test subjects who were asked to watch while the researchers pierced the hand of their romantic partner with a needle. The neuroscientists found that watching a loved one experience pain produced brain activity that was similar to that observed when the test subject experienced the pain personally.[39]

Yet even before the development of fMRI and similar technologies, there was little doubt most people are capable of empathizing with others' emotions, including others' joys and sufferings. The Milgram experiments themselves provided strong indirect evidence of empathy. To *homo economicus*, the only surprising thing about Milgram's results was that anyone was surprised by them. After all, Milgram's subjects were being *paid* to inflict pain on fellow human beings. Yet Milgram's results provoked widespread revulsion. In the eyes of the world, decent human beings were expected to show more empathy for their supposed victims.

Indeed, empathy is not confined to decent human beings. Some animals also show empathy, in everyday life and in formal experiments. Consider the well-documented case of Binti, a gorilla at Chicago's Brookfield Zoo. In 1996, when a human toddler fell eighteen feet into the moat surrounding Binti's gorilla exhibit, Binti gently picked up the unconscious child and carried him to the service gate to deliver him to the anxious zookeepers.[40] As early as 1959, psychologist Russell Church demonstrated that a hungry rat that had been trained to press a lever to get food pellets would refuse to do so if pressing the lever caused a second rat in an adjacent cage to simultaneously receive a painful electric shock.[41] (It is tempting to observe that Church's rats showed more empathy for their fellow rodents than Milgram's subjects showed for human beings, highlighting the irony of insulting someone by calling him "a rat.")

Of course, we cannot know what was going on in Binti's head, or between the furry ears of Church's subjects, any more than we can be sure what motivates people to follow their conscience. But Church's rats and Binti the gorilla *acted* like empathic altruists. Perhaps, like humans, they were more inclined to behave altruistically because the stakes seemed high.[42]

Such similarities among rats, humans, and gorillas carry interesting implications about the possible evolutionary benefits of altruism in social animals. Although apes and humans are kissing cousins from an evolutionary perspective, the lab rat is descended from the Norwegian rat, *rattus norvegicus*, a species whose ancestors diverged from ours scores of millions of years ago. That rodents and primates both demonstrate something that looks like empathy suggests empathy offers evolutionary advantages in social species. We explore this idea in the next chapter. Meanwhile, whatever its origins, empathy remains deeply imbedded in human nature, to the point where introductory psychology texts routinely devote substantial time to discussing its development. Given this importance, along with corroborating evidence from experimental games, we will incorporate altruistic empathy into our three-factor model as well by assuming that, along with instructions from authority and evidence of others' unselfishness, the size of the benefits to others from one's own unselfishness is a third important social determinant of other-regarding behavior.

THE ROLE OF SELF-INTEREST

So far, we have focused on how three social variables—instructions from authority (which triggers obedience), beliefs about others' behavior (which triggers conformity), and increasing the magnitude of the perceived benefits or costs to others (which triggers empathy)—play important roles in promoting unselfish prosocial behavior. This focus recognizes that social context plays a critical role in determining whether people behave in a selfish or an unselfish fashion. Yet saying "social context matters" is not the same as saying "personal payoffs don't." The rational choice model may be incomplete, but it is not irrelevant. In addition to the importance of social context, a second robust finding that has emerged from the gaming literature is that unselfish behavior depends not only on social variables, but on *personal payoffs as well*.

As the personal cost of acting unselfishly rises, people become less likely to indulge in unselfish behavior. Conversely, the lower the cost of unselfish action, the more likely unselfish action becomes. This relationship is most easily observed in social dilemma games, where studies find that as the personal cost of cooperating rises (that is, as the expected gains from defecting increase), the incidence of cooperation drops significantly. Sally's meta-survey, for example, found that doubling the reward from defecting decreased average cooperation rates by as much as 16 percent.[43] Such findings imply the supply function for unselfish behavior is, to use the language of economics, "downward-sloping." We are more inclined toward benevolent (spiteful) actions when benevolence (spite) is cheap. Conversely, when unselfishness is expensive, we are less inclined to "buy" it. George Washington made a similar observation when he noted that "few men have virtue to withstand the highest bidder."

This means that, as a practical matter, people rarely behave like perfect altruists who are utterly indifferent to their own welfare. (We might call this "Mother Theresa" altruism.) Rather than acting like selfless Mother Theresas, most people behave like intuitive utilitarians who take account of others' welfare, *along with their own*, in situations where the social variables call for prosociality. Put differently, we are "efficient altruists" who prefer to behave unselfishly when the benefits to others outweigh the costs to ourselves.

This notion fits well with most people's experience and intuitions. We would expect almost anyone to make a small sacrifice in order to save another human being from disaster, for example braking to avoid a jaywalker or calling 911 to report a serious accident. Most of us, however, would refuse to make a large sacrifice to spare someone else from mild nuisance (say, by taking an afternoon off from work to drive a neighbor to a convenience store on the next block). Indeed, we might be offended if our neighbor asked us to do such an inefficient thing.

KEEPING DOWN THE COST OF CONSCIENCE

It is vital to recognize that observing that people are more likely to act unselfishly when it doesn't cost them too much does not mean that unselfish behavior is unimportant and can be safely ignored in favor of the tried-and-true *homo economicus* approach. Just as saying "social context matters" is not the same thing as saying "personal payoffs don't matter," saying that people act more selfishly as the cost of unselfishness rises is not the same as saying it's safe to treat people as purely selfish actors. To the contrary, the fact that prosocial behavior is sensitive to personal cost heightens the importance of paying attention to conscience.

In particular, the inverse relationship between prosocial behavior and personal cost revealed by experimental gaming highlights the critical need to pay attention to "the cost of conscience" in our policy and daily affairs. Put simply, if we want people to be good, it's essential we don't tempt them to be bad. Unfortunately, an over-reliance on material incentives often creates temptations.

Consider an elementary school teacher in Georgia who has been promised a $2,000 bonus if he can raise his students' scores on some standardized test. Left to his own devices and paid a flat salary, the teacher might have devoted his efforts to helping his students become inquisitive, motivated, skilled learners. Tempted by the bonus, he may instead focus relentlessly on "drilling" them for the test. Worse, he may cheat by changing his students' answers on their scoring sheets—as appears to have actually happened, on a massive scale, in Atlanta.[44]

Conscience needs breathing room to work. But when we give it breathing room, we can expect most people will be willing to make at least a small personal sacrifice (when the social conditions are right) in order to behave prosocially. And there are many situations where a small act of unselfishness that costs the unselfish actor very little provides much larger benefits to others. Summed up over many different individuals and many different social interactions, the total gains from many such small acts of altruism can be enormous. We all benefit, and substantially, from living in a society where most people refrain from robbing each other even when the police aren't around. Not only can we stop worrying about keeping our drivers' licenses and children's photos, but we also don't have to put bars on our windows, armor our cars, pack heat, and hire bodyguards whenever we use the ATM machine. Similarly, a society where everyone works a bit harder and more honestly in their employment and at their professions than they really have to, is a more wealthy and productive society. Thus, even a limited human capacity for unselfishness can generate enormous benefits over long periods of time and large populations.

SUMMING UP: THE THREE-FACTOR SOCIAL MODEL OF CONSCIENCE

We are now in a position to make some observations about what, exactly, triggers the internal force laymen call conscience. In brief, the three-factor model of unselfish prosocial behavior does not abandon the notion that self-interest influences behavior. (Self-interest is, in a sense, a fourth factor in the model, albeit one that is economic rather than social in nature.) The three-factor model acknowledges, however, that while self-interest matters, it is not the *only* thing that matters. When given a reasonable degree of freedom from severe temptation in which it can operate, social context plays a critical role as well.

Social context causes people to act as if they have two personalities or modes of behavior. When our selfish Mr. Hyde personality dominates, we seek to maximize our own material welfare without regard to how our actions affect others. But when social context brings our prosocial Dr. Jekyll personality into play, we sacrifice for others and follow legal and ethical moral rules—at least as long as it doesn't cost us too much.

"Social context" can, of course, include an enormous variety of influences and factors. By restricting our attention to only three elements—instructions from authority, beliefs about others' unselfish behavior, and perceptions of how much others benefit from one's own unselfish action—the three-factor model inevitably offers a reductionist account of human nature. Sometimes a little reductionism is useful, however. Any attempt to model human behavior that tried to account for every possible influence that tempts us to be nice or nasty would be so cumbersome as to be useless. A balance must be struck between accuracy and simplicity. The three-factor model strikes a balance that offers greater accuracy than the *homo economicus* model (a one-factor model where the only variable that counts is personal gain), and greater simplicity and ease of use than the *homo sociologicus* approach of "it's all culture."

Although hardly perfect, the result offers lawmakers and regulators a number of useful insights into how they can use the phenomenon that Oliver Wendell Holmes dismissed—"conscience"—to change behavior. Of course, the model does not tell us exactly *why* people sometimes act as if they care about others and about following rules. Instead, it treats individuals as "black boxes" whose internal workings cannot be observed. Unable to see what goes on inside the box, we must content ourselves with observing the relationship between the social and economic variables that go into the box, and the behavior that comes out.

This approach still gives us a fair amount of room to make testable predictions about when and where people are likely to sacrifice for others—including testable predictions about when they will unselfishly follow rules. We can predict, for example, that when the three social variables work in tandem to support unselfishness (authority says cooperation is called for, you believe others would cooperate, you expect your cooperation to greatly benefit others), the vast majority of individuals will act in cooperative fashion. Conversely, the vast majority will act selfishly when all three social variables support selfishness (authority says selfishness is appropriate, you believe others would act selfishly, and you believe unselfish cooperation would provide only small benefits to others).

The approach is hardly perfect. There is always a chance that, even when the social stars are perfectly aligned to encourage unselfishness, some individuals might act selfishly, especially when the personal cost of unselfish action is high. Moreover, the three-factor model cannot tell us what happens when one of the factors contradicts the others. Consider the case of army warrant officer Hugh Thompson, a helicopter pilot during the Vietnam War. Thompson, upon observing American military officers slaughtering civilians in the village of My Lai, landed his helicopter and instructed his crew to hold their fellow Americans at gunpoint while he loaded villagers into the helicopter to fly them to safety. (The U.S. Army presented Thompson with the Soldier's Medal for heroism, albeit thirty years later.) Thompson was outranked in authority by Lieutenant William Calley, who ordered the massacre. Thompson also failed to conform his actions to those of the other soldiers participating in the killing spree. But obedience and conformity lost out to empathy. In an Associated Press interview thirty years after the massacre, Thompson explained his rescue quite simply: "These people were looking at me for help, and there was no way I could turn my back on them."[45]

The science of conscience, like the science of meteorology, must deal with probabilities more than certainties. (Forecast for Pittsburgh today: widespread decency, with scattered thoughtlessness during the afternoon rush hour.) Yet despite its relative imprecision, it has the great advantage of allowing us to make predictions about human behavior that will often prove more accurate than the predictions of the rational selfishness model. The *homo economicus* account of behavior is as precise and mechanical as a Swiss timepiece. By assuming people want only to maximize their own wealth, it allows us to make exact predictions about how people behave. Pay individuals to do something—whether it be donating blood or committing genocide—and they'll do more of it. Penalize them, and they'll do less. Unfortunately, although these predictions are unambiguous, they are also (as demonstrated not only by Hugh Thompson's heroism but also by hundreds of ultimatum, dictator, and social dilemma games) often incorrect.

Financial guru Warren Buffett has famously observed that "it is better to be approximately right than precisely wrong."[46] Most people outside academia follow the same philosophy. They want real solutions to real problems, not elegant mathematical equations. That is enough to make the three-factor model useful to lawmakers, regulators, and employers— indeed, to anyone who wants to understand and encourage prosocial behavior.

CHAPTER SIX

ORIGINS

> Any animal whatever, endowed with well-marked social
> instincts . . . would inevitably acquire a moral sense or
> conscience.
>
> —*Charles Darwin, The Descent of Man*

The previous chapter presented a three-factor model of social variables that trigger the internal constraints on selfish behavior we call "conscience." Part Three (chapters 7, 8, and 9) will demonstrate how this model can be used both to predict behavior, and to change it. The reader with a practical bent accordingly can abandon any further inquiry into the nature of conscience and move on to Part Three and the instrumental question of how to best combine law and conscience to influence behavior.

For the reader in less of a hurry, this chapter detours to explore the question: how, exactly, did conscience arise? What are the evolutionary roots of the Jekyll/Hyde syndrome?

Any discussion of these questions inevitably is somewhat speculative. Although the reality of unselfish behavior is amply demonstrated by experimental gaming, we weren't around to witness when or how it appeared on the scene, and the question of why humans evolved a capacity for unselfish action remains controversial. Evolutionary biologists have offered a number of different theories. These theories are worth exploring for at least three reasons.

The first reason is sheer curiosity. Human behavior tends to be of interest to humans. And although our understanding of how *homo sapiens* evolved a capacity to act unselfishly has advanced considerably since Darwin first offered his thoughts on the subject, there remains ample room for debate. This uncertainty should not discourage us from indulging in the intellectual pleasure of wondering how we managed to evolve toward "goodness."

Second, a better understanding of the biological origins of unselfish behavior can help overcome the common assumption that unselfish behavior must be rare because widespread altruism should be stamped out in the Darwinian struggle for "survival of the fittest." Although the Darwinian objection to altruism is often raised by nonexperts, the experts themselves have developed not one but several theories to explain how evolutionary pressures can favor altruistic behavior. These differing but mutually reinforcing theories should reassure any skeptic that, as the experimental evidence demonstrates, conscience can exist.

Finally, there is a third reason to inquire into the origins of our Jekyll/Hyde natures. It is possible that, if we can understand how and why conscience evolved, we may be able to better understand how it operates and what its limitations might be. In other words, evolutionary biology can not only help convince skeptics conscience exists; it may also be able to shed light on how conscience works.

Before going further, two words of caution are in order. First, many people view the idea that human behavior can have evolutionary roots with a certain amount of squeamishness. The idea smacks of determinism, the triumph of nature over nurture in the long-standing debate over whether our behavior is determined more by heredity or environment. To most biologists, however, the debate seems silly. Nature and nurture are both essential, and interact with each other in complex ways. Behavior is constrained by heredity *and* by environment, and cannot be understood fully without taking both into account. Thus, while some behavioral traits seem deeply ingrained (for example, fear of falling), others are the result of a complex interaction between genes and environment. As we shall see, this seems especially true of unselfish behavior, where evolutionary pressures have favored behavioral "plasticity"—the ability to act like either a saint or a psychopath, depending on circumstances.

Second, it is important to avoid the "naturalistic fallacy"— the assumption that because something is natural it is also desirable. Infanticide, for example, is common in the natural world and in many early human societies, but I have never met an evolutionary biologist who would not be horrified at the suggestion that this justifies killing babies. The same is true for selfishness and unselfishness. Both types of behavior are "natural." This tells us almost nothing about whether it is good public policy to promote selfish or unselfish behavior in any particular set of circumstances.

With these caveats in mind, we turn to the question of how a capacity for unselfish behavior has evolved in *homo sapiens.* One place to gain some insight into how unselfishness develops at the level of the species is by examining how the capacity for unselfish behavior develops at the level of the individual. So we turn to developmental psychology and the question: how does the typical person grow a "conscience"?

MORAL DEVELOPMENT IN INDIVIDUALS

Babies are selfish beasts. They demand food when they are hungry, whether it is convenient for Mom or not; they demand comfort when they wake at night, whether or not Dad is sleeping. No amount of pleading or respectful negotiation can placate them. Infants want what they want when they want it, and they howl until they get it, indifferent to the burdens their demands place on their caretakers.

Parents are not the only ones who have noticed this moral deficit. Although psychologists disagree on many things, they agree that humans enter the world as selfish beings. Freud believed infant behavior was regulated by a primitive, self-seeking "id," and that only as a child grows older does he or she develop an other-regarding, self-sanctioning "superego."[1] Piaget similarly viewed children younger than age five or six as egocentric beings unable to consider any perspective other than their own.[2] Lawrence Kohlberg, whose theories of moral development built on Piaget's and whose ideas are still widely cited by contemporary developmental psychologists, argued that children start with selfishness and develop a sense of morality only progressively. According to Kohlberg, very young children obey rules for the same reason that *homo economicus* does: to avoid a punishment or earn a reward.[3]

Experimental gaming confirms that other-regarding behavior does indeed increase with age, and the process goes on well into adulthood. When asked to play ultimatum games with M&Ms, kindergartners who receive low offers are far less likely to reject them, and so punish the offending proposers, than adults who play ultimatum games with money.[4] A study of 310 children ages seven through eighteen who played dictator and ultimatum games also found that younger children made significantly smaller proposals than older children: indeed, second-graders playing the dictator game tended to share almost nothing.[5] Proposals increased with age, as did the likelihood that a responder in an ultimatum game would reject a small offer. In other words, both altruistic and spiteful behavior seem to increase with age.

Nor does the process of becoming more prosocial stop after high school. Seniors and juniors at universities cooperate more in social dilemma games than freshmen and sophomores do.[6] A 2003 study examining how more than six hundred participants ranging in age from eight to over sixty behaved in trust games found that the incidence of altruistic reciprocation increased into, and beyond, middle age.[7] A 2004 study of human behavior in two natural "social dilemma" situations, a university fund-raising campaign and a television game show, also concluded there was a "correlation between age and other-regarding behavior."[8] The same author also reported that in a formal social dilemma experiment, over 35 percent of subjects fifty years or older contributed the social optimum, while only 12 percent of subjects younger than nineteen years of age chose to give the optimal amount.[9]

The pattern of altruism increasing with age seems to hold for most people. It is important to note, however, that not every individual seems capable of "maturing" morally in this fashion. Criminal psychologists believe that some portion of the human population (probably no more than 1 or 2 percent) consists of individuals who are not only born without a conscience, but seem incapable of developing one. Experts refer to this condition as "psychopathy" and suspect genetic origins in some cases.[10] Serial killer and cannibal Jeffrey Dahmer was said to have had a normal childhood, suggesting that nature rather than nurture must be blamed for his extraordinarily antisocial hobby.[11] We shall return to this idea later.

Meanwhile, whether or not some people are "bad seeds" when they leave the womb, even when an individual is born carrying the genetic material necessary to develop a full-fledged conscience, environmental factors can cause things to go awry. It is a truism among developmental psychologists that children raised by abusive, antisocial parents are at risk of maturing into abusive and antisocial adults themselves. In extreme cases, they may become psychopaths whose behavior mirrors that of their genetically challenged brethren.[12]

Things can also go wrong as a result of accident or disease. Consider the famous case of Phineas Gage, a twenty-five-year-old construction foreman for the Rutland and Burlington Railroad who suffered a traumatic brain injury in 1848 as a result of an accident with dynamite. The blast drove a piece of metal through Gage's face, brain, and skull, producing a horrible wound Gage survived and recovered from. The accident left Gage a changed man, however. Where he had once been kind, popular, and responsible, he became callous, isolated, unreliable, and prone to profanity and unseemly requests for sexual service.[13] The change in his behavior was all the more remarkable because his motor functions and intelligence seemed unaffected, suggesting that the area of his brain damaged in the accident—the prefrontal cortex—was particularly important to prosocial behavior. Similar and more extreme effects have been seen in other patients with prefrontal cortex injuries, especially children, who often mature into adults who are undependable, chronic liars, physically and verbally abusive, and lacking empathy. In effect, they remain stuck at Kohlberg's first stage of moral reasoning, unable to think about moral dilemmas in any terms other than their own expected punishments and rewards.[14]

Taken together, the evidence suggests that the vast majority of people leave their mothers' wombs primed to develop a "conscience," meaning a set of internalized constraints that cause them to follow rules and respect others even when external rewards and punishments are absent. We begin life, however, as egoists. Only after years of interaction, observation, and indoctrination do children start to behave in an unselfish fashion. The process takes time and goes on well into adulthood, perhaps over our entire lifespans. Nor is the process infallible. A blessedly small number of people seem genetically incapable of moving beyond the egoist stage. For others, negative environmental factors, whether in the form of abusive parents or a tragic accident of the sort that befell Phineas Gage, can retard the growth of conscience, or destroy a fully fledged conscience that had already emerged. Luckily, the vast majority of people escape such fates, becoming and remaining cooperative, prosocial employees, neighbors, spouses, and citizens—"good" men and women in contrast to Holmes' "bad."

But nature and nurture do sometimes create bad men and women, even if in thankfully small numbers. As long as this is true, altruistic behavior poses a problem from an evolutionary perspective. To this problem we now turn.

MORAL DEVELOPMENT IN SPECIES

Chapter 5 explored how four factors—three social variables (instructions from authority, perceptions of others' unselfishness, and beliefs about benefits to others), together with the personal calculus of cost and benefit—seem to play especially

powerful roles in determining unselfish behavior in laboratory experiments. It also considered how each factor corre-
sponds to a basic trait of human nature: *obedience*; *imitation*;
empathy; and (of course) *self-interest*.

From an evolutionary perspective, three of the four factors
are easy to explain. Self-interest has obvious value in motivating an organism to gather food, find a mate, and defend itself
from predators. Imitation also is useful to social animals: the
antelope that wanders away from the herd is easy prey, and
the young baboon that searches for water on its own rather
than following its tribe to the waterhole is likely to go thirsty.
Finally, there is ample reason to suspect that obedience to
authority can have adaptive value. Human children take an
extraordinarily long time, from a biological perspective, to
mature to the point at which they can fend for themselves.
Obeying authority improves a child's odds of surviving: the
youngster who never listens to his or her elders will not last
long. Obedience to authority also offers advantages in adulthood. Like their primate cousins, humans live in hierarchical groups with well-defined lines of authority, offering yet
another pressure, if more were needed, to develop the habit of
obeying the dominant "alpha" female or male.

Altruistic empathy is, however, quite a different story. From
the perspective of an evolutionary biologist, altruistic behavior
poses a riddle that is irresistibly appealing. The puzzle was
first noted by Darwin in *The Descent of Man*:

> It is extremely doubtful whether the offspring of the more
> sympathetic and benevolent parents, or of those who
> were the most faithful to their comrades, would be reared
> in greater numbers than the children of the selfish and
> treacherous parents belonging to the same tribe. He who

was ready to sacrifice his life, as many a savage has been, rather than betray his comrades, would often leave no off- spring to inherit his noble nature. The bravest men, who were always willing to come to the front in war, and who freely risked their lives for others, would on average per- ish in larger numbers than other men. Therefore, it hardly seems probable that the number of men gifted with such virtues, or that the standard of their excellence, could be increased through natural selection, that is, by the survival of the fittest.[15]

In other words, self-sacrifice does not seem a winning strategy for the individual organism. Other things being equal, one would expect any organism prone to altruistic behavior as a result of some random mutation to swiftly die out, and be replaced by less generous members of the same species.

At the same time, there is good reason to hesitate before we dismiss the possibility of altruism so quickly. If it can some- how survive, a penchant for altruistic cooperation can offer obvious advantages at the level of the group in terms of pro- moting survival in difficult environments. If you share your meat today and I share the berries I find tomorrow, neither of us goes hungry. If you help me scare off the cave bear today and I help defend you against the saber-toothed tiger tomor- row, we both survive instead of both becoming dinner. Work- ing together, we may be able to drive a mammoth off a cliff, acquiring far more meat by working in tandem than either of us could by acting alone. In contrast, if we refuse to cooperate with each other and behave opportunistically (hoarding our own food supplies and trying to raid each other's, refusing to work together to defend ourselves from predators or to hunt prey), we can expect life to look much as Thomas Hobbes described it: solitary, poor, nasty, brutish, and short. This is hardly a recipe for evolutionary success. ~ Hobbes

Thinking about evolution puts us in a bind. Selfishness is clearly the best strategy for an individual organism. At the same time, if every member of a group of organisms behaves selfishly, they lose the enormous advantages that can flow from cooperation and coordination, and fewer in the group survive to reproduce. Life, it turns out, is often a prisoner's dilemma. As a result, the problem of altruism has preoccupied evolutionary theorists for as long as there has been evolutionary theory.

Having killed many a tree in pursuit of the answer to the altruism puzzle, evolutionary biologists today have developed not one but several theories to explain how altruistic cooperation can evolve and survive in social species. We look at some of these theories next, starting with ideas that are widely accepted among experts and moving on to more controversial explanations. In the process, we shall not only see how altruistic cooperation can indeed exist in the face of Darwinian pressures, but we will also learn several lessons that may help us move toward our ultimate goal of being able to better predict and promote unselfish prosocial behavior.

KIN SELECTION

Egoistic animals that we are, people tend to think about "survival of the fittest" in terms of their personal survival. And yet, of course, none of us survives in the long run. Only our genes live on, in the bodies of our descendents. Survival of the fittest really means survival of the fittest *genes*.

This insight underlies the idea of altruism driven by kin selection. The theory of kin selection was first thoroughly developed by William D. Hamilton[16] and then popularized by Richard Dawkins in his 1976 bestseller *The Selfish Gene.* It predicts that altruistic behavior will be favored by natural selection only when it works to promote the survival of kin who share one's genes. Sometimes referred to as "inclusive fitness," the theory of kin selection predicts that the closer two individuals are related to each other genetically, the more likely they will make altruistic sacrifices to benefit each other, because such sacrifices, while putting the survival of the individual organism in doubt, promote the survival of the organism's genes.

The idea of kin-based altruism has obvious appeal. At the anecdotal level, we frequently see parents making altruistic sacrifices for their offspring. The idea of a "selfish gene" seems to go a long way toward explaining this kind of behavior. In biology, kin selection also has been used to explain the mystery of social insects like ants and bees, which live in colonies in which many members are sterile workers who do not reproduce at all (the ultimate act of self-sacrifice from a Darwinian perspective).

At the same time, in its pure form, kin selection implies that altruistic behavior should only be displayed toward those with whom we have close genetic ties. In humans and other diploid species, this means that we should see more altruistic behavior between siblings (who carry an average of 50 percent of the same genetic heritage) than toward cousins (12.5 percent genetic relatedness). The basic idea was nicely encapsulated in the 1930s by J.B.S. Haldane, who famously said, "I'd lay down my life for two brothers or eight cousins."[18] Yet we rarely see cooperative behavior follow this rigid mathematical formula. Many individuals behave altruistically toward step-siblings and adoptive siblings with whom they have no genetic relationships, while homicidal sibling rivalry between blood brothers can be traced back to Cain and Abel.[19]

While widely accepted, the idea of kin-selected altruism does not do a very good job of explaining altruism between strangers including the sort of altruistic cooperation seen in experimental games. Nor can it explain the dozens of people who die each year in the United States attempting to save nonrelatives' lives. In a fascinating empirical study of rescue attempts, legal scholar David Hyman concluded at least seventy-eight Americans die each year trying to rescue someone else, and that "proven cases of non-rescue" (that is, cases where an observer who could safely attempt rescue declined to help another in peril) "are extraordinarily rare" while "proven cases of rescues are exceedingly common—often in hazardous circumstances."[20]

Something more than kin selection is going on.

RECIPROCAL ALTRUISM

After kin selection, perhaps the most widely accepted theory of the evolution of altruistic cooperation is the theory of "reciprocal altruism."[21] In lay terms, reciprocal altruism means "you scratch my back and I'll scratch yours." By exchanging favors with each other, otherwise-selfish organisms make themselves better off. Vampire bats, for example, are famous for their reciprocal exchanges: when a bat is lucky enough to find a large mammal on whose blood it can gorge, on returning to the nest it will often regurgitate some of its meal to share with another vampire bat that was not as fortunate. The next night, if the generous vampire bat goes without a meal, it benefits from a similar donation. This mutual generosity, observed between kin and nonkin bats alike, is highly beneficial to the individual bats who participate in such exchanges.[22] (A vampire bat will starve if it goes sixty hours without a meal.)

For reciprocal altruism to work, however, two things are necessary. First, the organism must live in a group where it is able to interact with other members of the group on a repeated basis. (There is no point in doing a favor for another bat if it won't stick around to return the favor.) Second, the organisms must have enough cognitive capacity to recognize and keep track of their exchange partners. Indiscriminate altruism that is not returned confers no advantage. Vampire bats, it turns out, seem quite good at recognizing and favoring other bats that have helped them in the past.

It seems likely that both conditions—the opportunity for repeated exchange and the cognitive ability to keep track of exchanges—applied to our early ancestors. Anthropologists believe that before the rise of agriculture, most people lived in small groups or tribes. As a result, reciprocal exchange is probably a pretty good explanation for superficially altruistic behavior in such small groups. In its classic form, however, reciprocal altruism does not do a very good job of explaining "generalized reciprocity"—altruistic cooperation in modern urban societies among strangers who will likely never see each other again.

THE BIG MISTAKE theory

Reciprocal altruism can provide a more compelling explanation for generalized reciprocity when it is combined with another idea drawn from evolutionary theory, an idea we might dub the Big Mistake theory.[23] Consider again our ancestral environment of hundreds of thousands or even millions of years ago, when we tended to live in small tribes and to interact with strangers only rarely. In such circumstances, it might not make evolutionary sense to invest in the massive cognitive capacity needed to keep track of each and every favor one does for or receives from others. (Thinking burns quite a lot of energy.) Instead, it might be more efficient to follow a general rule of thumb: "I'll be nice to anyone in the expectation that, and as long as, they are nice back." In the claustrophobic environment of the tribe, it might also be efficient to simply assume that any misbehavior would likely be detected by one's fellows.

Now flash forward to the modern era. Many people now live in anonymous, urban, mobile societies where they frequently interact with strangers they'll never see again, and where misbehavior often would not be detected or punished. But from an evolutionary perspective, this urban environment is incredibly novel. We have lived among strangers for only a few hundred years; during most of human prehistory, we lived cheek and jowl with our familiars. As a result, we bring the cognitive habits of early tribal living to our anonymous urban society. Even when it is irrational, we behave toward strangers as if they will have an opportunity to reciprocate our kindness, and as if our own misbehavior would be detected and reciprocated. The phenomenon is captured by the old joke about the elderly professor who always went to his colleagues' funerals for fear that if he didn't, they wouldn't go to his.

If we still carry the evolutionary baggage of our ancestral environment—if we still follow the simple rule of thumb to start with cooperation and assume defection will be detected—the Big Mistake results. Put differently, "conscience" may be a form of cognitive error, a prosocial glitch in our thinking that prompts us to behave as if we expect to meet people again and as if we believe we are being observed—even when reason should tell us we will not and are not.

This idea can explain why, in experimental gaming, people are remarkably willing to cooperate with strangers, at least initially. People are so willing that many will adopt an unselfish strategy when asked to play a social dilemma game not with another person, but with a *computer*.[24] (Interestingly, people are more willing to cooperate with a straightforward, plastic-box computer than with a "sneaky" computer that poses as a human by speaking with a synthesized voice.)[25] This idea that we are prepared to cooperate with some, but not all, strangers—human or otherwise—provides the foundation for yet another theory to explain the evolution of altruistic cooperation. That theory is partner selection.

PARTNER SELECTION *theory*

When the idea of reciprocal altruism is combined with the idea of the Big Mistake, the result is a plausible explanation for how at least some people might have evolved a capacity to approach strangers with a cooperative attitude. Most of us no longer live in small tribal groups, however. Around the world, hundreds of millions of people now live in anonymous urban environments where they are frequently interacting with strangers whom they will never see again. Under such circumstances, one naturally wonders just how long a mistaken "cooperator" can last.

So we return to the problem first noted by Charles Darwin: even if altruists can somehow be created, how can they survive in a world where they must compete with egoists? Another possible answer lies in the idea of partner selection. The basic insight of partner selection models is that even in a modern urban society, people can exercise a great deal of choice over whom they interact with. If altruists can manage somehow to identify and interact only with other altruists—while excluding or avoiding interactions with egoists—the altruists can capture all the gains of their mutually "nice" behavior without having to tolerate the parasitic burden of the selfish egoists. This will be true not only in environments where small groups of people interact with each other on a daily basis, but in larger communities as well. All that is needed is some mechanism for altruistic "cooperators" to distinguish themselves from egoistic "defectors."

The idea that altruistic cooperators need a way to identify each other has given rise to an idea, suggested early on by William Hamilton[26] and expanded upon by Richard Dawkins,[27] called the "green beard effect." If the genes that allow for altruistic behavior are genetically linked to some other, more easily observed trait—like a so-called green beard—altruists will thrive because they will be able to identify and deal only with other green-bearded altruists, while shunning egoists and leaving them to deal, in an unpleasant and Hobbesian fashion, only with each other.

Of course, literal green beards are rare among humans and typically accomplished with chemical intervention. Nevertheless, there may be other observable human traits that signal a relatively altruistic nature with some reliability. Economist Robert Frank argues that one sign of a relatively prosocial person is a tendency to blush involuntarily whenever one is ashamed of oneself (for example, after telling a lie). On first inspection, a tendency to reveal one's guilt by blushing would seem disadvantageous. Yet it may allow prosocial, blushing altruists to find and interact with each other while avoiding coldhearted, nonblushing egoists.[28]

However we accomplish the task, most of us are indeed capable, to at least some extent, of sorting the prosocial wheat from the egoistic chaff, whether by body language, fleeting facial expressions, or some other cue. Indirect evidence of this ability can be found in a rare genetic condition, Williams-Beuren Syndrome (WS), where this ability is missing. Patients with WS display an indiscriminate friendliness and utter lack of social inhibition when dealing with strangers. Experimental fMRI studies of subjects with WS find differences in a region of the brain called the amygdala.[29] Other studies of patients who have suffered amydgala damage have found a similarly impaired ability to judge the approachability and trustworthiness of strangers.[30] This suggests the amygdala plays a role in helping us select trustworthy, cooperative partners.

Of course, once prosocial cooperators evolve the ability to identify each other, whether with green beards, blushes, or their amygdalas, we can expect that some selfish defectors may evolve the ability to simulate the cooperators. In other words, just as the cooperators evolve to distinguish themselves from the cheaters, the cheaters should evolve to better imitate the cooperators. The result is an evolutionary "arms race" in which both cooperators and defectors are constantly morphing in response to the other. The outcome is an equilibrium in which most people are altruists, but cheating egoists (Ponzi-schemer Bernie Madoff comes to mind) can never be eliminated entirely, only held down to an acceptably small proportion of the population. This picture comports nicely with the idea, discussed earlier, that a small percentage of the population consists of psychopaths who survive by preying on the rest of us—in Jeffrey Dahmer's case, literally.

GROUP LEVEL SELECTION

Kin selection, reciprocal altruism perpetuated by the Big Mistake, and partner selection are all well-accepted theories developed to explain the evolution of cooperative behavior. In recent years, however, two additional theories have been advanced that are more controversial. These two theories are group level selection and sexual selection.

In *The Descent of Man*, Darwin gave an example of group level selection:

> It must not be forgotten that although a high standard of morality gives but a slight or no advantage to each individual man and his children over the other men of the same tribe, yet that an increase in the number of well-endowed men and an advancement in the standard of morality will certainly give an immense advantage to one tribe over another . . . At all times throughout the world tribes have supplanted other tribes; and as morality is one important element in their success, the standard of morality and the number of well-endowed men will thus everywhere tend to rise and increase.[31]

In lay terms, group selection relies on the notion that even if altruistic cooperation is not advantageous for the individual organism, a group of organisms that practices altruistic cooperation will do better than another group whose members practice selfishness. As a result, groups made up of purely selfish organisms dwindle and die out, while tribes of unselfish cooperators thrive and grow.

Although superficially appealing, the idea of group level selection fell into disfavor in the 1960s as a result of critiques based on mathematical models that suggested that group level selection was unlikely to be very effective.[32] More recently, however, the idea of group level selection has enjoyed a renaissance, as typified by Elliot Sober and David Sloan Wilson's influential book *Unto Others: The Evolution of Unselfish Behavior*.[33] In particular, two important ideas have played a large role in increasing interest among evolutionary biologists in the idea of group level selection.

The first idea is that of "altruistic punishment." As seen in ultimatum games, unselfish behavior in the lab can take the form not of only altruism, but also spite. Indeed, the urge to punish those we see as overly selfish seems so deeply ingrained in human nature that subjects in experimental games will incur a personal cost not only to punish someone whom they perceive to have wronged themselves, but also to punish someone whom they perceived to have wronged another. A similar, real-life phenomenon has been reported by legal scholar Geoffrey Miller, who has compiled a remarkable database of cases where able-bodied persons intervened to berate or otherwise "punish" drivers who parked illegally in handicapped spaces.[34]

This sort of behavior, often called "third-party punishment" or "altruistic punishment," has been studied extensively by a number of modern theorists, including Ernst Fehr of the University of Zurich. In a wide variety of experiments, Fehr and others have demonstrated that experimental subjects are willing to incur a personal cost to punish another player who has refused to altruistically cooperate with a third party.[35] When people are willing to sacrifice not only to help others but also to punish someone who refuses to help others, *homo economicus* may no longer be at an advantage. When he tries to take advantage of altruists' cooperation, he finds himself punished by all the other altruists in the group. As a result, the phenomenon of spite can shift the evolutionary calculus away from selfishness and toward unselfish behavior.

At the same time, the idea of altruistic punishment seems to move the problem back a step. Why would anyone incur a cost to punish someone who harmed a third party? Doesn't this put the altruistic punishers at an evolutionary disadvantage? (If you berate an able-bodied driver for parking illegally in a handicapped space, the driver might be able-bodied enough to give you a black eye.) Shouldn't altruistic punishment be eliminated in the Darwinian race, just as altruistic cooperation should be eliminated?

Maybe not. As pointed out in a 2001 paper by John Henrich and Robert Boyd, although altruistic punishers suffer some cost when they police against egoists, there is an important asymmetry between altruistic cooperation and altruistic punishment.[36] The cost of altruistic cooperation is always borne entirely by the cooperator. In contrast, the cost of altruistic punishment may be shared by a number of punishers, so that individual cost declines dramatically as the percentage of altruistic punishers in a population increases. This means that, while natural selection tends to disfavor altruistic punishers just as it disfavors altruistic cooperators, its power is far weaker—so weak that group level selection may allow altruistic punishers to prevail. Altruistic punishment "juices" group level selection, making it more effective.

A related argument recently offered in favor of group level selection for altruism is the "culture-gene coevolution" argument.[37] The intuition behind the gene-culture coevolution argument is straightforward. Just as the presence of altruistic punishers can reduce or eliminate the advantages selfish defectors would otherwise enjoy from natural selection, the existence of cultural institutions that punish selfish defectors (as we will discuss in chapter 9, the penal system is one such cultural institution) strengthens group level selection to promote the evolution of altruism toward strangers. Tribes that can maintain cooperation through institutions that punish defectors do better than tribes without such sanctioning institutions.[38] As a result, the old mathematical critiques of group level selection no longer apply, and Darwin's original notion of group level selection may indeed be an important part of the explanation for the evolution of altruism.

COSTLY SIGNALING AND SEXUAL SELECTION

Finally, perhaps the most controversial theory of the evolution of altruism is the "costly signaling hypothesis." When most people think of evolution, they tend to think of natural selection—the tendency for nature to take weaker, more unfit organisms out of the picture through disease, starvation, or predation, while allowing stronger organisms to survive. The image is nature "red in tooth and claw," ruthlessly sorting the strong from the weak so only the strong survive to reproduce and leave descendents.

Yet, in addition to natural selection, theorists since Darwin have understood that there is another mechanism at work: sexual selection. It's not enough that you simply survive. If you want to have descendents, you must also have a way with the ladies (or with the gents, if you are female). This means that evolution favors not only organisms that survive nature's perils, but also organisms that do a good job of appealing to the opposite sex.

And how, exactly, does one appeal to the opposite sex? This question preoccupies not only teenagers but evolutionary biologists. One interesting possibility is that sexual selection favors individuals with "fitness indicators," physical attributes or behaviors that demonstrate you are a better, stronger, "fitter" source of genes than the next guy or gal. And one of the best and most reliable fitness indicators, ironically, is a noticeable handicap.[39]

The classic illustration of this "handicap principle" is the peacock's tail. From the perspective of natural selection, the tail is a serious drawback. Dragging around such a heavy, showy object can only increase the chances that you will be caught and eaten. But from the perspective of sexual selection, a flashy tail may be a tremendous advantage as a fitness indicator if it signals to the peahens that you are such a fine, strong mating partner that you can afford to drag a big tail around and still do just fine. A similar phenomenon may explain some human males' preoccupation with expensive sports cars, or dangerous hobbies like parachuting and rock climbing.

A generous nature may also be a fitness indicator. This argument has been offered to explain meat sharing by successful hunters in primitive societies.[40] The idea is that if you are a successful enough hunter that you can afford to give away large quantities of meat, you must have an especially good set of genes. Of course, costly handicaps only lead to reproductive success when they are observed, suggesting altruistic behavior is more likely when the altruist thinks others (especially others of the opposite sex) are watching. As a result, the costly signaling hypothesis, alone, may not do much to explain altruistic behavior in anonymous one-shot social dilemmas. It may be an important reinforcing factor, however, in explaining altruism in everyday life, where acts of kindness toward strangers may be observed by others in one's community.[41]

CONCLUSION: THREE LESSONS FROM EVOLUTION

Nonexperts often assume that evolutionary pressures tend to stamp out unselfish behaviors. As we have seen, however, evolutionary theorists have come up with not just one, but several, plausible explanations for how altruistic behaviors can evolve in social species. There is no need to choose among these explanations. Each and every theory likely has some validity in at least some circumstances. Family ties, reciprocity, irrational overestimation of the odds good behavior will be rewarded and bad behavior punished (the Big Mistake), partner selection, fear of altruistic third-party punishers or institutional punishment, and the desire to look good to members of the opposite sex, all likely play a role in explaining how humans—and perhaps other social species as well—have evolved something that looks like a conscience.

Whatever explanation seems to apply in any particular case, they all carry at least three important common lessons. The first is that evolution is not, in fact, inconsistent with widespread altruism. To the contrary, the enormous gains that flow from mutual cooperation can create strong evolutionary pressures to favor cooperation over competition. Many biologists believe, for example, that our basic cellular structure is a product of cooperative evolution. The nuclei of our cells contain mitochondria and other specialized "organelles" that may have evolved over a billion years ago from simple single-celled organisms without internal structures that parasitically invaded the membranes of other single-celled organisms. Today, this original parasite-prey relation has changed to one of mutual dependence, as our former parasites have evolved to become indispensable parts of our cells.[42]

A second lesson that can be drawn from evolution is that we should not be surprised if our altruistic behavior often "feels" subjectively selfish. If prosocial behavior is evolutionarily advantageous, it only makes sense to evolve an internalized reward system to promote it. Sex offers an obvious analogy. Although the evolutionary role of sex is procreation, nature has cleverly motivated us to engage in sexual intercourse by making it feel pleasurable. There is considerable evidence that cooperative behavior also produces feelings of subjective happiness and well-being. Subjects who choose to cooperate with each other in a trust game experience a rise in their levels of oxytocin, a hormone associated with maternal attachment and pair bonding in mammals.[43] Similarly, fMRI studies have found that subjects who cooperate with each other in playing a prisoner's dilemma show an increase in activity in their mesolimbic dopamine system, an area described as the brain's "reward circuit."[44] In ultimatum games, subjects who receive "fair" offers of 40 percent or more of the stakes from their proposers report feeling happier than subjects who receive "unfair" offers (less than 20 percent of the stakes), even when the absolute monetary value of the offers is the same.[45]

The third lesson about unselfish prosocial behavior that we can learn from evolutionary theory, however, is perhaps the most useful. Indeed, we shall put this lesson to work in Part Three of this book. In brief, altruistic cooperation tends to occur only with *other members of one's in-group*.

Sociologists have long noted that prosocial behavior tends to be directed only to those with whom one feels some sort of common bond. As sociologist William Sumner put it over a century ago, "[t]he insiders in a we-group are in a relation of peace, order, law, government, and industry, to each other. Their relation to all outsiders, or to others-groups, is one of war and plunder."[46] Evolutionary biology provides theoretical support for this observation. Whatever theory of the evolution of altruism one favors, all predict that altruistic behavior should be confined and not indiscriminate. The "in-group" toward whom one directs one's altruism may be very small (only close family members, according to kin selection) or very large (any human—indeed any entity—whom the Big Mistake leads us to believe might someday reciprocate a favor). But however we define our in-group, our conscience is concerned with the welfare only of those who fall within it.

Once again, the point was made by Darwin:

> The above view of the origin and nature of the moral sense, which tells us what we ought to do, and of the conscience which reproves us if we disobey it, accords well with what we see of the early and undeveloped condition of this faculty in mankind . . . [Moral virtues] are practiced almost exclusively in relation to men of the same tribe; and their opposites are not regarded as crimes in relation to the men of other tribes.[47]

This means we are only likely to see signs of conscience when people are dealing with others whom they believe are, or at least could be, members of their relevant in-group. Experimental gaming confirms this prediction. As noted in chapter 5, in addition to instructions from authority and beliefs about others' behavior and benefits, a fourth social variable that strongly influences other-regarding behavior in the laboratory is social distance. This suggests that conscience can only be expected to come into play when we are dealing with others with whom we feel some common association.

The good news is that our ideas about who belongs in our in-group seem quite flexible. Evolutionary biology again predicts this. Apart from kin selection (which defines the relevant in-group in narrow and fixed genetic terms), each of the theories of the evolution of altruism discussed in this chapter predicts that our notions about who is, or is not, a member of our in-group should be quite plastic. After all, you never know who (or what) might turn out to be a good reciprocator, a trustworthy partner, or an opportunity for a display of generosity that will signal one's fitness to possible sexual partners.

This behavioral plasticity may explain why many subjects choose cooperative behavior in experimental games even when researchers go to great lengths to ensure that the subjects are anonymous and play in conditions that socially isolate them both from each other and from the experimenter. It does not seem implausible that most people most of the time—or certainly most Western undergraduate and graduate students—are predisposed to arrive at the lab assuming that anyone they meet there automatically should be treated as an in-group member whose interests deserve at least some consideration. Only in extraordinary circumstances are we likely to dismiss another human's welfare as utterly irrelevant.

We turn to this hopeful idea next in Part Three, where we examine how our rough model of conscience offers insights into the workings of the law.

PART THREE

CHAPTER SEVEN

MY BROTHER'S KEEPER:
THE ROLE OF UNSELFISHNESS
IN TORT LAW

Am I my brother's keeper?

—*Genesis 4:9*

On a warm July evening in Broward County, Florida, Flor Osterman made a fatal mistake. She agreed to walk with a friend to the local convenience store to buy milk. Osterman, a forty-one-year old nurse, was walking with her friend on the right side of the road in a quiet residential area when she was struck from behind by a speeding car driven by Arnold Dale. Dale, a twenty-six-year-old resident of Pompano Beach, had just left a bar called Durty Kurty's where (Dale later admitted) he had downed several beers. Dale's car struck Osterman with such force that her left leg was severed from her torso and flung more than 90 feet down the road.[1]

Dale's car was seriously damaged in the collision. Nevertheless, he managed to drive home, where he called the police to report his car had "hit something." The Highway Patrol did not get to Dale's apartment for at least two hours. When they arrived, there were additional delays before they found a hospital that could administer a blood alcohol test. When

Dale's blood was finally drawn—more than four hours after he had left Durty Kurty's—he had a blood alcohol level of 0.10 percent. A toxicologist later testified that at the time of the accident, Dale's blood alcohol content was likely between 0.14 and 0.22 percent.[2]

THE PROBLEM OF EXTERNAL COSTS

Osterman's death offers a graphic illustration of how selfish decisions made by one person—in this case, Dale's decision to drive himself home from Durty Kurty's rather than calling a taxi—can have very bad consequences for other people. Economists refer to this as the problem of "external costs." External costs are endemic in modern societies. Tom's selfish decision to drive instead of walking adds to traffic congestion that delays Dick. Dick's selfish decision to mow his yard Sunday morning wakes his sleeping neighbor Harry. Harry's selfish decision to light a cigarette in a restaurant spoils Tom's meal. Nevertheless, Tom drives, Dick mows, and Harry smokes, because inconveniences suffered by others are "external" to their selfish decision-making.[3]

As Adam Smith famously argued, selfish behavior in the marketplace often benefits others, because the desire to acquire money inspires people to produce valuable goods and services others are willing to pay for. Selfishness thus provides "external" benefits. Outside the market, however, selfishness is often a vice rather than a virtue. This is especially true when a selfish desire leads one person to pursue a course of action that poses a grave risk of harm to another's life, limb, or property—for example, to drive drunk, sell tainted food, or negligently rush a surgical operation to get to the golf course more quickly.

How can we discourage people from selfishly creating risks that impose external costs on others? This question lies at the heart of the body of legal doctrine known as tort law. Tort law determines when and how much someone who accidentally injures another's person or property (the "injurer" or "tortfeasor") must pay damages to compensate the person who was injured (the "victim"). In the process, tort law creates material incentives for even the most selfish injurer to think twice before doing something that might harm others.

THE ECONOMIC APPROACH TO TORTS

Because the incentive effects of tort damages are so obvious, tort law has become a favorite subject for law and economics scholars. The economic analysis of tort law starts with two basic assumptions or beliefs. The first is that tort law's primary purpose is to discourage or "deter" accidents by giving potential injurers incentive to act with due care toward others.[4] The following discussion assumes that tort law is indeed mostly about deterrence, although legal scholars of a more philosophical bent sometimes argue that tort law also serves "corrective justice."[5] (Law and economics scholars often sniff at corrective justice arguments—Richard Posner has drily suggested that "[c]haracterization of the negligence standard as moral or moralistic does not advance analysis"[6]—but we shall see later how taking account of conscience offers insight into, and support for, some corrective justice arguments.)

The second basic assumption underlying the economic analysis of tort, and the idea we shall focus most of our attention on, is the familiar assumption that injurers are selfish actors who happily impose external costs on others. In other words, economic analysis of tort, like economic analysis in general, relies on the rational selfishness model. This second assumption, as we shall see, turns out to be in odd tension with the first. If the assumption of rational selfishness is accurate, then for a number of reasons the tort law system should do a pretty dreadful job of deterring negligence. Rather than being premised on the assumption of selfishness, many elements of the tort law system can only be expected to work if most people have a conscience.

Before exploring how tort law seems premised on conscience, however, it's worth spending some time to examine just how deeply economic theory has sunk its roots in the way modern experts think about tort. No better illustration can be found than in the definition of negligence developed in the famous 1947 case—decided decades before economic analysis became fashionable among academics—of *United States v. Carroll Towing Company.*[7]

NEGLIGENCE AND THE B < PL FORMULA

Carroll Towing is a landmark case in American tort law, discussed in virtually every torts casebook and every torts classroom. This is not, sadly, because the facts of the case are particularly interesting. *Carroll Towing* is a convoluted case in admiralty (shipping law) that revolves around the question of which party ought to be legally responsible for the accidental sinking of a flour-laden barge. The barge sank for at least two reasons. First, she broke away from her moorings in New York Harbor and was damaged as a result of the actions of the defendant's tugboat, the *Carroll*. Second, there was no watchman aboard the barge at the time to notice the damage, and as a result, after many hours the vessel took on so much water it sank. Thus, the main issue in the case was whether the owner of the barge was at least partly responsible for its own loss because it failed to ensure that a watchman was aboard the barge to take care of the vessel.

The opinion in *Carroll Towing* was written by Judge Learned Hand, one of the most influential judges of the twentieth century. (Learned's parents produced another venerably named son, Augustus, who also become a respected judge.) According to Learned Hand, whether or not the barge owners were legally responsible for some of the damage to the barge depended on whether their failure to keep a watchman on board amounted to legal negligence. Again according to Hand, the test for negligence was "a function of three variables: (1) the probability that [the barge] will break away; (2) the gravity of the resulting injury, if she does; [and] (3) the burden of adequate precautions."[8]

In other words, Hand defined negligence in terms of a social cost-benefit analysis that compared the probable social cost of an accident to the probable social cost of preventing it. Hand even suggested negligence could be determined by a mathematical formula:

> Possibly it serves to bring this notion into relief to state it in algebraic terms: if the probability [of an accidental injury] be called P; the [cost of the] injury, L; and the burden [of preventing the accidental injury], B; liability depends upon whether B is less than L multiplied by P: i.e., whether $B < PL$.[9]

Learned Hand thus saw negligence in explicitly economic terms, declaring conduct a basis for liability only when it resulted in an accident that imposed greater costs on society (discounted by the probability the accident might never have occurred) than the social costs of preventing the accident. Voilà—a judicial recipe for "incentivizing" selfish tortfeasors to avoid causing "inefficient" accidents.

THE NEED FOR ACCURATE DAMAGES

Hand formula

Hand's $B<PL$ negligence formula illustrates how deeply economic thinking has permeated modern tort analysis: some version of the Hand formula for defining negligence has been endorsed by courts in more than thirty states.[10] At the same time, closer inspection suggests that fundamental aspects of tort doctrine are difficult or impossible to reconcile with the idea that tort law's sole job is to create efficient incentives.

To understand this point, it is important to understand that in order for tort law to discourage purely selfish actors from negligence, it is not enough just to make negligent defendants pay damages. They must pay damages in the *right amount*.[11] When tortfeasors pay too little—if Dale only had to pay $1 for Osterman's death—incentives are too weak. When tortfeasors pay too much—if every driver who causes a fender-bender must pay $1 billion—the tort system "over-deters," leaving people afraid to drive their cars out of their own driveways for fear of causing an accident.

Implicit in Hand's $B<PL$ formula is the requirement that damages be set accurately, so they are neither greater nor less than the actual harm caused. Focusing on the question of damages makes it easier to see how fundamental aspects of tort law are at odds with the claim that most people are purely selfish. This is because, in the vast majority of tort cases, courts routinely set damages too low to deter purely selfish actors from negligently injuring others. But in a small subset

of cases—"punitive damages" cases—courts set damages too high. What can explain this pattern? Tort law, it appears, takes account of conscience.

WHEN DAMAGES ARE TOO LOW: THE PROBLEM OF UNDERENFORCEMENT

Conventional deterrence theory assumes people are purely selfish actors who don't hesitate to impose risks on others. Thus, the only way to get people to follow the Golden Rule and act like their "brother's keeper" is to make negligent tortfeasors pay for each and every penny of damage they cause when they do not. This account fails to address one of the most basic characteristics of the modern tort system. *Tort law does not require negligent tortfeasors to pay for all the damage they cause.*

Many different factors contribute to this pattern of underenforcement. One important factor is that many victims choose not to sue. There are many reasons why victims don't sue, including distaste for the legal system, the desire to avoid stressful and time-consuming litigation, and a stiff-upper-lip approach to dealing with personal setbacks. Many also don't sue because of the "American Rule" for dealing with attorney fees, which requires each party to a lawsuit to pay for his or her own attorney. From a plaintiff's perspective, this means that even if the lawsuit is successful, the victim recovers only a portion of the damages. As tort plaintiffs typically pay their lawyers 25–40 percent of any recovery, when the need to pay attorney fees is added to the inconvenience and stress of litigation, many victims prefer not to pursue legal action at all. One Harvard study reported that fewer than one in eight patients injured by medical malpractice makes a claim.[12] while another study by the RAND Corporation concluded that, apart from auto accidents, only a very small percentage of negligence victims actually make tort claims.[13]

Victims who do sue face other difficulties. To succeed in court, a tort victim must identify who injured her, obtain personal jurisdiction over the defendant, and prove to the court's satisfaction that the defendant was indeed responsible for the victim's loss, in circumstances giving rise to liability. Each requirement presents significant hurdles. The plaintiff may not be able to identify who harmed her. (Dale was only identified as the driver who struck Osterman because he turned himself in to the police.) The plaintiff may not be able to get personal jurisdiction over the defendant. (Dale might have fled to South America.) The plaintiff may not be able to prove the defendant was legally responsible for the harm. (Dale might have argued that Osterman ran into the road, and it was her own negligence that caused the fatal accident.)

Even when the plaintiff can prove liability, a variety of legal doctrines preclude plaintiffs from recovering for some kinds of losses. For example, in states that follow the rule of "contributory negligence," a finding that the plaintiff's carelessness contributed to the accident, no matter in how minor a fashion, defeats any claim for recovery against an admittedly negligent defendant who otherwise would liable.[14] In other states, defendants in deadly accidents are not required to pay for a deceased victim's "nonpecuniary" losses, such as pain or suffering experienced before death, or the lost chance to enjoy more years of living. (Hence the old joke about the lawyer who, upon receiving a call from a panicked client who says he has just run over a pedestrian, advises the client to put the car in reverse and finish the job.) For victims who survive, many states have passed laws that cap the amounts they can recover for nonpecuniary losses. California, for example, limits noneconomic damages in medical negligence cases to no more than $250,000.[15] A surgeon operating on a retiree in California—or anyone else who could not prove lost earnings—can safely assume $250,000 is the maximum she would have to pay for her negligence, no matter how horrific, painful, debilitating, or disfiguring the result.[16]

American tort law almost seems designed to allow tortfeasors to escape paying the full cost of the damage they cause. To make matters worse, tort's incentive effect is undermined further by the common practice of purchasing liability insurance. Insurance against being sued for negligence is readily available, and many people who engage in activities that pose risks to others (drivers, doctors, employers) routinely buy it. The threat of liability for negligence becomes much less of a threat when one knows that, in the event of a lawsuit, the insurance company will foot the bill. And while a negligent insured may lose coverage or have to pay higher premiums in the future, this incentive is indirect at best.

Finally, for many people, the threat of tort liability is nearly eliminated by lack of personal wealth. Dale was unable to pay the more than $1 million judgment the jury entered against him for Osterman's wrongful death, and simply declared bankruptcy.[17] Only the wealthy—doctors, lawyers, CEOs, corporations—typically can afford to pay damages in serious tort cases. Accordingly, it is only the wealthy for whom the tort system should provide significant incentive to avoid harming others.

The inevitable result, if people were purely selfish, would be runaway negligence. Asocial tortfeasors who anticipate they will escape paying for most of the harm resulting from their negligence will impose risks on others with wild abandon. Tort law should be largely ineffective at deterring costly accidents. Routine carelessness, with resulting death and injury, should be the norm.

Yet it is perhaps not too optimistic to suggest that routine negligence is not the norm in twenty-first-century America. Horrific injuries and dramatic accidents are rare enough to be reported in newspapers. Most people, most of the time, exercise at least some care not to harm others, despite the fact that the American tort system provides them with very limited incentive to do so. This idea is supported by case studies in other countries where tort liability has been suddenly removed (for example, Canada's move to a "no-fault" regime for auto accidents, or New Zealand's 1974 decision to abolish all tort liability for personal injuries and replace it with a state compensation scheme). In both cases, studies found that while accident rates rose, the increase was surprisingly modest.[18]

It does not seem to be the threat of tort liability, alone, that keeps most people from harming others. American tort law underenforces, but this has not translated into social chaos and runaway negligence. Later we will return to the question of why. First, let us consider the mirror image of the problem of underenforcement when damages are set too low: the problem of overenforcement and overdeterrence when damages are set too high.

WHEN DAMAGES ARE TOO HIGH: PUNITIVE DAMAGES AND OVERENFORCEMENT

American tort law generally allows tortfeasors to avoid bearing the full cost of their negligence. There is, however, an important exception to this rule: punitive damages cases. Punitive damages are just that—punitive—and require a defendant to pay a victim more in damages than the actual harm the victim suffered as a result of the defendant's negligence. In other words, punitive damages awards deliberately *overcompensate* certain victims.

Why should tort law undercompensate most accident victims, but deliberately overcompensate a select few? The answer rests not with the nature of the victim, but with the nature of the injurer, or more accurately, with the nature of the injurer's conduct. Punitive damages are not awarded to compensate victims, but to punish select injurers for "outrageous" behavior. As a result, punitive damages are only awarded in rare cases where a judge or jury finds a defendant's behavior amounted not to mere negligence, but to "gross negligence," "wanton negligence," "malice," "outrageous conduct," or "reckless indifference" toward the interests of others.[19]

From the get-go, punitive damages challenge the idea of law as price. Why should judges and juries be invited to inflict special punishment on injurers who disregard the rights of others, when *homo economicus* by his very nature thinks only about himself? Indeed, one common legal standard for imposing punitive damages—a finding that the defendant acted with "reckless indifference toward the welfare of others"—could simply be rephrased "the defendant acted as any sensible *homo economicus* would." Why heap special abuse on the head of the injurer who behaves like Holmes' "bad man" if we are all bad men and women—or, at least, if the law assumes we all are?

The idea of punitive damages also poses a challenge to deterrence theory because requiring injurers to pay damages that exceed the victim's losses should result in inefficient "overdeterrence." Consider the notorious decision by a New Mexico jury to award $2.7 million in punitive damages to a woman who was badly burned when she spilled a cup of McDonald's coffee on her lap. (The judge in the case eventually reduced this figure to $480,000.)[20] Suppose that, in the wake of this award, McDonald's, Burger King, Wendy's, and Seven-Eleven all decided to replace their coffee brewing equipment with a new technology that controlled coffee temperatures more effectively but also increased the cost of coffee to $10 a cup and ensured consumers could purchase only tepid brew. Such a result might be undesirable from the perspective both of business establishments that serve coffee, and consumers who buy and drink it.

Not surprisingly, law and economics scholars often criticize punitive damages,[21] questioning their social value.[22] This critique, paired with a public perception that punitive damages awards are "out of control," has encouraged lawmakers to cut back on the availability of punitive damages. Nearly a score of states have imposed caps or ratios on punitive damages awards.[23] The U.S. Supreme Court recently invoked the Due Process Clause to limit punitive damages in a high-profile case surrounding the negligent grounding of the oil tanker *Exxon Valdez* on the shores of Alaska's Prince William Sound.[24]

Nevertheless, punitive damages remain part of American tort law. Meanwhile, in the vast majority of cases, the tort system allows tortfeasors to escape paying for the full consequences of their negligence. These observations pose a challenge to the claim that tort law is designed to deter accidents by imposing carefully calibrated damages awards on selfish injurers.

TORT LAW AND THE ASSUMPTION OF PROSOCIAL BEHAVIOR

One possible answer to the twin puzzles of underenforcement and punitive damages is that tort law does not, in fact, assume that most people are selfish. To the contrary—and in direct rebuke to Oliver Wendell Holmes' "bad man" theory of the law—American tort law assumes most people have a conscience. What's more, it is the "bad man" who acts as if he does not, whom tort singles out for the special condemnation and punishment of punitive damages.

Put differently, tort law recognizes that if most people are passive altruists willing to try to avoid harming others, we can get by with weak external incentives to exercise care because most people have an internal incentive (conscience) to fill the gap. This explains why even when tort liability is eliminated, as when New Zealand eliminated personal injury suits, widespread mayhem does not result. Of course, the three-factor model predicts that people do not *always* consider others' welfare in making decisions. Social context plays an enormously important role in determining when people take account of others' well-being. But when it comes to avoiding harming others, social context in most modern societies strongly favors prosociality. We are taught from an early age not to hurt others or damage their property. We routinely observe those around us taking care to avoid injuring people and even other species ("I Brake for Animals"). The losses others suffer when they are accidently maimed or killed are obvious and dramatic.

Social context ensures that when it comes to accidentally harming others, most people behave more like the considerate Dr. Jekyll than the child-trampling Mr. Hyde. Of course, as we also saw in chapter 5, selfishness still can rear its head when the personal cost of acting unselfishly gets too high. Tort liability can be understood as a kind of safety net to support prosocial behavior in such situations. Absent tort liability, when the personal benefits of acting negligently become large, a potential injurer might be tempted to cut safety corners. Tort law steps in at this point to create a marginal, additional incentive that tips the balance back toward prosocial behavior.

This makes it unnecessary to require injurers to compensate victims for 100 percent of the harm they cause. Making tortfeasors pay for only a portion of the damage they cause gets most people to exercise due care. Meanwhile, underenforcement preserves plaintiffs' incentives to watch out for themselves. (The coffee drinker who can expect to bear part of the loss if she spills hot coffee on herself may be more careful when handling her coffee.)[25]

PROSOCIAL BEHAVIOR AND "CORRECTIVE JUSTICE"

Incorporating conscience into standard deterrence theory offers to close some of the intellectual gap between the law and economics school of tort law and its competitor, corrective justice theory. As the influential tort scholar Gary Schwartz has put it, "There are two major camps of tort scholars. One understands tort liability as an instrument aimed largely at the goal of deterrence. The other looks at tort law as a way of achieving corrective justice between the parties."[26] But if we take account of prosocial behavior, the two camps have more in common than they appear to have on first inspection.

Corrective justice theorists, for example, like to point out that judges instructing juries in negligence cases typically do not instruct jurors to apply the sort of "$B<PL$" cost-benefit analysis judges themselves employ in their opinions. Rather, judges instruct jurors to find negligence if the defendant's conduct failed to measure up to that of the "reasonable person." As Stephen Gilles has observed, this standard would

result in widespread negligence if the "reasonable person" were defined as a purely selfish individual not subject to liability.[27] The reasonable person standard only makes sense when interpreted to mean the reasonable *prosocial* person, who considers costs and benefits to others as well as costs and benefits to himself. This prosocial focus on social costs and benefits instead of individual costs and benefits looks, of course, very much like the standard set by Hand's formula.[28]

Similarly, corrective justice theorists sometimes argue that tort law's primary purpose is not to deter accidents but to restore the "balance of justice" that is upset when one person acts wrongfully by "[r]anking his own welfare as more important than the welfare of others."[29] Corrective justice theorists thus view a tortfeasor's state of mind as important: injuring another is never a good thing, but it becomes "unjust" and grounds for liability only when you injure someone because you view your own goals and desires as more important than their safety. This focus on a tortfeasors' subjective attitude seems pointless to analysts who follow the *homo economicus* model, which recognizes only one possible attitude ("maximize my own material interests"). Once we take account of socially contingent prosociality, however, the idea of using tort law to punish individuals who view their own interests as always trumping others' begins to make economic, as well as moral, sense. It also suggests an answer to the puzzle of punitive damages.[30]

PROSOCIALITY AND PUNITIVE DAMAGES

If people are prosocial, so that most are willing to exercise at least a modicum of care to avoid injuring others even absent material incentives, the tort system can deter negligence reasonably well despite systematic underenforcement. Prosocial-ity means there is no need to make sure that every victim who is injured is able to recover, and recover 100 percent of his loss to boot, to ensure adequate deterrence. Imperfect enforce-ment and limited compensation are good enough.

But what if some people actually fit the *homo economicus* mold? A tort system that systematically underenforces invites psychopaths to wreak havoc. To a purely selfish person, under-enforced tort laws invite routine negligence in the rational expectation that even if others are injured or killed as a result, the defendant will pay only a portion of the damages, and may escape liability entirely.

This is where punitive damages fit in. Punitive damages can be understood as a response to the problem of the rare individual who insists on acting like *homo economicus* even in social situations where context says "take care." This expla-nation fits neatly with the actual legal standard for punitive damages, which requires a finding that the defendant acted with "malice" or "indifference" toward others. Indifference toward others is, of course, Economic Man's only possible mental state. Thus, it is Economic Man for whom punitive damages are intended, and for whom punitive damages are needed to keep him in line and prevent him from system-atically taking advantage of the tort system's tendency toward underenforcement.

And who acts most like Economic Man? As we saw in chap-ter 6, true psychopathy is relatively rare, estimated to afflict only 1–3 percent of the human population. But humans are not the only entities that commit torts. Which raises the ques-tion: how effective should we expect our tort rules to be when they are applied not to humans but to a different sort of legal entity entirely—the corporation?

THE CORPORATION AS PSYCHOPATH

In 2004, a team of Canadian filmmakers released an award-winning documentary entitled *The Corporation*. The film, accompanied by a book of the same title,[31] had the provocative thesis that corporations are hazardous to human health. This is because (according to the filmmakers) corporations ruthlessly pursue profits, always choosing the course of action that brings the greatest financial return without regard to what others may suffer in terms of economic loss, pain, misery, or death. In other words, a business corporation acts like *homo economicus*—or, as *The Corporation* put it, with a formal psychological diagnosis, like "a psychopathic creature" that "can neither recognize nor act upon moral reasons to refrain from harming others."[32]

Newspaper headlines suggest corporations may indeed commit more than their share of asocial acts. They sell leaking breast implants (Dow Corning), tires that lose tread at highway speeds (Firestone), laptop computers that burst into flames (Sony), and cars that mysteriously accelerate, apparently of their own volition (Toyota). They foul the environment by dumping chemicals in rivers (General Electric), crashing oil tankers onto rocky shores (Exxon), and building offshore oil rigs that collapse (BP). They build chemical plants that explode, killing and maiming thousands (Union Carbide).

Still, closer inspection of the realities of corporate law and practice suggest that the claim that corporations are psychopathic is at least overstated. Thanks to the legal doctrine known as the "business judgment rule," corporate law does not in any real sense require a company's directors and officers to ruthlessly maximize profits. To the contrary, managers enjoy a wide range of legal discretion to donate corporate funds to charity, retain employees during economic downturns, spend money designing safer products, refrain from profitable pollution, and obey health, safety, and employment laws even when violations would not be detected. And while marketplace competition can create pressures to cut moral corners, those pressures are not always absolute. A successful firm with market power in its chosen niche—a Ben & Jerry's or Body Shop—has some economic breathing room to follow its corporate "conscience," at least until it gets bought out by a more ruthless and profitable rival.[33]

So there is reason to hesitate before assuming corporations always act like *homo economicus*. But to say that corporations do not always act like *homo economicus* is not the same thing as saying they always act like *homo sapiens*. Corporations may not be psychopaths, but they are not humans, either.

Some might object at this point that it is silly to ascribe either motives or personality disorders to corporations because they are legal fictions—invisible, insensate, and incapable of acting except through human proxies. According to this view, corporations behave much as humans do because they can only act through humans. To the extent law or conscience reins in human misbehavior, they also rein in corporate misbehavior.

THE PROBLEM OF "CORPORATION MAN"

This argument overlooks an important reality. Corporations are legal fictions, but they are also very real social institutions. More specifically, they are very real social contexts. The employee who walks through the front door of the corporate headquarters and takes the elevator upstairs to his office enters a world that provides a powerful mix of social signals about what behavior is expected, what others are doing, and how his actions affect others. That social context alters his behavior. If he does not become as purely self-interested as Economic Man, he may at least behave like his second cousin, Corporation Man. In other words, it is true corporations act only through "their" people. But corporations also influence how "their" people act.

Sometimes the corporate context shifts human behavior in a conscientious direction. Inside the firm, corporations often try to encourage trust, cooperation, and dedication to team goals through inspirational posters, motivational staff meetings, and team-building in its most obvious and hilarious form, the corporate retreat. (Human resources managers seem to have concluded that playing golf, fording rivers, and beating African drums encourage prosocial employee behavior.) When it comes to dealing with those outside the firm, however, the story may be quite different. Especially in large public companies, the corporate environment often channels human behavior in a direction that moves it closer to the psychopathic ideal of the *homo economicus* model. This is because businesses typically employ the familiar social levers of obedience, imitation, and empathy to encourage employees to think primarily about the welfare of those "inside" the corporation (executives, employees), not the well-being of those "outside" it (customers, the community, outside investors).

Beginning with obedience, corporations are hierarchical social environments in which employees are explicitly instructed by those above them in the chain of command. Typically these instructions are some variation on "increase profits." Although corporations may publish mission statements or undertake ad campaigns to portray themselves as socially responsible to the outside world—Anheuser-Busch claims it wants its beer-loving customers to "drink responsibly"—inside the firm, employees are urged to focus on the bottom line.[34] As for imitation, people in corporations spend their days surrounded by other people who are laboring mightily to increase profits, rather than to make the world a better place. Finally, the structure of the typical large corporation, which divides information among many different individuals with specialized responsibilities, is notorious for shielding individual corporate participants from full knowledge of the negative consequences their decisions have on others. One need only recall Kathy Lee Gifford's tearful remorse on learning Wal-Mart had used illegal child labor to produce clothing bearing her designer label, to appreciate how the corporate structure can shield empathic individuals from the harmful effects of their activities.

Some corporations may also act psychopathically due to "selection bias"—that is, due to the unusual types of human personalities they attract and employ. The tobacco industry, for example, creates such obvious risks to others' lives and health that it is difficult to keep the firm's human employees from recognizing the negative social consequences of the business. Tobacco firms may nevertheless staff themselves by hiring unusual individuals who, by nature or nurture, have little interest in others' welfare. (This was the premise of the dark comedy *Thank You For Smoking*, a 2005 film in which Aaron Eckhart played the role of a charming but psychopathic lobbyist for Big Tobacco.) As mentioned in chapter 3, one study has found that students who choose to major in business cooperate less in social dilemma experiments than students who major in psychology.

When we consider the factors of social context and employee selection, it no longer seems either sensible or safe to assume that legal and moral rules that constrain most people from misbehaving will also constrain corporations. To the contrary, even if corporations are not utterly psychopathic, their behavior should still hew more closely to the purely self-interested behavior predicted by the *homo economicus* model than the behavior of a typical, well-socialized *homo sapiens* would.

That observation suggests an intriguing possibility. To make sure the tort law system does a good job of deterring costly accidents, we may need to develop different legal rules for different entities. In particular, we should have different legal rules for natural persons and for corporations.

DIFFERENT LAWS FOR DIFFERENT ENTITIES

Conventional economics generally does not distinguish between the behavior of legal entities and the behavior of real people. This is because conventional economics assumes both act the same way. Both are purely self-interested and seek to maximize material rewards—profits in the case of corporations, personal wealth in the case of people. As a result, the law and economics literature on torts generally does not distinguish between people and corporations in terms of how they respond to legal sanctions. It typically assumes that a single, uniform system of tort rules should apply equally, and be equally effective, for both.[35]

Taking account of the human potential for prosocial behavior offers a different perspective. Most people have an "internal" incentive, in the form of conscience, to take modest care to avoid harming others. Corporations may lack this incentive. Thus, we may want to beef up external incentives for corporations, developing different legal rules for natural persons and for corporations.

One obvious starting point for such a project might be to reexamine the traditional tort pattern of undercompensating victims. Damages rules that undercompensate victims do not necessarily pose a problem when we are dealing with humans, the vast majority of whom tend to act more like Dr. Jekyll than Mr. Hyde when it comes to damaging others' persons and property. For natural persons, partial liability may be enough, when added to the internal sanction of conscience, to motivate most to take care to avoid harming others.

But the same undercompensation pattern may produce too little deterrence when applied to corporations. Corporations lack a conscience to weigh in when deciding whether to harm others for profit. As a result, if they are not required to pay all the costs that flow from their negligence, they will be negligent more often. We may want special damages rules for corporations to ensure they fully compensate victims. Put bluntly, we may want corporate defendants to pay victims more in damages than human defendants must pay.

This is not a Robin Hood proposal designed to redistribute wealth from rich corporations to poor human victims. It is based entirely on concern for economic efficiency, and particularly the need to ensure that conscienceless corporations fully "internalize" the otherwise-external costs they impose on others. Interestingly, there are signs American tort law already is evolving in this direction. Antitrust law, which is applied almost exclusively to corporations and other business entities, requires businesses found liable for antitrust violations to pay "treble damages" calculated at three times the actual harm caused by their anticompetitive activities.[36] The Racketeer Influenced and Corrupt Organizations Act, or RICO (which also, as its name suggests, applies to organizations) similarly provides for treble damages.[37] Such rules can be thought of as a legislative variation on punitive damages designed to deter business organizations from routinely exploiting the reality that many victims do not sue. From a defendant corporation's perspective, treble damages raise the "P" and the "L" in Learned Hand's $B<PL$ formula in a fashion that counteracts the reduction in "P" and "L" resulting from other aspects of the tort system that favor underenforcement.

To someone who believes people and corporations both self-interestedly maximize wealth, treble damages rules that require misbehaving corporations to pay larger damages for the same injury than a human defendant would pay may seem nonsensical. To someone willing to acknowledge a behavioral difference between the two types of entities, however, having different rules for corporations and natural persons not only makes sense—it may be essential for tort law to deter costly accidents.

CONCLUSION: TORT LAW'S PROSOCIAL FOUNDATIONS

Tort law has always provided a comfortable home for law and economics, in large part because tort rules serve such an obvious economic function. Whether or not it is "just," it is generally efficient to deter drunk driving, medical malpractice, and sales of tainted food.

At the same time, the rules of tort law present a variety of puzzles for the idea of "law as price." If tort law's goal is deterrence, for example, how can the system work when so many aspects of the tort law either discourage victims from suing, or limit the damages that defendants pay when victims do sue? If tort law is based on the assumption of selfishness, why impose punitive damages on defendants who show indifference to others?

By taking account of conscience and the three-factor model, we can find answers to these legal puzzles. In modern societies, social context encourages us not to destroy others' persons and property. This means that, despite incomplete enforcement and limited damages, underenforced tort law provides sufficient additional incentive to discourage most people from negligently injuring others, because most already have internal incentive in the form of conscience. The additional threat of tort liability is only icing on the prosocial behavior cake. Punitive damages address the rare situation where the cake seems to be missing, reserving special punishment for the defendant who, despite social context, shows callous indifference to others.

Paying attention to conscience can not only help us understand the tort system better; it may also guide us in improving that system. In particular, human beings have evolved a capacity for prosocial behavior only after hundreds of thousands or even millions of years of living in social groups under circumstances where cooperation often proved advantageous. There is no reason to assume corporations, which have been around for only a few centuries, have evolved the same capacity. Indeed, it would be a shocking coincidence, beyond all laws of probability, if they had. If we want to make our tort law system as effective as possible at preventing costly accidents, we should recognize this reality.

CHAPTER EIGHT

PICKING PROSOCIAL PARTNERS: THE STORY OF RELATIONAL CONTRACT

> Covenants, without the Sword, are but Words, and of no
> strength to secure a man at all.
>
> —*Thomas Hobbes*

Lynn Joy was a business consultant. In 1996, she was hired by
the Chicago office of the Hay Group, an international management consulting firm. By 2001, Joy was earning an annual
base salary of $210,000. By 2002, she was fired.[1]

According to the Hay Group, Joy was fired because she
failed to meet her annual quota in client billings. Hay
claimed this meant Joy's employment had been terminated
for cause. The meaning of the word "cause" was important,
because Joy's employment contract with Hay provided that
if she were terminated without cause she was entitled to one
year's salary in severance pay. In Hay's view, Joy's failure to
meet her billing quota was cause, and she was not entitled to
the $210,000 severance provided by her contract. Joy sued for
breach of contract. Her case found its way to the U.S. Court
of Appeals for the Seventh Circuit and the desk of Judge Richard A. Posner.[2]

THE BENEFITS OF SELFISHNESS IN
MARKET EXCHANGE

Even more than in tort law, the rational selfishness model of behavior dominates how most contemporary experts think and write about contracts.[3] On first inspection this seems quite sensible. Even if some social contexts trigger unselfish behavior, market exchange is one context where we expect people to look out for themselves. As lawyers and judges put it, most people buying and selling cars, wheat futures, and six-packs of Coca Cola are dealing with each "at arm's length." Conscience is irrelevant: selfishness is appropriate and expected.

Moreover, selfish exchange usually produces a happy outcome for both parties. When a speeding driver runs over a pedestrian, loss and injury to the pedestrian result. But when two people selfishly trade some combination of goods, services, and money with each other, the trade usually leaves both better off. This was, of course, exactly the point the Scottish economist Adam Smith sought to make with his famous parable of the market's "Invisible Hand":

> It is only for the sake of profit that any man employs capital in the support of industry; and he will always, therefore, endeavor to employ it in that industry of which the produce is likely to be of the greatest value, or to exchange for the greatest quantity of money or of other goods . . . he intends only his own gain, and he is in this, as in many other cases, led by an invisible hand to promote an end which was no part of his intention . . . By pursuing his

own interest he frequently promotes that of the society more effectually than when he really intends to promote it.[4]

HOW CONTRACT LAW PROMOTES MUTUALLY BENEFICIAL EXCHANGE

Which brings us to the role contract law plays in promoting the exchange of goods and services. People do not need a contract for every exchange; no one needs a formal contract to buy a loaf of bread. You give the baker your money, and the baker gives you the bread.

Contracts become useful, however, when parties want to arrange an exchange that requires one or both to promise to do something in the future. Consider the risks involved in buying goods from a mail-order catalog or making a loan. Without an enforceable contract, the goods that arrive in the mail might look completely different from those shown in the catalog (if the goods arrive at all), and the loan might never be repaid. Knowing this, many people would be reluctant to buy goods from catalogs or make loans. Many mutually beneficial exchanges that rely on promise might not take place, leaving us collectively and individually worse off.

Contracts make exchanges based on promise safer and more attractive. Economic theory predicts, however, that this only works when the contracts are actually enforced. Someone or something must make sure contract promises are kept, by force if necessary. As Thomas Hobbes described the problem in 1651 in *Leviathan,* "Covenants, without the Sword, are but Words, and of no strength to secure a man at all."[5]

In the modern world, the threat that a court will make you pay damages for breach of contract is the "sword" that motivates selfish individuals to keep contract covenants they would prefer not to keep. This understanding of contract law's purpose makes the *homo economicus* model of self-interested behavior seem, on first inspection, both an accurate and an appealing way to analyze contract law. Even if people are not always motivated by self-interest, they tend to be motivated by self-interest when they exchange goods and services. What's more, enforcing the promises made in self-interested exchanges generally benefits both exchanging parties. So, why not assume rational selfishness in contract law? Why bother worrying about conscience?

THE PROBLEM OF INCOMPLETE CONTRACTS

In fact, the *homo economicus* model may be all we need to analyze simple "discrete" contracts, like a contract to purchase one hundred boxes of nails. Just as in tort, however, closer inspection reveals important areas where conscience plays an essential role in explaining how contract really works.

This is most obvious when we consider what legal scholars call "incomplete" contracts: contracts that fail to address some potential issue or dispute that may arise between the parties. Even the most lengthy and detailed contract cannot address absolutely every question that might arise during the course of performing some exchanges. For example, a contract between a homeowner and a building contractor to remodel a kitchen is likely to discuss the scope of the work to be performed, the color and type of materials to be used, and the price to be paid for the work. It is unlikely, however, to discuss what should happen if the house burns to the ground in the middle of the

contracts / incompleteness

remodel, or if extensive termite damage is discovered. Similarly, Joy's employment contract specified a severance package if she were fired without cause. The contract did not address, however, whether failing to meet a billing quota amounted to "cause."

Contracts are incomplete for a number of good reasons. One is that humans aren't omniscient. As contracts scholar Mel Eisenberg has put it, "contracts concern the future, and are therefore always made under conditions of uncertainty."[6] Problems can arise while performing a contract that neither party thought of, much less discussed in the contract.

Complexity also leads to incompleteness, because complexity makes negotiating and drafting contracts expensive. Suppose the homeowner and contractor could somehow anticipate every issue that might arise in the course of remodeling the kitchen, from a defect in a batch of paint to nationwide quarantine due to a flu pandemic. A formal contract that addressed each and every possible contingency would be prohibitively expensive and time-consuming to draft, and probably too heavy to carry. Rather than try to draft a complete contract, the parties might reasonably content themselves with a short, incomplete contract that addresses only the most important and obvious aspects of their proposed exchange and leaves other matters to be dealt with in the future should they arise.

Finally, contracts can be incomplete because they deal with matters that, while important to the parties, are difficult to "verify," meaning they are difficult to prove in court. For example, suppose the contract between the homeowner and the contractor includes a clause specifying that the cabinetry work in the kitchen should be of "high quality." As long as the workmanship is not obviously defective, it might be prohibitively expensive and even impossible for the homeowner to demonstrate the quality of the cabinetry work to a judge. This means that, as a practical matter, the "high quality" clause is not enforceable, and possibly not worth including in the contract. A judge might conclude the cabinetry work is high quality, or she might not: neither side can be sure.

THE UBIQUITY OF INCOMPLETE CONTRACTS

Because uncertainty, complexity, and unverifiability are endemic, incomplete contracts are everywhere. Even a relatively simple contract—say, to buy a car—contains gaps. (What if the car does not get as good gas mileage as advertised?) In the words of influential law and economics scholar Steven Shavell, "[c]ontracts typically omit all manner of variables and contingencies that are of potential relevance to the contracting parties."[7] Contracts scholar Robert Scott goes further: "[a]ll contracts are incomplete."[8]

But to paraphrase George Orwell, some contracts are more incomplete than others. Legal experts describe contracts as falling along a spectrum of completeness.[9] At one end lie "discrete" contracts—simple, easily described, nearly complete contracts for exchanges between parties who never expect to deal with each other again. A contract to purchase a used car is an example of a discrete contract. At the other end of the spectrum lies "relational" contracts that involve complex, long-term, uncertain exchanges—for example, a contract to construct a commercial office building, or to code specialized software for a new business venture, or to employ a management consultant like Lynn Joy.

Because, of course, an incomplete relational contract was exactly what Judge Posner had to deal with in *Joy v. Hay Group*. Joy's employment contract did not define the important term "cause." As a result, Posner noted, the "precise meaning that the word bears in the contract cannot be determined just from reading the contract. . . . [t]he present case is not one in which the written contract appears to have a clear meaning."[10] Joy's employment contract, although it involved an exchange of great economic significance to the parties, was incomplete.

This incompleteness is especially striking because Joy's consulting expertise lay in the field of executive compensation. As Posner drily observed in ruling that Joy was entitled to a trial, "[i]t is a considerable irony that a firm that is in the business of consulting on executive compensation failed to draft a contract that clearly specified the compensation rights of one of its own executives."[11]

The incompleteness of Joy's contract may have been ironic, but it was hardly uncommon or unpredictable. Drastic incompleteness is a hallmark of most relational contracts. An empirical study of the employment contracts of Fortune 500 CEOs, for example, found that nearly a third had no written employment contract at all, and another third had only bare-bones contracts that spelled out their pay but very few of their duties.[12] This is typical of relational contracting. A relational contract will often do little more than touch on the most obvious and important issues likely to arise as the exchange goes forward, leaving all else to be decided by mutual agreement between the parties as the relationship unfolds. As Robert Scott describes it, these contracts "appear to be 'deliberately' incomplete."[13]

COURTS AS INCOMPETENT ENFORCERS OF RELATIONAL CONTRACTS

Relational contracts pose serious enforcement problems for courts. How can a judge enforce contract "terms" the parties never actually agreed upon?[14] In the words of legal scholar Eric Posner (Judge Richard Posner's son), parties to relational contracts "lack the clairvoyance needed to give courts proper guidance if a dispute arises, and courts lack the genius that would be needed to enforce contracts properly in the absence of such guidance."[15] Just as uncertainty, complexity, and unverifiability defeat the contracting parties' ability to draft a complete contract ex ante, they defeat a court's ability to figure out the best way to settle disputes over incompleteness ex post.

This means courts often "resolve" relational contracts disputes—say, between two business partners over a failed venture, or between a building contractor and a homeowner over construction delays—in much the same way flipping a coin "resolves" the dispute. Although the court will certainly reach a decision, the parties cannot anticipate what the decision will be, or which side it will favor. To quote Eric Posner again, courts can be "*radically incompetent* when it comes to meeting the demands placed on them by relational contracts."[16]

Litigation in relational contract cases accordingly often resembles the medieval practice of trial by combat described in Sir Walter Scott's romance *Ivanhoe*. When the Templar knight Brian de Bois-Guilbert accuses the beautiful jewess Rebecca of the crime of sorcery—in particular, of enchanting de Bois-Guilbert into a most un-Christian lust—the question of Rebecca's guilt is determined not by a judge or jury, but by a joust between Bois-Guilbert and Rebecca's armored champion Ivanhoe. Ivanhoe wins the joust, and Rebecca wins the case.[18] Litigants in modern relational contract disputes—business disagreements, employment disputes, landlord-tenant cases, service contract disputes—use lawyers rather than knights to fight their battles. As in trial by combat, however, the outcome of the engagement is unpredictable, and often depends more on the skill and aggressiveness of one's champion than the merits of one's claims.

THE PUZZLE OF RELATIONAL CONTRACTING
WITHOUT ENFORCEMENT

Relational contracts accordingly pose a challenge to the claim that contract law's primary function is to allow selfish actors to commit themselves to perform their promises. Courts can enforce the explicit terms found in simple, discrete contracts. But they cannot be counted on to enforce the nonexistence "terms" that are found, if they can be said to be found at all, only in the enormous gaps left in relational contracts. Indeed, it may be only a slight exaggeration to say the primary consequence of a formal contract in a relational exchange is that each of the parties has the ability to make the other miserable by dragging them into court.

This observation raises the question of how relational exchanges work. Purely selfish actors will exploit the large gaps in relational contracts and refuse to perform their promises, because they calculate the odds a court will punish their misbehavior are less than 100 percent and perhaps as low as 50 percent. The risk of being punished is reduced further by the possibility that the victim, recognizing that a lawsuit would be expensive and might not succeed, might not to sue. Thus, a purely selfish building contractor, for example, might hire unskilled workers, use inferior materials, cut permitting corners, or even demolish the homeowner's kitchen and then claim that it cannot be rebuilt except at twice the agreed-upon price, calculating that the homeowner would not be able to sue her successfully.

Anticipating this, purely selfish actors would avoid relational exchanges with other purely selfish actors. Yet real people do enter incomplete relational contracts. In fact, many of

[handwritten marginalia]: faulty contractors/chancery court

the most economically important exchanges in modern life—long-term supply contracts, joint business ventures, apartment leases, building contracts, employment agreements, service contracts—involve relational contracts.' Somehow, despite the infirmities of courts and judges, people feel it is safe to engage in relational exchanges—at least, safe enough relational exchanges take place. What's more, many contracts employed in relational exchanges are not only incomplete, they seem more incomplete than they really need to be. Joy and the Hay Group, as professional management consultants specializing in executive compensation, were capable of drafting a contract that would have given Judge Posner more guidance on what exactly constituted "cause" sufficient to forfeit Joy's claim to severance. Instead, they opted for a bare-bones contract—why?

THE LIMITED POWER OF REPUTATION

Contract experts sometimes argue that opportunistic behavior in contracting is deterred not by fear of the legal system, but by fear of loss of reputation. In particular (the reputational argument goes), when people are "repeat players" in a business, even purely selfish actors will hesitate to exploit the yawning gaps in relational contracts if word of their misbehavior might get around to future customers and suppliers. As the famed economist Oliver Williamson has put it (with the typical economist's dramatic flair), "reputation effects attenuate incentives to behave opportunistically in interfirm trade—since the immediate gains from opportunism in a regime where reputation counts must be traded off against future costs."[19]

Concern for reputation may indeed discourage corporations and other large, long-lived business entities from opportunis-

Young is old reputation costs [handwritten marginalia]

tic behavior in markets where they repeatedly do business. The strength of reputation to hold opportunism in check is more questionable, however, when dealing with shorter-lived humans. When you're getting started in a career or business, for example, you can't rely on reputation to reassure others it's safe to deal with you. Nevertheless, newly minted lawyers somehow get their first clients, budding business executives get their first salaried positions, and novice doctors find their first patients. At the other end of a career, reputation becomes an increasingly unreliable guarantee as one nears retirement, when the potential cost of a reputational hit decreases dramatically. Aging doctors should neglect their patients.

Another problem with relying on reputational concerns to motivate contract compliance arises from the difficulty outside observers have determining which party was at fault when a relational deal breaks down. If Joy claimed she failed to meet her client quota because the Hay Group had done a poor job of advertizing her services, it would be difficult for an outsider to determine which side's reputation should be tarnished. Finally, if reputational concerns suffice to explain how relational exchange can work despite judicial incompetence, why do people entering relational exchanges need formal contracts at all?

RELATIONAL CONTRACTS AND THE JEKYLL/HYDE SYNDROME

There is reason to doubt that reputation can always, or even often, motivate purely selfish actors to keep their promises in relational exchanges. As Oliver Williamson has conceded, "the efficacy of reputation effects is easily overstated."[20] Nor, as we have seen, can parties to relational contracts rely on the court system to enforce their covenants. How, then, can *homo economicus* participate successfully in relational exchange?

Perhaps *homo economicus* can't—at least, not with another *homo economicus*. So let us consider another possibility. Contract law may do a lousy job of encouraging relational exchange between purely selfish parties. It may do a pretty good job, however, of encouraging relational exchange between *prosocial* partners. Although conventional economic theory holds that contract law encourages exchange by allowing self-interested actors to commit themselves to perform their promises, the true story of relational contract may be just the opposite—not a tale of self-interest, but a tale of prosocial partners who trust each other and, to at least some extent, unselfishly look out for each other's welfare.

The key to understanding this idea is to understand that, when two people contemplate entering a relational contract, each wants protection against the possibility the other might try to take opportunistic advantage of the many gaps that necessarily exist in the contract. Courts can't reliably fill the gaps, because uncertainty, complexity, and unverifiability leave them "radically incompetent." Reputational concerns sometimes can check opportunistic behavior, but reputation alone often is not enough. So parties entering relational contracts may often be forced to rely on a third, alternative check on opportunistic behavior—their contracting partner's conscience.

Suppose, for example, some unanticipated problem or opportunity arises while two parties are performing a contract. Two selfish parties who ruthlessly seek to turn every situation to their own advantage will instantly find themselves locked in conflict, because each will want to foist the entirety of any loss from changed circumstances on the other, while

claiming the entirety of any possible gain. In contrast, prosocial contract partners willing to consider each other's welfare
can work out a resolution far more easily—say, by splitting
the unanticipated gain or loss—because they share, to at least
some extent, the common goal of promoting their mutual (not
merely individual) welfare. Nor do prosocial partners need to
reduce every detail of their bargain to writing. They trust each
other to focus on promoting their mutual welfare, rather than
on selfishly searching for loopholes. Finally, even when some
aspect of performance is unobservable or unverifiable, a contract partner who cares about her counterparty's well-being
will try to perform.

Put simply, one of the implicit "terms" of a relational contract is an agreement each party will suppress her Mr. Hyde
persona and adopt a Jekyll-esque attitude toward her contract
partner, taking account of her partner's welfare as well as her
own in making decisions about how to perform. This idea
echoes arguments that have been advanced by contract scholars from the law and society school critiquing the individual-
istic law and economics approach. Ian Macneil, for example,
has argued it is impossible to understand relational contracts
by focusing only on the formal terms negotiated by the parties. Rather, Macneil argues, a relational contract is just that—
a relationship—characterized by (among other attributes)
"role integrity," "flexibility," and "reciprocity."[21]

This is not too far from saying that the hallmark of a relational contract is that both parties perceive the contract as a
social situation that calls for at least some degree of unselfish behavior. The spectrum from simple discrete contracts to
complex, incomplete relational contracts can be recharacter-
ized as spectrum from Hydish behavior toward one's part-

ner to Jekyllish behavior. This approach offers a number of insights into the questions of how relational exchanges really work, and how contract law and contract lawyers can make them work better.

THE IMPORTANCE OF PARTNER SELECTION

One of the most important lessons about relational contracts that can be gleaned from the empirical evidence on prosocial behavior is that the key to a successful relational contract may be picking the right contract partner. Two members of the species *homo economicus* would refuse to enter a relational contract with each other, because they would each anticipate the other will, absent adequate judicial or reputational sanction, take opportunistic advantage of the contract's incompleteness. Similarly, a prosocial individual should refuse to enter a relational exchange with a recognizably selfish partner, because the selfish actor will only take advantage of the prosocial partner's cooperative tendencies. No loving parent would advise his child to enter an important relational contract—whether for employment, a business partnership, or a marriage—with *homo economicus*.

If, however, two prosocial individuals can somehow identify and negotiate a relational contract with each other, they can each look forward to what is likely to prove a mutually beneficial exchange. Thus, the first step in any relational exchange is finding an appropriately prosocial exchange partner. (Even Chicago School scholar Richard Epstein advises that sensible people "pick [their] partners first and worry about the contract later, not the other way around.")[22] But observing that partner selection is essential to relational contracting naturally raises the question: how does one identify a counterparty willing to temper self-interest?

As we saw in chapter 6, a small percentage of the population seems incapable of acting unselfishly, even when the social situation clearly calls for prosocial behavior. No sensible person would knowingly arrange an important relational exchange with such a psychopath. Psychopaths, however, rarely advertise their asocial tendencies.

A weaker version of the same problem is posed if nonpsychopathic individuals differ in their predispositions to cooperate. Although most people seem capable of prosocial behavior in social situations that clearly call for it, some social situations are ambiguous. A contract can be an ambiguous social situation, because purely self-interested behavior is socially acceptable in discrete contracting, and where a particular contract falls along the spectrum from "discrete" to "relational" is not always clear. As a result, there is an enormous advantage in relational exchange to choosing a partner who tends to view even ambiguous social situations as calling for cooperative behavior. But how to identify such a partner?

Chapter 6 explored how the problem of partner selection has captured the attention of evolutionary biologists, who have suggested as one solution the "green beard effect": altruists may be able to identify other altruists because altruism is genetically linked to a more easily observed trait, like a tendency to blush when caught telling a lie. Interestingly, one type of "green beard" that seems to identify prosocial tendencies is a willingness to assume *others* are prosocial. Empirical studies have repeatedly found that a greater willingness to make oneself vulnerable to others—that is, a greater willingness to trust—is statistically associated with a greater willingness to refrain from exploiting others—that is, a greater willingness to behave trustworthily.[23]

Being willing to trust accordingly can signal one's own trustworthiness. Conversely, distrusting others "outs" the relatively selfish and untrustworthy, allowing the prosocial to either avoid dealing with them, or to demand relatively complete and enforceable contracts when they do.

THE IMPORTANCE OF SOCIAL FRAMING, WITH A NOTE ON HOW LAWYERS CAN ALLEVIATE "CROWDING"

Showing a willingness to trust one's contract partner can do more, however, than simply signal one's own capacity for prosocial behavior. In addition to suggesting an inherently trustworthy nature, a willingness to make oneself vulnerable in an incomplete contract may also be an important sign of how one views the social context created by the particular contract in question.

Chapter 5 discussed how even people predisposed to behave prosocially default to self-interest in social contexts where selfishness seems appropriate. Contracting, of course, can be an ambiguous social context. Is the contract in question a discrete contract where selfish behavior is appropriate and expected? Or is it a relational contract calling for trust, cooperation, and mutual regard for each other's interests? In extreme cases (buying a used car versus negotiating a prenuptial agreement) the distinction is clear. In other cases—say, an employment contract—the contract may have both discrete and relational elements.

In an ambiguous contracting situation, the individual who hopes to rely on her contract partner's conscience must make it as clear as possible that the situation is indeed one that calls for mutually considerate rather than arm's-length behavior. To some extent this can be done explicitly. But verbal reassurances about one's own fidelity and good intentions are, as economists say, "cheap talk." Actions speak louder than words. And what messages, exactly, do one's actions send about the nature of a contractual relationship when one shows up with a lawyer and an inch-thick contract larded with fine print?

This "signaling" problem has long been understood by family lawyers, who find that couples planning to marry often avoid prenuptial agreements not because they are confident they won't divorce, but because they feel that asking for a prenuptial agreement shows a lack of trust that could poison the marriage.[24] Experimental gaming supports these couples' reluctance. As we have seen, one of the most important social cues for prosocial behavior in experimental games is whether the subjects believe that others are, or would, behave prosocially in the same game. The bride or groom who asks for a "prenup" is inevitably signaling that she or he views the marriage relationship as somewhat arm's-length, a stance that invites the fiancé to adopt a similarly self-interested posture.

This possibility is an example of the phenomenon social scientists call "crowding out" or "motivational crowding."[25] The basic idea is that if we treat a contract partner as purely self-interested, we signal that we believe the social context is one where selfishness is appropriate and expected. This signal raises the odds our partner will in fact behave self-interestedly. In one classic study of motivational crowding, researchers studied ten day-care centers where parents occasionally arrived late to pick up their children, forcing the teachers to stay after closing time. The researchers convinced

daycare example

six of the centers to introduce a new policy of fining the parents who arrived late. The result? The number of late arrivals increased significantly.[26]

From an economic perspective, these results seem bizarre. How can raising the cost of an activity prompt people to "buy" more of it? The answer, according to crowding out theory, is that by changing the social context to look more like a market, fining parents who arrived late decreased the "psychic cost" of arriving late, signaling that lateness was not a selfish social faux pas but a market decision parents were free to make without worrying about the teachers' welfare. By emphasizing external material incentives, the day-care centers crowded out "internal" incentives like guilt and empathy.

The desire to avoid crowding out prosocial motivations may explain the odd phenomenon, noted earlier, of relational contracts that seem even more incomplete than the parties need them to be. Joy and the Hay Group, as experts in executive compensation, had the knowledge and experience necessary to recognize that the definition of "cause" was an important element of their contract. Nevertheless, they refrained from defining it. It does not seem unlikely that they did so out of concern that showing too great an interest in spelling out the exact meaning of "cause" would signal, on Hay's part, an unseemly interest in being able to discharge Joy, and on Joy's part, an unseemly interest in being able to avoid being discharged.

This perspective also reveals that, however much individuals negotiating relational contracts may complain that involving lawyers obstructs the process, lawyers can play an essential role in smoothing the path toward a successful relational exchange. This is because lawyers are valuable scapegoats when one party to a relational contract wants to spell out some term or condition in greater detail. "It's not that I don't trust you," says the landlord to the tenant, or the prenuptial-seeking bride to her groom, "and it's not that I think anything will go wrong. But my lawyer says I have to do this."

Blaming lawyers this way allows parties to relational contracts to accomplish something extremely valuable: they can communicate to each other their specific hopes and expectations for the relationship—exchanging information that can prevent them from mistakenly embarking upon a relational exchange that doesn't really serve both parties' needs—without undermining their mutual expectations for a trusting, prosocial interaction. Meanwhile, the lawyers get something of value as well (their fees). Adam's Smith invisible hand can work its wonders in the market for legal services just as it can in other markets.

HOW RADICALLY INCOMPETENT COURTS CAN HELP: THE ROLE OF JUDICIAL EXHORTATION

So far we have looked at the question of how prosocial exchange partners can use conscience to rein in opportunistic behavior from a perspective that assumes courts are, to use Eric Posner's striking phrase, "radically incompetent" at enforcing relational contracts. This naturally raises the question of why the parties to relational exchanges bother to involve the legal system by using formal contracts at all. Part of the answer, obviously, is that there may be aspects of even a highly relational exchange that remain relatively discrete, and can be easily reduced to writing by the parties and enforced by the courts. But courts can play another useful role as well, one that has nothing to do with their ability (or lack thereof) to create reliable material incentives for performance.

In particular, instructions from authority are another social cue that plays a powerful role in triggering prosocial behavior in experimental games. Courts and judges are nothing if not sources of authority. This suggests judges can encourage parties to relational contracts to act prosocially through the simple and remarkably cheap expedient of *telling them that's what they ought to do.*

This idea echoes a modern strain of legal scholarship that argues that, in addition to providing incentives, law can also serve an "expressive" function and change human behavior simply by sending authoritative messages about what sorts of values and behaviors are appropriate.[27] According to expressive law theorists, when lawmakers make public statements in judicial opinions and in statutes about what type of conduct is proper and expected, people will try to conform to these authority-articulated norms of behavior even in the absence of material punishments and rewards. Expressive law theory is usually applied to criminal law, or to constitutional law doctrines like the Equal Protection or Establishment clauses. (Chapter 9 will reexamine the role of expressive theories in criminal law in greater detail.) But law may play an important expressive function in contract cases as well.

In particular, as contracts scholar Erin O'Hara has observed, judges often write in contract cases that implied into every contract is the obligation for each party to act in "good faith."[28] Like the meaning of the word "cause" in Joy's employment contract with Hay Group, the meaning of "good faith" is notably vague. As a result, it can be impossible for contract parties to determine in advance when they will be deemed to have either met, or violated, their good faith obligations. In other words, courts can be radically incompetent at enforcing judicially implied good faith obligations, just as they can be radically incompetent at enforcing other incomplete aspects of relational contracts.

Nevertheless, judicial opinions exhorting contracting parties to act with "good faith" and "honesty in fact" may promote unselfishness in relational exchanges by helping create a social context in which parties to relational contracts feel an internal obligation to behave prosocially toward their partners. As O'Hara puts it, "contract law serves a type of expressive function by communicating to tradesmen that certain standards of decency will be required of their conduct."[29] By simply telling parties to relational contracts they ought to show concern for their partner's welfare, courts can increase the odds they will, without imposing material sanctions.

This observation explains the moralizing language courts often employ in relational contract cases. This pattern has been noted especially by business law scholars describing the "fiduciary" duties imposed on business partners and corporate officers and directors. One of the most interesting things about fiduciary duty cases is that judges often describe a fiduciary position as a kind of contractual commitment to renounce selfishness and treat the beneficiary's interests as more important than one's own. As Justice Cardozo put it in the often-cited case of *Meinhard v. Salmon*, a fiduciary has "put himself in a position in which the thought of self was to be renounced, however hard the abnegation."[30]

At the same time, courts are notoriously reluctant to go beyond moralizing in "duty of care" cases brought against negligent corporate fiduciaries, who are generally protected from liability by a doctrine called the "business judgment rule."[31] Corporate scholar Edward Rock concludes that "we should understand . . . fiduciary duty law as a set of parables or folktales of good and bad managers and directors, tales that collectively describe their normative role."[32] If corporate managers and directors behaved like *homo economicus*, courts could tell endless morality tales of this sort, without ever changing fiduciaries' actual behavior. But if, as the experimental gaming evidence suggests, many people can resist self-interest when instructed to do so by a respected authority, such judicial "expressions" can change behavior even when unaccompanied by material sanctions.

HOW RADICALLY INCOMPETENT COURTS CAN HELP MORE: THE ROLE OF VENGEANCE

By focusing on the possibility that courts can discourage at least some opportunistic behavior in relational contracting by sending authoritative signals about its inappropriateness, we find a partial answer to the question of how "radically incompetent" courts can nevertheless play a useful role in relational contracting. But if helping frame social context is all the courts can do, we are left with the problem of why parties to relational exchanges bother with formal contracts at all. After all, if judges' primary role is simply to exhort the parties to relational contracts to behave themselves, judges can exhort, and parties can listen to their exhortations, without having to actually involve courts in deciding the outcomes of disputes in relational contract cases.

Yet parties do invite radically incompetent courts to decide disputes in relational contract cases, however randomly. Perhaps this simply reflects a mistake on the part of the contracting parties: perhaps, if they were wiser, they would include a clause in their contract providing that any disagreement not explicitly addressed by the contract should be decided by flipping a coin. Flipping a coin is far cheaper than hiring lawyers to engage in months or years of litigation.

Nevertheless, parties to relational contract disputes do choose to end up in court, with results that can resemble the fictional case of Jarndyce and Jarndyce from Charles Dickens' *Bleak House*: endless litigation that drains both sides of time, energy, and money. From an economic perspective, this behavior appears irrationally self-destructive. Litigation in relational contract cases is a negative-sum game rational and selfish parties should refuse to play. Recognizing this, some legal scholars suggest that reputational concerns can explain parties' willingness to engage in negative-sum litigation. Eric Posner, for example, has suggested that even radically incompetent courts can play a useful role in promoting relational exchange if contracting parties can use costly lawsuits to cultivate a reputation for being willing to "punish" faithless contract partners. Even though bringing a lawsuit hurts the nonbreaching party as much as it hurts the breaching party, the nonbreaching party may rationally conclude this cost is worthwhile if it helps the nonbreaching party acquire a reputation for vengefulness that discourages future exchange partners from behaving opportunistically.[33]

Eric Posner's theory is engaging and, in some cases, plausible. But it cannot explain litigation brought by someone who does not expect to be a "repeat player" entering similar relational contracts with others in the future. Something more is going on in these cases. The evidence from experimental gaming sheds light on what that "something" might be.

Ultimatum games demonstrate that unselfish behavior can take the form not only of a willingness to incur a cost to help others, but also a willingness to incur a cost to hurt them.

Spitefulness is not as attractive a personality characteristic as altruism. Nevertheless, as discussed in chapter 4, a willingness to spitefully punish someone who refuses to behave prosocially can have second-order effects that go a long way toward discouraging opportunistic behavior in others. If a party entering a relational contract can credibly signal to her partner her potential for spite, this may discourage the partner from trying to take unfair advantage of the contract's incompleteness, because of the risk the spiteful partner, if crossed, will vengefully file suit despite the personal cost. This basic idea, as Robert Frank has pointed out, offers an evolutionary explanation for spite: a predisposition toward vengefulness is an advantage if it discourages others from "messing" with you.[34]

A belief that one's contract partner might spitefully sue thus can discourage opportunistic breaches of relational contracts even if courts are, to use Eric Posner's phrase, radically incompetent. The prospect of going to court promotes honorable behavior between relational contract partners in much the same way the prospect of a duel is used to promote honorable behavior between aristocrats. Even a psychopath would hesitate to take advantage of a gentleman with a thin skin and an itchy trigger finger.

CONCLUSION: MORE THAN INCENTIVES

Over a century ago, Oliver Wendell Holmes wrote that to the bad man without a conscience, "[t]he duty to keep a contract at common law means a prediction that you must pay damages if you do not keep it,—and nothing else."[35] Many modern experts agree with Holmes' view, and see contract law primarily as an incentive system designed to encourage rational and selfish parties to enter and perform arm's-length exchanges.

This approach can work well for simple discrete contacts. It founders, however, on the rock of relational exchange. In relational contract cases, courts perform their "incentivizing" role only poorly, if at all. The sword of the law is wielded by the shaky hand of a judicial system that seems as likely to strike down the victim as the wrongdoer.

What contribution, then, can contract law make toward encouraging relational exchange? By focusing on the importance of unselfish behavior to successful relational exchange, we can see not only why prosocial partners are willing to make themselves vulnerable to each other in the first place, but also how contract law can encourage them to treat each other well by sending authoritative signals about the appropriateness of good faith and mutually considerate behavior. We can also see how, when things go awry, even incompetent courts can play a useful role by providing relational contract victims with a vehicle for vengeance.

CHAPTER NINE

CRIME, PUNISHMENT, AND COMMUNITY

Obviously crime pays, or there'd be no crime.

–*G. Gordon Liddy*

Robert DiBlasi was an unlucky man. An unemployed father of two, he had a history of depression and drug abuse and also had been diagnosed with AIDS. July 13, 1998, proved an especially unlucky day for DiBlasi. He strolled into a supermarket in Pomona, California, put a $5.69 package of Duracell batteries into his pocket, and picked up a coconut cream pie. DiBlasi then went to a cash register, where he paid for the pie, but not the batteries. DiBlasi was caught, convicted of shoplifting, and sentenced to thirty-one years to life in prison.[1]

CRIMINAL LAW AS PRICE?

DiBlasi's case illustrates how our criminal justice system relies on conscience. To appreciate this counterintuitive claim, it is useful to start with a question: Why did the State of California send DiBlasi to jail, for what was likely to prove the rest of his life, for stealing a package of batteries worth only $5.69?

DiBlasi's sentence should puzzle any good economist, because economists view criminal law, as they view all law, as a system of incentives. (As the best-selling economist Steven Levitt puts it, "criminals, like everyone else, respond to incentives.")[2] According to this view, just as tort liability deters costly accidents by making tortfeasors pay damages, criminal law deters by making criminals "pay" for costly crimes with time in jail. Nobel Prize winner Gary Becker nicely captured this idea when he said criminal punishment can be "considered the price of an offense . . . for example, the 'price' of stealing a car might be six months in jail."[3]

But does it really make sense to think of a thirty-one-years-to-life sentence as the "price" for stealing a package of batteries? DiBlasi received his long sentence because he did his shoplifting in California, which in 1994 adopted the harshest "three strikes" law in the nation.[4] In 1984, DiBlasi had been convicted of residential burglary. In 1989, he had been convicted of assault with a deadly weapon in connection with a car accident in which (DiBlasi claimed) the victim did not sustain any injury.[5] Then California adopted its three-strikes law. DiBlasi's 1999 petty theft put him over the three-strikes limit, and he was "out."

The idea of "law as price" seems hard to reconcile with DiBlasi's being given a life sentence for shoplifting almost ten years after he had committed (and paid the "price" for) his other relatively minor crimes. As influential criminologist John Braithwaite has put it, the economic analysis of criminal law is "theoretically sophisticated" but also "transparently false."[6] To see the truth in Braithwaite's observation, let us consider other aspects of criminal law that demonstrate there is more going on here than just incentives.

THE PUZZLE OF PRISON

Because most people prefer not to spend time in jail, the threat of imprisonment deters crime. But is there any reason to think prison is a particularly good—meaning, to an economist, particularly efficient—deterrent?

The State of California could have punished DiBlasi in a number of different ways. Rather than sending him to jail, California could have made him pay a fine; forced him to clean up trash along the highway; required him to wear an ankle monitor that gave him a painful electric shock if he went into a store; or sentenced him to spend his evenings listening to the music of Barry Manilow. (This last punishment is regularly employed by a Colorado judge dealing with troublesome teens.)[7] A thoughtful lawmaker choosing among possible punishments would consider not only how effective a punishment might be at discouraging crime, but also how much it costs society to impose the punishment. And when it comes to cost, we can hardly do worse than prison.

Prisons are notoriously expensive to run. For example, it costs over $25,000 annually to house an inmate in the California penal system.[8] This means that, if DiBlasi serves out his minimum sentence of thirty-one years, California's taxpayers will pay at least $775,000 to punish him for stealing a $5.69 pack of batteries. Prison also keeps prisoners idle, depriving society of the value of their labor. (DiBlasi might prefer idleness to work, but why indulge him? Why not make him put in fifty hours a week on a road gang or prison farm?) Finally, imprisoning criminals provides no material benefit to victims, whose only consolation for being assaulted, stolen from, or otherwise abused is whatever dubious pleasure comes from knowing "justice was done."

From a purely economic perspective, it makes far more sense to punish offenders with hefty fines.[9] Of course, a criminal without significant wealth may not be able to pay a fine, an important qualification we shall return to in a moment. But when an offender does have assets, a large fine not only punishes him, it also encourages him to work harder to restore his lost wealth. Putting him in prison just adds him to the rolls of the unemployed. Moreover, money from fines can be used to compensate victims, vaccinate children, reduce the federal debt, and promote other worthy causes. Money spent on prison walls, guards, and concertina wire brings little joy to others.

But what about the many criminals too poor to pay the large fines that would accompany serious crimes like battery or rape? These offenders are, as lawyers put it, "judgment-proof." As a result, law and economics scholars often argue that criminal law relies on prison to punish major crimes because most criminals can't afford to pay significant fines.[10]

But the criminals-can't-afford-to-pay-fines argument quickly runs into at least three serious problems. The first is that not all criminals are poor. Although wealth permits a rich defendant to mount a lively legal defense, once convicted, she will be sent to jail like the rest of us. (Perhaps, admittedly, a nicer jail.) Consider the example of successful businesswoman Martha Stewart, imprisoned for obstructing an investigation into possible insider trading. Why lock her up instead of simply confiscating her money? Imprisoning rich and poor alike seems odd from an economic perspective, because society saves money by punishing the rich with fines.

Second, if wealth limitations make fines ineffective for deterring crimes, why don't wealth limitations make tort dam-

204 • CHAPTER NINE

ages ineffective at deterring negligence? Indeed, because you can purchase insurance against tort liability, monetary damages should be even worse at discouraging negligence than fines are at discouraging crimes. Yet when it comes to torts, we still rely on damages. We almost never throw doctors who commit malpractice, or negligent drivers who cause accidents, into jail.

The third response to the claim most criminals can't pay fines is to point out that, even for impecunious offenders, there remain plenty of alternative punishments that cost less than imprisonment. We could follow the example of the *Bounty's* Captain Bligh, and punish convicted criminals with floggings. Floggings cost society far less than keeping convicts in jail, and after offenders recover from their whippings, they can get back to work. Better yet, we could brand their foreheads or cut off their ears. The pain is equivalent, the recovery still quicker.

As disincentives go, prison seems extraordinarily wasteful. This may explain why theorists discussing "law as price" like to use examples of minor regulatory crimes, like speeding or illegal parking, that are typically punished with fines.[11] Lawyers, however, label such "crimes" *malum prohibitum,* meaning acts that are bad only because they are formally prohibited. Archetypal criminal offenses like rape, robbery, and murder are *malum in se* (bad in themselves). *Malum in se* crimes lie at the heart of the criminal law, and they are typically punished with imprisonment. Prison, in turn, makes no economic sense.

THE PUZZLE OF CRIMINAL INTENT

A second aspect of criminal law that illustrates its deep attention to the role of conscience is the criminal law's concern—it might even be described as obsession—with what was going on in the criminal's head when she committed the crime. Did the accused murderer intend to fire the rifle at his hunting partner, or did he pull the trigger accidently? Did the accused burglar break into the home intending to steal jewelry, or did she plan only to borrow the telephone to report a serious accident?

As we saw in chapter 7, apart from the unusual case of punitive damages, tort law does not much care about a defendant's state of mind. Indeed, some tort liability is "strict," meaning the defendant's state of mind is legally irrelevant. (It doesn't matter whether the manufacturer of a defective toy intended to give a child lead poisoning; it only matters that the toy poisoned the child.) The second common form of tort liability, negligence, requires a finding that the defendant imposed an unreasonable risk on others. But "unreasonable" is defined objectively. No matter how sincerely a speeding driver may believe he was operating his vehicle safely, he is liable if the jury concludes that, judged by an objective standard, his driving was unreasonably dangerous.

Criminal law, in contrast, pays close attention to what's going on between the ears of the accused. Many acts only become crimes when performed with a wrongful motive. (Purposely shoving someone on a crowded sidewalk is a battery, but accidently bumping into someone is not.) Other criminal acts are deemed more or less serious depending on the defendant's subjective intent. (Assault with intent to murder is a more serious crime than simple assault.) Finally, an accused's state of mind matters in sentencing. (A judge may reduce the sentence of a defendant who was distraught when he committed his crime, and now regrets his actions.)

As Richard Posner has observed, this focus on the criminal's subjective state of mind "is puzzling to the economist: one can read many books on economics without encountering a reference to 'intent'."[12] *Homo economicus,* after all, has only one intent: to maximize his own material welfare. It is only to be expected that he will evaluate any course of action, up to and including murder, in terms of expected costs and benefits to himself. If the benefits exceed the costs, *homo economicus* will commit the crime, viewing the risk of punishment as the price he must pay to serve his own interests. Thus, it makes no sense for criminal law to focus on subjective intent the way it does. All lawmakers need to do is set the penalty for committing a particular crime high enough, and make sure enforcement is certain enough, and people will be deterred from crime except in the rare case where a crime benefits the criminal more than it harms the victim. (In that case the crime is an "efficient" crime that, like an efficient accident, should not be prevented.)

The theory of rational selfishness accordingly predicts that penal codes should focus only on objective consequences, not on subjective intent, which is hard for observers to measure, easy for criminals to misrepresent, and not always tied to any actual harm. Yet criminal law does the opposite. It punishes intent more than consequences. Intent is so central to criminal liability that a person with bad intent can be sent to jail even if she harms no one. This happens when offenders are imprisoned for attempts, unsuccessful conspiracies, and other "inchoate" crimes that never succeed. The incompetent would-be terrorist whose defective car bomb never explodes will still, if caught, and convicted, go to jail.

THE PUZZLE OF THE TORT/CRIME DISTINCTION

Finally, a third aspect of criminal law that seems to incorporate the idea of conscience is the notable distinction between criminal law and tort. Both fields are concerned with controlling the external costs one person's actions (negligence, crime) impose on others. Yet tort law is enforced through private lawsuits; criminal law is enforced by state prosecutions. Tort law relies on monetary damages to deter; criminal law makes heavy use of imprisonment. Tort law largely ignores a defendant's subjective intent; criminal law pays close attention. Tort law only makes people pay when they actually harm others; criminal law punishes attempts and conspiracies that harm no one.

If the two areas of law deal with the same basic economic problem, why are they so different? Some economics-oriented scholars suggest the differences stem from the fact that tort law does not seek to completely prevent but merely to "price" risky behavior that may be socially desirable, while criminal law seeks to entirely deter whole categories of behavior that are almost never socially beneficial.[13] Supposedly, this explains why criminal law punishes repeat offenders like DiBlasi more severely, and also why being imprisoned carries a stigma that paying damages does not.[14] But this argument only moves the question back a step. If a crime is priced correctly in terms of its penalty, and someone chooses nevertheless to commit the crime, doesn't this mean the crime in question is an "efficient crime" that benefits the criminal more than it harms the victim? And why punish a repeat offender more severely, instead of recognizing that he may be the rare individual for whom the benefits of crime outweigh the social costs? Finally, how can a criminal penalty carry a stigma if it is only a price?

IS CRIMINAL LAW MISTAKEN?

At a very deep level, the rules of criminal law simply don't mesh with the assumption of selfishness. Even law and economics guru Richard Posner—who in his earlier academic work tried as hard as anyone could to fit criminal law into an economic frame—has conceded that economic explanations for criminal law are "not . . . entirely satisfactory."[15] Economist George Stigler goes further. According to Stigler, the fault lies not in economics, but in the law itself. "The use of criminal sanctions is erratic," Stigler writes, and "there is a widespread failure to adopt rational criteria."[16]

The gap between the idea of "law as price" and the actual rules of criminal law has kept the law and economics approach from permeating nearly as deeply into the thinking of criminal law experts as it has permeated thinking about tort and contract. Criminologists talk about punishments as disincentive, but they talk about punishments in other, distinctly uneconomic ways as well.[17] For example, prison is often justified as a means of incapacitating dangerous individuals and removing them from society. (The British used to transport convicts to Australia; today we "transport" to prison, or in extreme cases, transport with extreme prejudice by means of lethal injection.) The idea of incapacitation raises problems for an incentive-based approach to criminal law. Why should the standard penalties deter most of us but not all? Either the standard punishments are too weak, and most of us obey the law for some deeper reason, or the punishments are strong enough but criminals don't respond correctly to incentives.

A second common theme in criminology that has enjoyed support from time to time is the idea of "rehabilitation," the hopeful view that the penal system can change the character of criminals in a way that makes it safe to return them to society. *Homo economicus*, however, is incapable of being rehabilitated. He is, and always will be, happy to follow any course of action, legal or illegal, that maximizes his own material welfare.

Finally, a third common idea in criminal law scholarship is the idea of punishment as social retribution for evil acts. But punishing someone for any reason other than to promote better behavior in the future suggests an odd and uneconomic preoccupation with reducing the criminal's subjective well-being, rather than increasing one's own. Suppose, for example, a man secretly murders and then takes the place of his identical twin. If a court finds the defendant was driven by a unique and bizarre psychological impulse and, having run out of twins, will never murder again, and if no one else knows about the crime, what is the point of sending the murdering twin to jail? Punishing him by definition imposes a cost on him. If this cost is not offset by a greater deterrence benefit to the larger society, punishment is inefficient.

To make sense of the ideas of incapacitation, rehabilitation, and retribution, we must go beyond rational selfishness and incorporate conscience into our thinking. As we shall see, this approach explains a number of important and otherwise-baffling aspects of criminal law. It also solves the three puzzles described earlier: criminal law's use of imprisonment, its focus on intent, and the nature of the tort/crime distinction. Finally, it offers a road map not only for understanding criminal law better, but for using criminal law more effectively.

RETURN TO THE JEKYLL/HYDE SYNDROME

Chapter 5 described the Jekyll/Hyde syndrome, our tendency to shift between selfish and unselfish behavior in response to social context. The rational selfishness model, however, assumes only one mode of behavior is possible: we always act like Mr. Hyde. This implies there is no difference between the motives and attitudes of criminals, and the motives and attitudes of law-abiding citizens. As Gary Becker has explained it, "The approach . . . assumes that a person commits an offense if the expected utility to him exceeds the utility he could get by using his time and other resources at other activities. Some persons become 'criminals,' therefore, not because their basic motivation differs from that of other persons, but because their benefits and costs differ."[18]

In Stevenson's novella, however, Dr. Jekyll's basic motivations differed greatly from Mr. Hyde's. Hyde was a psychopath of "wonderful selfishness" who was "wholly evil."[19] Jekyll, in contrast, cared about himself but sometimes cared about others, too, so that Jekyll was "commingled out of good and evil."[20] This duality in human nature is the key to understanding criminal law. In brief, when it comes to *malum in se* crimes, society says we must act like Dr. Jekyll. We are expected to follow the rules even when self-interest tempts otherwise. An individual who steals, rapes, and murders whenever it suits him is acting like Hyde in a social context where he should act like Dr. Jekyll. Something has gone seriously wrong. The criminal's Hyde persona dominates in situations where his Jekyll persona should be in charge.

Modern societies are not set up to endure such individuals. Our workplaces, peaceful neighborhoods, and public stores and restaurants all depend, to greater or lesser degrees, on our capacity for unselfish prosocial behavior. Although we care about our own material gains, most of us also care about following basic social rules, and refrain from fraud, theft, and mayhem even when we would personally benefit from such activities. Like Jekyll, we have "balancing instincts, by which [we] walk with some degree of steadiness among temptations."[21] Hyde not only succumbs to temptation, he does not to try to resist it. A person who always acts Hydish poses a danger to the rest of us, just as Hyde posed a danger to the inhabitants of nineteenth-century London. Mr. Hyde must either be transformed into Dr. Jekyll or removed from society.

The remainder of this chapter explores the relationship between the Jekyll/Hyde syndrome and criminal law. As we shall see, the reality of prosocial behavior explains criminal law's fondness for imprisonment, its concern with subjective intent, and the nature of the tort/crime distinction. It also supports the ideas of incapacitation, rehabilitation, and retribution. Perhaps most important, it can help us use criminal law more effectively.

PRISON AS A SOLUTION TO MR. HYDE

Prison, as we have seen, is an expensive punishment. At least one thing can be accomplished by throwing offenders into jail, however, that can't be accomplished by fining them, flogging them, or cutting off their ears. Jail removes offenders from society. Prison "incapacitates" inmates, making it impossible for them to harm those outside the prison walls.

Why should we need to incapacitate certain people? If criminal law worked only through incentives, and if those incentives failed to deter crime adequately either because enforcement was too uncertain or punishments insufficiently severe, the problem could be solved by hiring more police and making punishments more unpleasant. Even the death penalty can be made worse by finding more gruesome and painful ways to put offenders to death—say, by burning them, or disemboweling them alive. (The two methods can even be combined, as in one reported eighteenth-century case where a murderess was executed by placing her in an iron cage with sixteen wildcats and suspending the cage over a raging fire:

the wildcats supposedly attacked the accused and pulled out her entrails.)[22]

Given the availability of such cheap and effective deterrents—although one wonders how much it would cost to procure sixteen wildcats—why use prisons? The answer becomes apparent if we recognize that we don't actually want to have to design a penal system with punishments certain enough and severe enough to deter a population of asocial, conscienceless pyschopaths—and in most cases we don't need to.

Sociologists believe most people don't commit crimes not primarily out of fear of being caught and punished, but out of conscience: that is, because they think they ought not to.[23] This wonderful state of affairs allows society to save money on law enforcement through "underpolicing"—hiring relatively fewer police officers, prosecutors, and judges, and imposing relatively light sentences, at least on first-time offenders. Crime may pay, but mild and haphazardly enforced criminal penalties that would not deter *homo economicus* are enough to keep most people from a life of crime, in the same fashion that (as we saw in chapter 7) weak and patchy rules of tort liability deter most negligence.

This cost-saving system runs into trouble, however, when it encounters the rare individual who insists on acting like Hyde even in social situations that call for Dr. Jekyll. Purely asocial individuals can be expected to take advantage of underpolicing by committing crimes. The only way to keep them from routinely resorting to theft, fraud, and battery is to do what the State of California eventually did with DiBlasi: incapacitate him by imprisoning him. This explains why the law doles out longer sentences to repeat offenders. Repeat offenses don't trigger harsher penalties because they are more costly. After all, a store owner's loss is the same when batteries are stolen by a first-time offender. Repeat offenses do, however, suggest the offender is one of those rare individuals who, for reasons of nature or nurture, acts like Hyde in social situations where most of us act like Dr. Jekyll. Because such individuals cannot be deterred by the usual weak and uncertain criminal penalties, they need to be incapacitated.

The observation that repeat offenders may have different basic attitudes and motivations from the rest of us raises the question: how do these individuals become stuck in Hyde mode? As we saw in chapter 6, psychopathy can be a product of genes, trauma, or disease (including addiction, which seems to have played a role in DiBlasi's case). Depending on the cause, some psychopathic individuals may be beyond remediation. But as we also saw in chapter 6, even people who are capable of acting prosocially toward those whom they regard as members of their "in-group" may show cold indifference to the welfare of those they see as outside their group. The hallmark of genocides—the systematic killing of Jews and Gypsies during the Holocaust, the Japanese Army's rape of Nanking, the Rwanda massacres—is the dehumanization of the ethnic or cultural group that is the target of the genocide.

This unhappy observation supports a rather more optimistic, albeit uneconomic, idea in criminology: the idea of rehabilitation. Some criminals may show indifference to others' rights not because they are incapable of prosocial behavior, but because they define their "in-group" narrowly in terms of family or fellow gang members. If this narrow perception of group membership can be expanded—and numerous experiments in social psychology, not to mention the examples of sports teams and military training, suggest group affiliations are easily manipulated[24]—perhaps the right sorts of experiences in prison might lead some offenders to expand their view of their in-group to include their fellow citizens. Reinforcing a criminal's sense of belonging to the broader society thus may promote more prosocial behavior. When this happens, we say a prisoner has been rehabilitated.

By the same token, out-group perceptions may also explain why many people seem indifferent to the horrific conditions convicts often endure in jail, including overcrowding, lack of medical care, and physical and sexual abuse by guards and other prisoners. This indifference may reflect a belief that convicts are no longer members of the in-group known as civilized society. Just as a criminal may perceive strangers as out-group members whose interests do not deserve consideration, law-abiding citizens may view convicts as out-group members whose interests are of no concern. The underlying attitude seems to be something like "if you won't play nicely with us and act like an in-group member, then we won't treat you like an in-group member either: go play with the other criminals."

Unfortunately, this approach may not do a particularly good job of persuading convicts to expand their notions of in-group membership. There is an inevitable tension between using prison as a deterrent and using it for rehabilitation. Harsh confinement conditions that may be essential to deter a true psychopath may simultaneously prove counterproductive for nonpsychopathic convicts, if ill treatment makes them feel less connected to society. A penal system that emphasizes not only incapacitation, but also harsh treatment, may make rehabilitation difficult or impossible.

PROSOCIALITY AND THE IMPORTANCE OF INTENT

Just as the Jekyll/Hyde syndrome sheds light on criminal law's use of prison as a sanction, it also offers insight into criminal law's focus on the accused's state of mind. To lawyers, the hallmark of *malum in se* crimes like fraud, rape, and murder is "malice," defined as the mental state of indifference or hostility toward the welfare of others. (Indifference toward others is, of course, the very definition of *homo economicus*.) Lovemaking is not rape, and a tragic accident is not a murder. Criminal law pays attention to intentions in this way because, in an underpoliced society, a person who shows "malicious" indifference toward others in situations where the social signals say he should show concern is a serious threat. State of mind matters because (contrary to Gary Becker's claim) criminals have motives quite different from, and dangerous to, the rest of us.

This is not to suggest that otherwise law-abiding persons can't be tempted to commit crimes. As we have seen in experimental games, people behave more selfishly as the personal rewards from selfishness increase, suggesting that when the stakes are high enough, most of us are capable of acting like Hyde even in social contexts that say "Jekyll." The difference between the criminal and the law-abiding citizen may only be a matter of degree. Criminals may simply shift into Hyde mode more readily than most of us do.

But in a society that wants to save on law enforcement costs by underpolicing, someone who shifts into Hyde mode too easily is a threat. This is why a person who generally cares about others' welfare but injures another by accident is not a criminal, and tort rather than criminal law applies. Criminal punishment is reserved for those who show indifference to others in social situations where indifference is inappropriate.

This focus on punishing indifference and promoting concern for others can also be seen in the important roles remorse and apology play in criminal law. Criminal defendants who apologize and express remorse are treated more leniently by prosecutors, judges, and parole boards.[25] The theory seems to be that criminals who seem to sincerely regret harming others are more likely to be prosocial Jekylls who have gone astray than utterly asocial Hydes, and present less of a danger to society. Richard Posner himself, having apparently become sensitized to conscience by his years on the bench, describes this idea in one of his judicial opinions. "A person who feels genuine remorse for his wrong . . . is on the way to developing those internal checks that would keep many people from committing crimes even if the expected costs of criminal punishment were lower than they are."[26]

THE JEKYLL/HYDE SYNDROME AND THE TORT/CRIME DISTINCTION

Finally, focusing on the essential role conscience plays in discouraging criminal behavior sheds light on the third puzzle we have mentioned—the tort/crime distinction. If tort and criminal law both are only incentive systems designed to deter selfish individuals from harming others, it becomes difficult to explain why the two areas of law differ so greatly. Once we take account of the Jekyll/Hyde syndrome, however, it becomes apparent that tort and criminal law differ because they in fact deal with two quite different problems.

Tort law deals with otherwise-prosocial individuals who miscalculate a risk or fail to recognize a danger. Criminal law deals with a much more serious threat: purely selfish individuals who just don't care.[27] This helps explain why criminal laws are enforced by the state rather than through private lawsuits. While most *malum in se* crimes are also grounds for a private suit, criminal prosecutions are brought by professional government prosecutors, and the only benefit a crime victim typically enjoys from a defendant's criminal conviction is a sense of satisfaction. The use of state resources to prosecute crimes can be understood by recognizing that to the extent that a criminal lacks a Jekyll persona, he poses a danger not only to his immediate victim, but to everyone else around him. This makes a criminal conviction a "public" good, like a park or highway, that benefits large numbers of people and justifies the expenditure of public resources.

The idea of criminal law as a government-funded public good also provides insight into the evolutionary puzzle, discussed in chapter 6, of how unselfish prosocial behavior could evolve. In brief, a criminal law system that allows Dr. Jekylls to identify and remove Hydes from their midst promotes "gene-culture coevolution."[28] The existence of a police force, even in the primitive form of a "Big Man" who settles tribal disputes, changes the human environment in a fashion that allows pro-social individuals to do better than purely selfish individuals. Thus, a criminal law system tips the evolutionary calculus in favor of prosociality.

Of course, evolution works slowly, over thousands or even hundreds of thousands of years. Yet the cultural institution of an "official" punisher who enjoys social privileges in return for taking on the burden of keeping miscreants in line is also quite ancient. According to primatologist Frans de Waal, even chimpanzee tribes select a dominant male (a "Big Chimp") to keep order and settle fights: "Dominant chimps generally break up fights either by supporting the weak against the strong or through impartial intervention."[29] If early humans followed the same pattern as our chimpanzee cousins, gene-culture coevolution for prosocial behavior may have been at work for even longer than we've been a species.

Thinking about the evolutionary roots of prosociality also sheds light on the role retribution plays in criminal law. On first inspection, retribution seems inefficient. As Jeremy Bentham pointed out nearly two centuries ago, punishment for punishment's sake, rather than to deter future crimes, just

adds more misery to the world.

adds more misery to the world.[30] Nevertheless, among laymen, the desire for retribution seems to be as or more important in motivating people to punish criminals than the desire for deterrence. One study found, for example, that college students asked to recommend sentences in response to a series of fictional crime vignettes were more likely to recommend a harsh sentence for a crime that seemed especially morally objectionable, than for a crime that seemed especially hard to deter.[31] Some experts suggest that "all humans seem to share a fundamental urge to punish transgressors—not simply those who inflict a personal injury on each of us, but also those who harm other members of our family or group."[32]

Evolutionary biology offers an explanation for this "instinct to punish." As discussed in chapter 6, one possible solution to the puzzle of how altruists win out against egoists in the Darwinian struggle for survival lies in the idea of "altruistic punishers" willing to punish someone who harms a third party. Given the presence of enough altruistic punishers, selfish behavior that incurs their collective wrath may become so costly that egoists find themselves at an evolutionary disadvantage. This idea does not necessarily make retribution either a desirable, or a useful, attribute of criminal law in a society that can rely on formal enforcement institutions rather than vigilantism to maintain order. But it at least makes the impulse to use criminal law as a vehicle for social vengeance more understandable.

USING PROSOCIAL BEHAVIOR TO IMPROVE CRIMINAL LAW

So far we have focused on how taking account of conscience helps explain aspects of criminal law that seem difficult or impossible to reconcile with the idea of "law as price." In the process, we have seen why criminologists—in contrast to tort and contracts scholars—tend to think of criminal law not only in terms of the incentives it creates but also in terms of non-economic goals like incapacitation, rehabilitation, and retribution. This improved understanding of criminal law is valuable in and of itself. But the scientific literature on prosocial behavior offers a bigger reward: the opportunity to promote law-abiding behavior more effectively.

As we saw in chapter 5, prosocial behavior increases when the personal sacrifice involved becomes smaller. Because the risk of criminal punishment raises the "cost" of committing a crime, it simultaneously lowers the "cost" of law-abiding behavior. Thus, criminal sanctions do indeed create incentives that deter offenses.

But the evidence explored in chapter 5 also demonstrates that tweaking the calculus of personal cost and benefit is just part, and perhaps not the largest part, of the story when it comes to explaining prosocial behavior. Conscience plays a vital role, and conscience in turn depends on social context. This suggests prosociality can be promoted not only through incentives, but also by manipulating social context and in particular by pulling the three familiar social levers of obedience, imitation, and empathy. Lawmakers willing to pay attention to these three social cues can deter more crime at a lower cost—a goal any economist would applaud.

INSTRUCTIONS FROM AUTHORITY: ON "EXPRESSIVE" CRIMINAL LAW

Let us begin with the role of obedience to authority. Psychologist Stanley Milgram showed how people tend to do what authority tells them to, an instinct for obedience Milgram employed to make his experimental subjects do things they believed hurt others. The instinct for obedience can also, however, be employed for the more beneficial purpose of inducing people *not* to harm others. Tell people it is wrong to steal, rape, and murder, and they become less likely to steal, rape, and murder—even when their material incentives remain unchanged.

This idea is reflected in an important strand of criminal law scholarship that argues that criminal law performs something Chicago law professor Cass Sunstein has dubbed an "expressive" function.[33] (The expressive theory of law was first mentioned in chapter 8.) Expressive law theorists argue that the fact that a particular behavior is declared to be a crime as well as a tort (although almost all *malum in se* crimes are also torts, this isn't true the other way around) sends the official message: "this is very bad behavior, and the authorities are telling you in the strongest terms not to do it." As criminal law expert Dan Kahan puts it, defining an act as a crime carries a "social meaning" that can independently alter behavior even in the absence of material incentives.[34]

This suggests yet another advantage to punishing criminals with prison time rather than fines. Prison is a punishment reserved almost exclusively for *malum in se* offenses. This means, Kahan argues, "[im]prisonment is an extraordinarily potent gesture of moral disapproval . . . Fines, in contrast, condemn much more ambiguously."[35]

Focusing on criminal law's expressive function leads to a further insight. In brief, it seems reasonable that instructions from authority are most likely to be followed when the authority in question is a "respected" authority, meaning the person being instructed views the authority as located within her "in-group." The hallmark of in-group membership, in turn, is mutually prosocial behavior—including prosocial behavior by the instructing authority, toward the persons being instructed. An authority perceived as indifferent or hostile is an "out-group authority" whose naked commands, unbacked by sanctions, are less likely to be followed. Legal scholar Tracey Meares, an expert in the problem of law enforcement in disadvantaged minority communities, puts it this way: "Individuals care about how they are treated by government authorities because treatment provides important indicators to individuals about how the authority in question views the group to which the individual evaluator perceives herself belonging."[36]

The importance of in-group identification in ensuring obedience to authority helps explain why it can be so difficult to control crime in communities whose members perceive themselves as different from, or outside of, a larger and possibly hostile society. The classic example is criminal gangs. To harness criminal law's expressive power, it may be essential to persuade gang members and potential gang members that they are welcome into, and should cast their lot with, the general citizenry. Similarly, any law enforcement policy that treats members of an identifiable subgroup more harshly—the controversial practice of "racial profiling" comes to mind—is likely to undermine respect for that authority among members of the disfavored group, resulting in a diminished sense of moral obligation to obey the law.

CONFORMITY AND "BROKEN WINDOWS" POLICING

In addition to instructions from authority, a second important social cue for triggering prosocial behavior in experimental games is the perception that others are behaving, or would behave, prosocially. Most people would hesitate before dropping a candy wrapper on a spotless floor. Conversely, otherwise law-abiding people who normally would never think of breaking a store window and stealing a television might find themselves tempted to join in when everyone around them is looting. (Empirical studies confirm that mass looting does, in fact, often draw in people without any prior criminal record.)[37]

The idea that criminal behavior begets more criminality and that social order begets more order underlies the influential "broken windows" theory of policing, which emphasizes strict enforcement of rules against minor "quality of life" crimes like public drunkenness and panhandling as a means of discouraging more serious crime. Broken windows theory got its name from the title of an influential article by James Q. Wilson and George L. Kelling published in 1982 in *The Atlantic Monthly*.[38] According to Wilson and Kelling, "if a window in a building is broken and left unrepaired, all the rest of the windows will soon be broken. . . . [O]ne unrepaired broken window is a signal that no one cares, and so breaking more windows costs nothing."[39] New York City, Chicago, and Los Angeles have each adopted some version of the broken windows approach by pursuing zero-tolerance policies of aggressive enforcement of laws against loitering, graffiti, and so forth, with subsequent declines in serious crime.[40]

Criminologists debate whether these crime reductions have been caused primarily by broken windows policing or by some other factor, such as an aging population or declining use of crack cocaine.[41] The experimental gaming data, however, support broken windows theory. What's more, the data suggest a causal link between broken windows policing and declining crime rates that is different from, and more direct than, the causal links often emphasized by experts.

In particular, expressive law theorists suggest broken windows policing works either by removing offenders from a

broken windows theory

neighhorhood, or by raising expectations that sanctions will be imposed because observers conclude visible social order must be evidence of a heightened police presence.[42] Each of these causal links makes sense, but the experimental evidence suggests a third mechanism by which visible social order reduces crime: simple conformity.

The human tendency to mimic others' behavior explored in chapter 5 implies that when people see others obeying the law, this makes them more willing to obey the law themselves— even when the people involved, and their collective perceptions of the likelihood of enforcement, remain unchanged. This simple "monkey see monkey do" hypothesis not only helps explain how broken windows policing works, it offers insights into how to make it work better.

In particular, if broken windows policing works because it convinces people that there must be lots of police around keeping an eye on them, there is no harm, and possibly much benefit, to a highly visible police presence. We might station a uniformed officer on every corner. If, however, broken windows policing works by sending the message that other people are law-abiding Jekylls rather than criminal Hydes, a highly visible police presence may be counterproductive, sending the unfortunate message that one's fellow citizens are not to be trusted and must be watched closely. Plainclothes policing might be the better option. In other words, the phenomenon of "crowding out" conscience may apply not only in contract negotiations, but on our public streets.

Empirical studies of tax compliance support the view that high-visibility enforcement measures that emphasize penalties instead of moral obligations can, indeed, encourage more tax violations. For example, research has found that taxpayers who are given information emphasizing the "tax gap" between the taxes due the government and taxes actually paid tend to declare less income and to claim more deductions. "The inference that evasion is widespread dominates any inference relating to the likely punishment for such behavior."[43]

The idea that knowing other people are breaking the law discourages law-abiding behavior suggests yet another advantage to imprisoning offenders, rather than fining or flogging them. Consider again the case of Robert DiBlasi, sentenced to thirty-one years to life for stealing a package of batteries valued at $5.69. Even if DiBlasi stole batteries every day for thirty-one years, the total social loss ($64,832) would be substantially less than the social cost of imprisoning him for the minimum thirty-one years ($775,000). How can such a prison sentence be cost-justified?

The answer lies in recognizing that by imprisoning DiBlasi, California did more than stop him from committing other, possibly more serious crimes (incapacitation). It also stopped law-abiding citizens from observing DiBlasi committing crimes,[44] reducing the odds they would imitate his behavior. In other words, crime is contagious. Prison quarantines chronic lawbreakers, removing them from society and reducing the chance the rest of us will be "infected." Curfews accomplish the same objective, although by quarantining the general population rather than restricting the freedom of the criminal.

EMPATHY, BENEFITS TO OTHERS, AND THE PROBLEM OF "VICTIMLESS" CRIME

Finally, let us turn to the third social variable in our three-factor model of prosocial behavior: perceived benefits to others. As we have seen, our Jekyll selves are intuitive utilitarians who weigh benefits to others against costs to ourselves in choosing to act prosocially. The more we believe our sacrifice helps others, the more willing we are to sacrifice.

Choosing not to commit a profitable or pleasurable crime is a form of self-sacrifice. And without a clear sense that some- one will benefit from our restraint, self-sacrifice becomes unlikely. This insight goes a long way toward explaining why it is so difficult to control "victimless" crimes like prostitu- tion, gambling, polygamy, euthanasia, and the use of recre- ational drugs and alcohol. The hallmark of a victimless crime is that everyone who participates in it does so voluntarily. This makes it difficult to explain why victimless crimes are harm- ful, and how we benefit others when we choose to respect vice laws.

The three-factor model accordingly predicts we face at least two significant, and perhaps insurmountable, obstacles to enforcing vice laws. First, unless the police happen to be watching, many people won't respect a law that criminalizes behavior that does not have a perceived victim. The most obvi- ous example may be the failure of Prohibition.[45] Before auto- mobiles became fast and ubiquitous, drunks were perceived to pose little danger to anyone but themselves. This meant many people were disinclined to adopt a moralistic attitude toward drinking alcohol simply because it was declared illegal from 1920 to 1933. Although estimates vary, the evidence sug- gests Prohibition, despite great resources devoted to enforce- ment, had only a modest impact on alcohol consumption.[46] Similarly, since the 1970s, the United States has pursued a "War on Drugs" characterized by aggressive enforcement and increasingly harsh sentences even for low-level offenders.[47] Yet chemical testing of urban sewage for residue chemicals excreted by drug users shows that cocaine use is far more common in Los Angeles than in London and Milan, where the penalties are much milder.[48]

Second, when there is no clear social harm from violating a law, not only will citizens be less willing to follow the law, police and politicians may be less willing to enforce it. Although Prohibition during the 1920s and 1930s and the War on Drugs today are notable exceptions, "enforcement agencies tend to monitor and punish these consensual crimes [gambling, prostitution, polygamy] in a lax and inconsistent manner."[49] Because prosocial behavior is more likely when we believe it benefits others, it is easy to understand why a police officer eager to arrest a reckless driver or bank robber has far less enthusiasm for arresting a well-behaved pot smoker or polygamist.

This should give pause to any lawmaker or enforcement agency that wants to prevent people from doing things they believe are harmless. When both citizens and police don't see "vice" as dangerous to others, vice laws will neither be obeyed nor well enforced. The only hope of discouraging so-called victimless crimes is to convince both citizens and police such crimes are not truly victimless.

Education and public relations accordingly are key. This approach has been employed in enforcing laws against polygamy, where enforcement efforts are often justified as necessary not to regulate sexual conduct, but to protect under-aged girls from exploitation by older men. When state authorities in Texas raided the Yearning for Zion ranch, a rural compound of a polygamist Mormon splinter sect,[50] the governor defended the raid not as a means of enforcing Texas' anti-polygamy laws but as necessary to protect the children in the compound from sexual abuse.[51] Similarly, emphasizing the dangers of second-hand smoke encourages compliance with smoking bans, and educational campaigns emphasizing how dog feces contribute to water pollution encourage dog owners to clean up after their pets.

The unavoidable corollary is that just as policymakers can encourage people to obey the law when they emphasize its social benefits, they discourage compliance when they question a law's wisdom. In the 2008 elections, Democratic vice presidential candidate Joseph Biden displayed an intuitive understanding of how to motivate tax compliance when, in a television interview, he said about raising income taxes: "It's time to be patriotic. Time to jump in. Time to be part of the deal. Time to help get America out of the rut." Republican vice president candidate Sarah Palin showed a tin ear for encouraging citizens to obey the law when she responded to Biden's remarks at a political rally by claiming that "raising taxes is about killing jobs and hurting small business and making things worse."[52] To the extent Palin's audience heard her as suggesting tax evasion is not only a victimless crime, but actually helps the economy, the unintended but unavoidable effect should be more tax cheating.

CONCLUSION: CRIMINAL LAW AS A PREFERENCE-SHAPING POLICY

Criminal law has always paid close attention to conscience, as shown by its use of imprisonment, its focus on subjective intent, and the tort/crime distinction. Indeed, in a world populated entirely by conscienceless psychopaths, criminal law couldn't work. After all, if everyone were willing to commit crime when it paid, this rule would apply to police and to judges. Laws could not be enforced because the enforcers would be too corrupt. Police would spend their time shaking down innocents for cash, and criminals would avoid jail by bribing judges.

Not surprisingly, criminal law scholars have shown a collective reluctance to embrace the notion that criminal law works only through incentives. In addition to taking the ideas of incapacitation, rehabilitation, and retribution seriously, some scholars argue that criminal law works not only by creating incentives but also through its "expressive" function, sending social signals that change behavior. This argument is consistent with the three-factor model, which suggests that the capacity to adopt a Dr. Jekyll persona when the social situation calls for it lies at the heart of the distinction between criminals and law-abiding citizens. Criminal law exists to address the problem of individuals who ignore social signals and act like Mr. Hyde in contexts that call for Dr. Jekyll. Thus, by paying attention to social signals, we may be able to use criminal law to channel behavior more effectively.

In the words of Ken Dau-Schmidt, one of the earliest legal scholars to focus on criminal law's expressive function, "in addition to creating disincentives for criminal activity, criminal punishment is intended to promote various norms of individual behavior by shaping the preferences of criminals and the population at large."[53] In other words, by changing social context, criminal law *changes what people want*, in the process shifting their behavior from purely selfish and asocial to unselfish and law-abiding.

When Dau-Schmidt wrote about this idea in 1990, he noted with some regret that economists seemed reluctant to analyze criminal law as a "preference-shaping" tool because "a complete model of societal preference-shaping policy requires specification of the preference-shaping technology."[54] In other words, the idea that law can change our preferences (and with them, our behavior) without actually imposing sanctions is not very useful until we know exactly how the changing process works. Today, however, we know quite a bit about how to "shape preferences," or at least how to use social context to encourage people to act as if their preferences have changed. Thus, the three-factor model not only helps us understand criminal law better, it also helps us use it more effectively.

authority +
conformity
empathy

PART FOUR

CONCLUSION

CHARIOTS OF THE SUN

Each man takes care that his neighbor shall not cheat him.
But a day comes when he begins to care that he does not
cheat his neighbor. Then all goes well—he has changed his
market-cart into a chariot of the sun.

—*Ralph Waldo Emerson*

On June 19, 2008, a sober-faced, forty-three-year-old banker named Bradley Birkenfeld stood before the bench of federal judge William Zloch in the U.S. District Court in Fort Lauderdale, Florida. Birkenfeld was a U.S. citizen who had been raised in the Boston area. He had spent much of his adult life, however, in Europe, working for various banks including the Swiss bank UBS. On Birkenfeld's most recent trip back to the United States to attend a high school reunion, he had been arrested at Logan Airport by federal authorities. Now he was in the courthouse in Fort Lauderdale to plead guilty to conspiracy to defraud the Internal Revenue Service (IRS).

Birkenfeld wasn't arrested for cheating on his own taxes. Rather, he was arrested because while at UBS, he had made a profession of advising wealthy U.S. clients how to cheat on theirs. In his statement to the court in connection with his guilty plea, Birkenfeld detailed how he and other UBS bankers had advised their U.S. clients to create concealed offshore accounts; to stash watches, jewelry, and artwork purchased with hidden funds in Swiss safe deposit boxes; and to use Swiss credit cards to prevent the IRS from tracking their purchases. He described how he had helped one especially important client, Orange County billionaire and real estate magnate Igor Olenicoff, avoid paying over $7 million in U.S. income taxes by hiding $200 million in offshore accounts. Birkenfeld also testified about how he had acted as a mule for his wealthy clients, carrying checks out of the United States for deposit in accounts in Switzerland and Liechtenstein, and on one occasion smuggling diamonds in a tube of toothpaste.[1]

Birkenfeld admitted to Judge Zloch that he had known what he was doing at UBS was illegal and he had worried about his involvement. When Zloch asked why Birkenfeld had nevertheless participated in the scheme, Birkenfeld replied softly, "I was employed by UBS ... I was incentivized to do this business."[2]

SAINTS AND PSYCHOPATHS

It is tempting to contrast Birkenfeld's decision to help his clients evade taxes with the decision made by Franco Gonzales, described in chapter 1, to return the $203,000 in cash that Gonzales found lying unattended in a Los Angeles street to its rightful owner. Birkenfeld had a background of privilege. His father was a neurosurgeon in the Boston area; he had gone to college at a private university in New England; he was employed by a prestigious investment bank; he had acquired a fair amount of personal wealth. Franco Gonzales, in contrast, had been raised in poverty in rural Mexico by his mother, who cleaned houses. Gonzales had little or no formal education or savings, and worked as a dishwasher in a Chinese restaurant.

It would be easy to jump to the conclusion there must be some fundamental character difference between the two men. Gonzales seems moral, virtuous, a man of conscience. Berkenfeld in contrast seems selfish and unprincipled, a classic "bad apple."

This book has shown such a view would be mistaken. Gonzales is not a saint. Nor is Berkenfeld a psychopath. Although Gonzales certainly is to be applauded for his decision to return the money he found, his scruples did not extend to complying with U.S. immigration laws: at the time he found the money, Gonzales had entered and was living in the United States illegally. Similarly, there is no evidence Berkenfeld ever tried to cheat his wealthy clients. Consider how easily he could have kept the diamonds in the toothpaste tube for himself, claiming he had lost them. Surely Berkenfeld had just as much financial incentive to steal from his clients as he had to help them, at great risk to himself, evade their taxes. The thought does not even seem to have occurred to him.

Like most of us, Gonzales and Berkenfeld each proved capable of both ethical unselfish action and unethical, self-serving behavior. Each man had a conscience that sometimes—only sometimes—stopped him from pursuing his own ends at others' expense. Part Two of this book explored this fundamental duality in human nature, examining how in response to social cues people will shift rapidly between prosocial, Dr. Jekyll-like behavior and selfish, Mr.-Hydish patterns of action, often without being aware their behavior has shifted. Sometimes we are cooperative, conscientious, and considerate. Other times we are not.

LAW AND CONSCIENCE

This book has argued that an understanding of and appreciation for the Jekyll/Hyde syndrome is essential to a full understanding of how rules—including but not limited to legal rules—channel human behavior. There are not enough police in the world to keep a society of conscienceless psychopaths (if you could call such a thing a "society") from relentlessly preying on itself. Nor is it clear whom you could safely hire in such a world to act as police. Civic order depends on our collective capacity to act like Dr. Jekyll and "internalize" rules, following them even when external sanctions are weak or missing.

Moreover, Part Two of this book demonstrated that people do not shift between their Mr. Hyde and Dr. Jekyll personas at random. The change is triggered, rather predictably, by certain noneconomic cues and variables collectively described as "social context." Our laws must work in—and also comprise part of—our social context. Thus, Part Three examined how the three-factor model developed in Part Two helps us make greater sense of the rules of tort, contract, and criminal law, and also helps us use those rules to shape behavior more effectively.

The result is that one of the most important lessons legal experts can glean from the emerging science of prosociality is that when Oliver Wendell Holmes advised them to think of law only from the perspective of the bad man without a conscience, he was giving poor advice indeed. Rather than ignoring conscience, lawmakers will get better results if they put conscience into harness. This is especially true when it comes to promoting unselfish prosocial behavior that takes the form this book has labeled "passive altruism," meaning ethical restraint from taking advantage of others' vulnerability. We may not necessarily want to encourage everyone to put five dollars in a beggar's cup. But at the least, we want them to refrain from stealing money from the cup when the beggar's back is turned.

The law plays an important role in promoting this sort of unselfishness, not only by creating incentives, but also by signaling what conduct is appropriate and expected; by encouraging prosocial behavior in others; and by educating us about how our own choices help or harm those around us. To understand and use law more effectively, we must take account of the many ways law changes behavior, above and beyond creating material incentives.

The potential rewards from paying attention to conscience are far larger than just a better understanding of law. To maintain order and promote productivity, modern societies rely not only on formal law but also on complex webs of nonlegal rules, including workplace rules; religious rules; ethical rules; and the community "rules" of polite and cooperative behavior that Robert Ellickson called "social norms." Just as lawmakers and regulators can put conscience to work, so can employers, reformers, educators, and civic and religious leaders.

The payoffs may be enormous. After all, most people do not view rules as ends in and of themselves. We use rules as a means toward the ultimate end of our own collective well-being. And in our quest for a peaceful and prosperous society, we may put rules to work best when we put them to work in tandem with conscience. When more people show concern for others' welfare, there are fewer nasty altercations, costly accidents, and expensive lawsuits to occupy the time of lawyers, judges, and jurors. When more corporate executives and employees work hard and honestly, our economy grows and there are fewer business scandals. And when more people prefer to obey the law even when the police aren't looking, there is less crime and less need for costly crime prevention measures like burglar alarms and barred windows. (By 2012, the Department of Labor predicts, the United States may have more people employed as private security guards than as high school teachers.)[3]

Thomas Hobbes, perhaps the first political economist, ignored the role that conscience plays in promoting social order. Many of his modern intellectual descendants, in their relentless focus on material incentives, can be accused of the same omission. Yet not only logic, but also mounting empirical evidence, suggests that we need more than the right material incentives to create thriving communities. We also need conscience.

CONSCIENCE AND PROSPERITY

The idea that unselfish prosocial behavior contributes to our collective economic well-being is hardly novel. John Stuart Mill wrote in 1848, "There are countries . . . where the most serious impediment to conducting business concerns on a large scale, is the rarity of persons who are supposed fit to be trusted."[4] In his classic 1958 study, *The Moral Basis of a Backward Society*, political economist Edward Banfield similarly concluded that poverty in Southern Italy was directly attributable to what he dubbed "amoral familism," meaning a collective cultural unwillingness to trust or keep commitments to anyone beyond immediate family.[5]

But the connection between conscience and prosperity is attracting special attention today. Beginning in the 1990s, experts in economic development have increasingly argued that differences in legal and economic institutions alone do not suffice to explain differences in prosperity among nations. Cultural patterns of cooperative, trustworthy behavior also seem to be important, contributing to economic growth by promoting market exchange and investment and discouraging opportunism and illegality.[6]

A growing body of empirical evidence supports the link. One interesting study by Paul Zak and Stephen Knack relies on the World Values Surveys that have been conducted over the decades in several dozen countries. One of the questions routinely asked in the Surveys is "[g]enerally speaking, would you say that most people can be trusted, or that you can't be too careful in dealing with people?" Average responses to this question vary from a low of less than 6 percent of Peruvians who think people can be trusted, to a high of more than 61 percent of Norwegians who express trust in others. Zak and Knack compared average responses to the "trust" question on the Survey with national economic growth rates (measured by per capita income growth) and investment (measured by investment as a percentage of gross domestic product). A belief that others are trustworthy proved to be positively and significantly correlated with both. A 15-point increase in the percentage of the population expressing trust in others was associated with a nearly 1 percent increase in annual economic growth, and an approximately 2 percent increase in investment, even after controlling for factors like per capita income and education.[7]

Other studies show similar results. For example, an earlier study by Knack and Philip Keefer found that national economic growth rates could be positively correlated with the self-reported law-abidingness of respondents in each nation: in countries with higher growth rates, respondents were more likely to answer that it was "never" justifiable to cheat on taxes or fraudulently claim government benefits. Similarly, Knack and Keefer found greater law-abidingness was associated with greater willingness to help others. Self-reported ethical behaviors were highly correlated with national differences in the results of an experiment in which wallets containing $50 in cash and the putative owner's address were "accidentally" dropped in the street in cities around the globe. The "lost" wallets were returned, cash included, significantly more often in countries where survey respondents reported that it was never justifiable to cheat on taxes or fraudulently claim government benefits.[8]

Although causation is always difficult to establish, the link between prosocial behavior and economic growth crops up repeatedly. Stock market returns are significantly higher in countries where people report greater trust in others.[9] Similarly, when Europeans are asked to rank the trustworthiness of people from other nations, the results are positively correlated with the amount of trade and investment between the two countries involved.[10]

The link between prosperity and prosocial behavior can be found in logic as well as statistical evidence. As Thomas Hobbes described the problem, when every man is for himself,

> there is no place for industry; because the fruit thereof is uncertain; and consequently no culture of the earth; no navigation, nor use of the commodities that may be imported by sea; no commodious building; no instruments of moving, and removing, such things as require much force; no knowledge of the face of the earth; no account of time; no arts; no letters; no society; and which is worst of all, continual fear, and danger of violent death; and the life of man, solitary, poor, nasty, brutish and short. [11]

CONSCIENCE AND HAPPINESS

Hobbes' famous observation hints at another great advantage of cultivating conscience. Conscience not only brings greater wealth, it brings greater happiness. Only a moment's thought reveals how others' prosocial behavior contributes to our own quality of life. If our fellow citizens were all conscienceless psychopaths, we would have to devote enormous time and resources to—and endure enormous amounts of stress and anxiety from—the need to protect ourselves and our property from their depredations. Every homeowner would keep firearms and snarling dogs for protection; the accumulation of wealth would be impossible without the services of armed guards (not that you could find guards worth trusting); kidnapping for ransom would be a major industry. If no one had a conscience, our lives indeed would be solitary, nasty, brutish, and short—and no conscienceless king or government could be trusted to make them otherwise.

Thus, we should be grateful most of our fellow citizens seem to have a conscience. But one person's decision to act prosocially may not only contribute to others' happiness, it may also contribute to her own. Doing volunteer work has been shown to improve happiness, self-esteem, and overall life satisfaction.[12] Researchers also have found a connection between self-reported happiness and ethical behavior, even when factors like income, age, and education are controlled for.[13] We can even see a biological link. Cooperating with another in an experimental game raises levels of oxytocin, a "feel good" hormone usually associated with breast-feeding and mate-bonding, while fMRI scans show that mutual cooperation in experimental games activates reward circuits in the brain. (Interestingly, these reward circuits are not activated when subjects cooperate in games with computers.)[14]

Promoting prosocial behavior brings psychological as well as monetary benefits. As John Stuart Mill observed, "the advantage to mankind of being able to trust one another, penetrates into every crevice and cranny of human life: the economical is perhaps the smallest part of it."[15]

Of course, it is important to acknowledge not all forms of unselfish behavior benefit society. Sometimes unselfish action is employed to benefit some subgroup at the expense of the larger community. One could imagine, for example, a conscientious gang member whose loyal and trustworthy behavior toward his fellow criminals leaves the rest of us worse off.

Moreover, it is also important to remember that legal sanctions and conscience are not the only tools we can use to promote prosocial behavior. Fear of retaliation and reputational concerns also play important roles. When he deals with others with whom he expects to interact again, even *homo economicus* will sacrifice short-term self-interest to preserve the opportunity for favorable future exchange. In addition to law and conscience, reputation can be thought of as a third leg of the three-legged stool that supports a prosperous and peaceful society.

But take away one leg of a three-legged stool, and the stool no longer stays upright. Take away conscience, and law and reputation, by themselves, may no longer suffice to ensure a civil society.

CONSCIENCE IN DECLINE

This possibility should concern us, for evidence is piling up that unselfish prosocial behavior is declining in the United States. In recent years we have been exposed to seemingly endless political and business scandals, from Enron's massive accounting fraud and President Clinton's dalliance with Monica Lewinsky at the turn of the millennium, to Bernie Madoff's multi-billion-dollar Ponzi scheme and former Illinois governor Rod Blagojevich's attempt to sell a vacant Senate seat today. Many Americans have begun to feel, at an intuitive level, our society is suffering from ethical decay. The empirical data support this intuition.

In his influential bestseller, *Bowling Alone: The Collapse and Revival of American Community*, sociologist Robert Putnam documents in alarming detail how actively altruistic behaviors like giving blood, working in a political campaign, or donating to charity have declined over the past four decades.[16] Meanwhile, the percentage of Americans who identify "a job that contributes to the welfare of society" as an important element in a good life declined from 38 percent in 1975 to 32 percent in 1996, while the percentage who identify making "a lot of money" as important has risen from 38 percent to 63 percent.[17]

Even more disturbing, the economically essential phenomenon of passive altruism—refraining from breaking rules or taking advantage of others—is also on the wane. A study of students at nine major U.S. state universities found that from 1964 to 1996, there was a substantial increase in participation in serious cheating behaviors. Self-reported incidents of copying from another student increased from 26 percent to 52 percent, while the use of crib notes rose from 16 percent to 27 percent.[18] In his book, *The Cheating Culture: Why More Americans Are Doing Wrong to Get Ahead*, David Callahan writes that employment firms and human resources officers report fraudulent job applications are reaching crisis proportions; a 2002 review of nearly 3 million job applications by a large firm that performs background checks found that 44 percent contained falsehoods.[19] Even our driving manners have gotten worse. In 1979, 71 percent of motorists made a full or rolling stop at stop signs at monitored intersections in suburban New York. By 1996, only 3 percent made any kind of stop at the same intersections.[20]

The idea that prosocial behavior is decreasing finds additional support in longitudinal surveys that show a remarkable drop in Americans' perceptions of the trustworthiness of their fellow citizens. In the late 1950s and 1960s, 55–60 percent of Americans described their fellow citizens as trustworthy. By the 1990s, this figure had declined to the mid- to upper 30s.[21]

Why do Americans seem, more and more, to be acting like amoral Mr. Hydes, and less like conscientious Dr. Jekylls? Some experts suggest rising economic inequality is the culprit, because it undermines the perception of common ingroup membership that (as we saw in chapter 6) provides the foundation for prosocial behavior.[22] There is some evidence to support this idea. Income inequality, for example, is negatively related at the national level to expressions of trust in others in the World Values Survey.[23] In the United States, however, the timing seems off. As Robert Putnam has noted, the decline in Americans' prosocial behavior began in the 1960s, some decades before the recent period of rising economic inequality.[24]

What about the diminishing role of organized religion in American life? Because formal religious instruction typically includes instruction in moral codes, organized religion and prosocial behavior may be linked in some fashion. But the connection is uncertain and poorly understood. For example, Italy, which is religiously homogenous, has enormous North-South differences in social capital and interpersonal trust.[25] Moreover, on a global scale, relatively nonreligious nations like Norway, Sweden, China, and Finland score highest for interpersonal trust, while Brazil, Peru, Turkey, and Philippines (where organized religion plays a far more important social and political role) score the lowest.[26] Nor has the rise of evangelical Christianity in the United States slowed the national decline in prosocial behavior.[27]

Robert Putnam, who has made perhaps the most careful study of American's declining prosociality of any scholar alive today, identifies still another contributing factor: our increasing reliance on television and other forms of electronic entertainment. Electronic entertainment keeps people indoors and isolated, away from public places and from each other. It encourages narcissism, materialism, and envy. (Consider the Fox network's hit show *American Idol,* or ABC's *Who Wants to Be a Millionaire?*) Finally, electronic entertainment often portrays or even glorifies asocial behavior. The popular video game *Grand Theft Auto* invites its players to commit theft, mayhem, and murder, while the hero of Showtime's television drama *Dexter* is a psychopathic serial killer.

According to Putnam, however, the single biggest factor in explaining our increasingly Hydish behavior seems to be something Putnam labels "generational change." By this, Putnam means the replacement through attrition of an older generation raised during the Great Depression and hardened in the refiner's fire of the Second World War by subsequent generations (Baby Boomers, Generation X-ers, Millennials) that seem far less inclined toward altruism, civic engagement, and trust in others. For some reason, Putnam writes, "being raised after World War II was quite a different experience from being raised before that watershed. It is as though the post-war generations were exposed to some anti-civic X-ray that permanently and increasingly rendered them less likely to connect with the community"—and, as the evidence shows, also less likely to behave in an unselfish prosocial fashion.[28]

One can easily see how the generation of Americans raised before and during World War II may, through the process of meeting their historic collective economic and military challenges, have developed a stronger sense of common in-group affiliation and a keener appreciation for the importance of self-sacrifice than subsequent generations raised in the relatively peaceful and prosperous years that followed. The scientific and empirical evidence surveyed in this book suggests, however, still another aspect of the post-war experience that may have contributed to Putnam's "anti-civic X-ray." That element is the increasing dominance of the rational selfishness model in our nation's universities, government offices, and corporate headquarters.

THE DANGERS OF OVERSELLING
HOMO ECONOMICUS

The assumption that people are selfish has been embedded in economics from the beginning. From at least Hobbes' day, economic thinkers have emphasized self-interest in explaining human behavior. This seems appropriate in a well-regulated marketplace, where selfish behavior is common and contributes to social welfare. The *homo economicus* approach is a wonderful tool for analyzing problems like monopoly, surplus, and shortage.

Outside anonymous markets, however, the assumption of rational selfishness may be of questionable value in helping us address social problems like failing schools, rising crime, poor medical care, political corruption, or CEO malfeasance. Nevertheless, the assumption of selfishness dominates discussion in these policy areas as well, as witness contemporary lawmakers' and reformers' relentless invocation of catch phrases like "accountability" and "incentives." Economic thinking has become so omnipresent that popular books urge laymen to adopt it as a way of life. The most obvious example may be Steven Levitt and Stephen Dubner's 2005 blockbuster, *Freakonomics: A Rogue Economist Explores the Hidden Side of Everything* (2005). According to Levitt and Dubner, "incentives are the cornerstone of modern life."[29] Or, as Levitt and Dubner also put it, "Morality . . . represents the way that people would like the world to work—whereas economics represents how it actually *does* work."[30]

This book begs to differ. Emphasizing the power of material incentives and ignoring conscience not only hampers our ability to address certain social problems, it can make those problems worse.

THE FIRST DANGER: TEACHING SELFISHNESS IS A SELF-FULFILLING PROPHECY

To understand the first risk we run by ignoring conscience, we might start by asking the question: when an entire generation, including that generation's business and political leaders, is repeatedly instructed that people are selfish and respond reliably only to material incentives, how is that likely to affect behavior? To answer this question we need only return to the three-factor model. If unselfish prosocial behavior depends on the social cues of instructions from authority, beliefs about others' unselfishness, and the perception that others benefit from one's unselfish actions, emphasizing the *homo economicus* model undermines all three.

When our respected authorities—professors, policymakers, experts—repeatedly tell us to assume people are selfish, this implies that selfish behavior is always permissible and even appropriate. Sometimes the message is explicit. A *Financial Times* columnist recently took a business executive to task for turning down a pay raise, scolding that "[f]or a capitalist economy to work, we all need to believe that more money is better than less money."[31] Conservative humorist P. J. O'Rourke advised graduating college students in a *Los Angeles Times* editorial to "Go out and make a bunch of money," "Don't be an idealist," "Get politically uninvolved," and "Forget about fairness!"[32] Less blatant but more pernicious, repeatedly invoking the phrase "rational self-interest" implies (not so subtly either) that someone who acts unselfishly is *ir*rational.

Moreover, formal instruction in the *homo economicus* model encourages us to believe people generally behave selfishly. By discounting the role and importance of unselfish behavior, economists unavoidably signal that most people, most of the time, pursue their own ends at others' expense. (As economist Gordon Tullock has put it, "the average human being is about 95 percent selfish.")[33] To the extent this stereotype influences our expectations of others' behavior, the three-factor model predicts that it will reduce our willingness to sacrifice for others, including our willingness to ethically refrain from taking advantage of them.

Finally, what about the third social variable emphasized in the three-factor model, perceptions of benefits to others? Formal instruction in economics may encourage more selfish behavior for the simple reason that economics often teaches (to quote the fictional Gordon Gekko from Oliver Stone's 1985 movie *Wall Street*) that "greed is good." Adam Smith's parable of the market's invisible hand provides perhaps the most famous example of this lesson, painting Economic Man as an unintending altruist who does good for others by doing well for himself.[34] Chicago School law professor and now federal judge Frank Easterbrook similarly described greed in one of his judicial opinions ~~as~~ *Or said* the "engine that propels a market economy."[35] Of course, even the most avid free-market economist admits selfishness sometimes leads people to impose inefficient external costs on others. But the standard economic solution to externalities is government regulation—not conscience, which is viewed as rare, quirky, unreliable, and perhaps nonexistent. Thus, economics teaches that selfishness generally benefits others and when it doesn't, it is the government, and not our sense of right and wrong, that should intervene.

The three-factor model accordingly predicts that focusing on the power and prevalence of selfishness should increase the incidence of selfish behavior. There is some evidence to support this: economics majors are famous for cooperating less in social dilemmas than non-economics students do. One classic study, for example, has reported that economics students contributed only 24 percent of their initial stakes in a social dilemma game, while non-economics students contributed 49 percent.[36] Another study has concluded that at least some of this difference in behavior seems to be due to studying economics, which seems to suppress cooperative behavior in experimental games.[37] It may have not been a coincidence that Bradley Birkenfeld, the UBS banker who made a profession of helping his clients evade U.S. taxes, majored in economics as an undergraduate.

THE SECOND DANGER: OVEREMPHASIZING INCENTIVES SUPPRESSES CONSCIENCE

There is a second negative consequence of relying too much on the *homo economicus* model, however, that may have contributed even more to the decline in Americans' prosocial behavior than the propagation of the idea of rational selfishness. This is the way the widespread belief in the power of selfishness has led reformers, policymakers, academics, consultants, and business managers alike to rely increasingly on material incentives to manage human behavior. Are investors getting poor returns on their portfolios? Change executive compensation rules to emphasize "pay for performance." Are American schoolchildren falling behind in their performance on standardized tests? Tie school budgets and teacher salaries to test scores.

The three-factor model predicts that by overemphasizing material incentives, we may be flirting with disaster. To understand the problem, it is important to begin by accepting that it is extremely difficult in real life to design incentive systems that always reward only beneficial—and never harmful—behaviors. When teacher pay is determined by students' test scores, a teacher can profit from excluding poor-testing students from her classes, or from helping her students cheat on their tests. Similarly, chapter 1 described how Congress's 1993 decision to modify the tax code to tie executive pay to corporate performance led to the widespread adoption of stock option plans like the ones that "incentivized" executives at Enron and Worldcom to undertake massive accounting frauds. More recently, bonuses based on short-term profits motivated executives at Bear Stearns, Lehman Brothers, and insurance giant AIG to embrace trading risks that nearly brought down their companies and the American economy. As yet another example, consider how UBH "incentivized" Bradley Birkenfeld to bring in new clients, but neglected to ensure he attracted them only by offering lawful banking services.

In many and perhaps most cases, it is impossible to create incentive systems that don't have potential to reward unethical behavior. A *Dilbert* cartoon lays out the problem. In the cartoon, a manager tells an employee during a job review, "Here are your regular goals and here are your stretch goals." When the employee asks the difference, the manager replies: "The regular goals can be achieved by sacrificing your health and your personal life. The stretch goals require all of that plus some sort of criminal conduct."

The difficulty of designing Hyde-proof incentives leads to danger, because as we learned in discussing the three-factor model in Part Two, social cues only reliably trigger unselfish prosocial behavior when unselfishness is not too personally costly. Conscience needs breathing room to work. When the potential rewards from unethical action get too large, many if not most of us can be expected to act unethically. This means that if we want to promote unselfish prosocial behavior, it's not enough to give people the proper social cues. We must also make sure that we do not inadvertently raise the "cost" of conscience. Put simply, *if we want people to be good, we must not tempt them to be bad*. And over-reliance on material incentives almost always leads to temptation.

Emphasizing material rewards can suppress conscience in a second fashion as well. As we saw in chapter 8, asking people to focus on extrinsic incentives can have the unfortunate effect of "crowding out" internal incentives like trustworthiness, honor, and concern for others' welfare. This is because, by emphasizing material incentives, we move the three familiar social levers of authority, conformity, and empathy in a direction that encourages selfishness. For example, offering a material incentive to induce someone to do something inevitably sends the unspoken signal that selfish behavior is both expected and appropriate to the task at hand. It suggests that others in the same situation are behaving selfishly. Finally, it implies selfishness must somehow be beneficial. Otherwise, why is it being rewarded?

Once we recognize how material incentives can suppress conscience, not only by creating temptations for unethical conduct but also by signaling that selfishness is appropriate, we can better understand what Bradley Berkenfeld meant when he told a federal judge that UBS had "incentivized" him to help his wealthy clients evade U.S. taxes. Berkenfeld was not trying to communicate simply that he had broken the law because it was personally advantageous for him to do so; no judge would listen sympathetically to a claim that self-interest excuses illegality. Rather, Birkenfeld was saying that by "incentivizing" him to help his clients evade taxes, UBS had created a social context that gave him *permission* to break the law.

Emphasizing material incentives, it turns out, does more than just change incentives. At a very deep level, it changes people. By treating people as if they should care only about their own material rewards, we ensure that they do.

CULTIVATING CONSCIENCE: BEYOND HOMO ECONOMICUS

It would be a grave mistake to put down this book thinking either that the *homo economicus* model should not be taught in our schools and universities, or that lawmakers and employers should never use material incentives to change behavior. That is not the message intended in these pages. Rather, the message is that the *homo economicus* model is not the *only* model of human behavior that should be taught. Similarly, material incentives are not the *only* tools we should use to change behavior—and when we do use incentives, we should be careful to ensure they do more good than harm.

It is time to take conscience as seriously as a powerful force that is essential to our economic, social, and political lives. Accumulating data indicate that Americans—historically more inclined toward trust, civic engagement, and law-abidingness than citizens of many other nations—increasingly are acting more asocially. Just as for many years vocal skeptics questioned the accreting evidence of climate change and global warming, skeptics can question and discount the emerging evidence of "conscience cooling." Just as in the case of climate change, however, if the evidence that Americans are becoming increasingly asocial and selfish is correct, ignoring the evidence may prove disastrous.

Conscience seems an important ingredient in the recipe for economic growth and personal satisfaction. Moreover, as we have seen, one important trigger for unselfish prosocial behavior is the perception others also are unselfishly prosocial. The alarming corollary is that a perception others are acting selfishly triggers more selfish behavior. Once we come to believe our fellow citizens are mostly selfish, we behave mostly selfishly ourselves, in a downward spiral that destroys wealth and well-being.

We must hope our society has not reached some tipping point where declining prosociality becomes an irreversible, self-fulfilling prophecy. Some experts predict that once a nation becomes too poor in trust and cooperation, stagnation and decline inevitably follow. "If trust is sufficiently low, growth stalls."[38] Savings, investment, and exchange disappear, and with them, peace and prosperity.

It is thus essential for all of us to understand and appreciate the force of conscience. But it is especially important for lawmakers, law enforcement officers, and law professors. Legal rules play an important role in promoting unselfish prosocial behavior, not only by creating incentives, but also by signaling what sort of conduct is appropriate and expected; by influencing the behavior of those around us; and by educating us about how our own choices help or harm others. Understanding how law and conscience interact not only allows us to harness conscience to make law more effective—it also invites us to use law to promote conscience.

We make a grave mistake if we follow Oliver Wendell Holmes' advice that "if you want to know the law . . . you must look at it as a bad man, who cares only for the material consequences which such knowledge allows him to predict, and not as a good one, who finds his reasons for conduct . . . in the vaguer sanctions of conscience."[39] Rather, we should listen to Holmes' contemporary, Supreme Court Justice Louis Brandeis. Although Brandeis and Holmes often agreed in their judicial opinions, they held quite different views about the role that morality plays in law. Holmes, as we have seen, thought law should be viewed from the perspective of the bad man. Brandeis believed (in the words of his biographer Alpheus Thomas Mason) "that no small part of the law's function is to make men good."[40]

The scientific evidence supports Brandeis over Holmes. Conscience exists. It is both a powerful force, and an endemic one. It can be destroyed, to our collective loss. But conscience can also be cultivated. Law plays a vital part in that process.

NOTES

CHAPTER 1: FRANCO'S CHOICE

1. Hector Becerra, "Ballad of the Poor Samaritan," *Los Angeles Times*, August 2, 2002.
2. Margaret M. Blair and Lynn A. Stout, "Trust, Trustworthiness, and the Behavioral Foundations of Corporate Law," *University of Pennsylvania Law Review* 149 (2001): 1735–1810.
3. Michael Kosfeld et al., "Oxytocin Increases Trust in Humans," *Nature* 435 (2005): 673–76.
4. Ibid., table 1, fig. 3.
5. Phil Trexler, "Masked Man Waits in Line; Robs Stow Bank," *The Beacon Journal*, January 8, 2009, http://www.ohio.com. A second problem with "cooperation" is that it does not necessarily imply concern for others' welfare: even a purely selfish person might cooperate if he found himself at the wrong end of a gun.
6. David Callahan, *The Cheating Culture: Why More Americans Are Doing Wrong to Get Ahead* (Orlando, FL: Harcourt, 2004).
7. Robert D. Putnam, *Bowling Alone: The Collapse and Revival of American Community* (New York: Simon & Schuster, 2000).
8. Francis Fukayama, *Trust: The Social Virtues and the Creation of Prosperity* (New York: Free Press, 1995); Stephen Knack and Philip Keefer, "Does Social Capital Have an Economic Payoff? A Cross-Country Investigation," *Quarterly Journal of Economics* 112 (1997): 1251–88; Paul J. Zak and Stephen Knack, "Trust and Growth," *Economic Journal* 111 (2001): 295–321.
9. Guido Calabresi and Douglas Melamed, "Property Rules, Liability Rules, and Inalienability: One View of the Cathedral," *Harvard Law Review* 85 (1972): 1089–1128.

CHAPTER 2: HOLMES' FOLLY

1. David J. Seipp, "Holmes's Path," *Boston University Law Review* 77 (June 1997): 545–46.
2. Paul A. Freund, *Oliver Wendell Holmes*, vol. 3, *The Justices of the United States Supreme Court 1789–1969: Their Lives and Major Opinions*, ed. L. Friedman and F. Israel (New York: Chelsea House and R. R. Bowker, 1969).

3. Steven J. Burton, ed., *"The Path of the Law" and Its Influence: The Legacy of Oliver Wendell Holmes, Jr.* (Cambridge and New York: Cambridge University Press, 2000).

4. Oliver Wendell Holmes, Jr., "The Path of the Law," *Harvard Law Review* 10, no. 8 (March 25, 1897): 460.

5. Ibid., 459, 461.

6. Ibid., 462.

7. Ibid., 461.

8. Seipp, "Holmes's Path," 519–21.

9. Holmes, "The Path of the Law," 459.

10. Thomas Hobbes, *Leviathan*, ed. C. B. MacPherson (1651; Harmondsworth, UK: Penguin Books, 1968), 54.

11. Adam Smith, *An Inquiry into the Nature and Causes of the Wealth of Nations* (1776; Chicago: Encyclopedia Britannica, 1952), 7.

12. John Stuart Mill, "On the Definition of Political Economy," in *Essays on Some Unsettled Questions of Political Economy* (1836; London: The London School of Economics and Political Science, 1948), 137.

13. Francis Y. Edgeworth, *Mathematical Psychics* (London: C. Kegan Paul & Co., 1881), 16, quoted in Jack Hirshleifer, "The Expanding Domain of Economics," *American Economic Review* 75, no. 6 (December 1985): 54.

14. Gary S. Becker, "Nobel Lecture: The Economic Way of Looking at Behavior," *Journal of Political Economy* 101, no. 3 (June 1993): 385–409; Hirshleifer, "The Expanding Domain of Economics," 53–68.

15. Ronald H. Coase, "The Problem of Social Cost," *Journal of Law & Economics* 3 (1960): 1; Guido Calabresi, *The Cost of Accidents: A Legal and Economic Analysis* (New Haven: Yale University Press, 1970); Richard A. Posner, *Economic Analysis of Law*, 5th ed. (New York: Aspen Law & Business, 1998).

16. Steven M. Teles, *The Rise of the Conservative Legal Movement: The Battle for Control of the Law* (Princeton, NJ and Oxford: Princeton University Press, 2008), 216.

17. Ibid., 181–82.

18. Ibid., 112–13.

19. Posner, *Economic Analysis of Law*, 3–4.

20. Steven E. Landsburg, *The Armchair Economist: Economics and Everyday Life* (New York: Free Press, 1993), 3.

21. Holmes, "The Path of the Law," 459.

22. Posner, *Economic Analysis of Law*, 5.

23. Burton, ed., *"The Path of the Law" and Its Influence*, 4.

24. Paul Milgrom and John Roberts, *Economics, Organization and Management* (Englewood Cliffs, NJ: Prentice Hall, 1992), 42.

25. For examples, see Becker, "The Economic Way of Looking at Behavior," 386; Posner, *Economic Analysis of Law*.

26. Harold Demsetz, "Rationality, Evolution, and Acquisitiveness," *Economic Inquiry* 34 (July 1999): 492.

27. Ibid.

28. Robert C. Ellickson, *Order Without Law: How Neighbors Settle Disputes* (Cambridge, MA: Harvard University Press, 1991), viii.

29. Ibid., 245.

30. For examples, see Robert Cooter, "Models of Morality in Law and Economics: Self-Control and Self-Improvement for the 'Bad Man' of Holmes," *Boston University Law Review* 78 (1998): 903–30; Richard H. McAdams, "The Origin, Development, and Regulation of Norms," *Michigan Law Review* 96 (1997): 338, 400; Eric A. Posner, *Law and Social Norms* (Cambridge, MA: Harvard University Press, 2000).

31. See Robert Cooter, "Expressive Law and Economics," *Journal of Legal Studies* 27 (June 1998): 585–608.

32. Lawrence E. Mitchell, "Understanding Norms," *University of Toronto Law Journal* 49 (Spring 1999): 189.

33. Eric Posner, "Efficient Norms," in *The New Palgrave Dictionary of Economics and the Law,* ed. Peter Newman (New York: Stockton Press, 1998), 2:20.

34. Kenneth G. Dau-Schmidt, "Economics and Sociology: The Prospects for an Interdisciplinary Discourse on Law," *Wisconsin Law Review* 1997, no. 3 (1997): 399; Ellickson, *Order Without Law,* 6–8.

35. Leda Cosmides and John Toobey, "Cognitive Adaptations for Social Exchange," in *The Adapted Mind: Evolutionary Psychology and the Generation of Culture,* ed. Jerome H. Barkow, Leda Cosmides, and John Toobey, 163–228 (New York: Oxford University Press, 1992).

36. Steven Pinker, *The Blank Slate: The Modern Denial of Human Nature* (New York: Viking, 2002).

37. No Child Left Behind Act of 2001, Public Law 107-110, *U.S. Statutes at Large* 115 (2001): 1425–2096.

38. James E. Ryan, "The Perverse Incentives of the No Child Left Behind Act," *New York University Law School* 79 (June 2004): 937–44.

39. David N. Figlio and Lawrence Kenny, "Individual Teacher Incentives and Student Performance" (NBER Working Paper Series no. 12627, National Bureau of Economic Research, Cambridge, MA, October 2006), 1; Dale Ballou, "Pay for Performance in Public and Private Schools," *Economics of Education Review* 20 (2000): 51–61; Dan Goldhaber, "Teacher Quality and Teacher Pay Structure: What Do We Know, and What Are the Options?" *Georgetown Public Policy Review* 7 (Spring 2002): 81–89.

40. Figlio and Kenny, "Individual Teacher Incentives and Student Performance," 1.

41. U.S. Department of Education, "Overview: No Child Left Behind Act Is Working," http://www.ed.gov/nclb/overview/importance/nclbworking.html (accessed November 10, 2008).

42. Ryan, "The Perverse Incentives of the No Child Left Behind Act," 961–63.

43. Figlio and Kenny, "Individual Teacher Incentives and Student Performance," 1–2.

44. Noel D. Campbell and Edward J. López, "Paying Teachers for Advanced Degrees: Evidence on Student Performance from Georgia," http://ssrn.com/abstract=1147162 (forthcoming in *Journal of Private Enterprise*), 5.

45. Shaila Dewan, "Georgia Schools Inquiry Finds Signs of Cheating," *New York Times*, February 12, 2010.

46. Michael C. Jensen and William H. Meckling, "Theory of the Firm: Managerial Behavior, Agency Costs and Ownership Structure," *Journal of Financial Economics* 3, no. 4 (October 1976): 305–60.

47. For a recent example, see Lucian Bebchuk and Jesse Fried, *Pay Without Performance: The Unfulfilled Promise of Executive Compensation* (Cambridge, MA: Harvard University Press, 2004).

48. Jeffrey D. Bauman, Alan R. Palmiter, and Frank Partnoy, *Corporations Law and Policy: Materials and Problems*, 6th ed. (St. Paul, MN: Thomson West, 2007), 816–17.

49. Ibid., 817.

50. Margit Osterloh and Bruno S. Frey, "Corporate Governance for Crooks? The Case for Corporate Virtue," ZEW Working Paper no. 164, http://ssrn.com/abstract=430062, 2; Judith Samuelson and Lynn A. Stout, "Are Executives Paid Too Much?" *Wall Street Journal*, February 25, 2009.

51. See, e.g., Michael C. Jensen, Kevin J. Murphy, and Eric G. Wruck, "Remuneration: Where We've Been, How, We Got to Here, What Are the Problems, and How to Fix Them," Harvard NOM Working Paper no. 04-28; ECGI-Finance Working Paper no. 44/2004, http://ssrn.com/abstract=561305.

52. Steven D. Levitt and Stephen J. Dubner, *Freakonomics: A Rogue Economist Explores the Hidden Side of Everything* (New York: William Morrow, 2005).

53. Landsburg, *The Armchair Economist*.

54. Tim Harford, *The Undercover Economist: Exposing Why the Rich Are Rich, the Poor Are Poor, and Why You Can Never Buy a Decent Used Car* (New York: Oxford University Press, 2005).

55. David Friedman, *Hidden Order: The Economics of Everyday Life* (New York: HarperBusiness, 1996).

56. Tyler Cowan, *Discover Your Inner Economist: Use Incentives to Fall in Love, Survive Your Next Meeting, and Motivate Your Dentist* (New York: Plume, 2007).

CHAPTER 3: BLIND TO GOODNESS

1. Benjamin Wolman, *The Sociopathic Personality* (New York: Brunner/ Mazel, 1987), 42.
2. American Psychiatric Association, *Diagnostic and Statistical Manual of Mental Disorders*, 4th ed. (Washington, DC: American Psychiatric Association, 2000), 704; hereafter *DSM-IV*.
3. Paul Pringle and Hemmy So, "An Unlikely Friendship that Finally Unraveled," *Los Angeles Times*, August 19, 2006.
4. APA, *DSM-IV*, 704.
5. U.S. Census Bureau, "State & County QuickFacts: Los Angeles (city), 2006," Population, 2006 Estimate, http://quickfacts.census.gov/qfd/ states/06/0644000.html; ibid., Land Area, 2000 (square miles).
6. Gabriel Kahn, "Top Cop in Los Angeles Says Cutting Crime Pays," *Wall Street Journal*, November 29–30, 2008.
7. Sylvia Nasar, *A Beautiful Mind: A Biography of John Forbes Nash, Jr., Winner of the Nobel Prize in Economics 1994* (New York: Simon & Schuster, 1998), 105.
8. David Sally, "Conversation and Cooperation in Social Dilemmas: A Meta-Analysis of Experiments from 1958 to 1992," *Rationality and Society* 7 (1995): 60.
9. Nasar, *A Beautiful Mind*, 119.
10. Sally, "Conversation and Cooperation in Social Dilemmas"; Robert H. Frank, Thomas Gilovich, and Dennis T. Regan, "Does Studying Economics Inhibit Cooperation?" *Journal of Economic Perspectives* 7 (1993): 159–71. Unselfish behavior is similarly routine in a sequential type of prisoner's dilemma called a "trust game," described in chapter 1. "Investors" typically cooperate with "trustees" by turning over some or all of their stakes, and trustees typically return the favor by altruistically returning slightly larger amounts to the investors. Paul J. Zak and Stephen Knack, "Trust and Growth," *Economic Journal* 111 (2001): 295–321.
11. Catherine Newman, "I Do. Not: Why I Won't Marry," in *The Bitch in the House: 26 Women Tell the Truth About Sex, Solitude, Work, Motherhood, and Marriage*, ed. Cathi Hanauer and Ellen Gilchrist (New York: Harper Collins, 2002), 67.
12. Donald E. Brown, *Human Universals* (Philadelphia: Temple University Press, 1991), 130–41.

13. Charles Darwin, *The Descent of Man*, in *Great Books of the Western World*, vol. 49, *Darwin*, ed. Robert Maynard Hutchins (London: Encyclopedia Britannica, 1952), 322.
14. Matt Ridley, *The Origins of Virtue: Human Instincts and the Evolution of Cooperation* (New York: Penguin Books, 1996), 38.
15. Percy Bysshe Shelley, *A Defense of Poetry*, ed. Albert S. Cook (Boston: Ginn and Company, 1890).
16. Leda Cosmides, "The Logic of Social Exchange: Has Natural Selection Shaped How Humans Reason? Studies with the Wason Selection Task," *Cognition* 31 (1989): 187–276.
17. Leda Cosmides and John Toobey, "Cognitive Adaptations for Social Exchange," in *The Adapted Mind: Evolutionary Psychology and the Generation of Culture*, ed. Jerome H. Barkow et al. (New York: Oxford University Press, 1992), 163–228; Robert Wright, *The Moral Animal: Evolutionary Psychology and Everyday Life* (New York: Vintage Books, 1994), 204.
18. Lee Ross and Andrew Ward, "Psychological Barriers to Dispute Resolution," *Advances in Experimental Social Psychology* 27 (1995): 279.
19. Jane J. Mansbridge, ed., *Beyond Self-Interest* (Chicago: Chicago University Press, 1990), 141.
20. Richard Dawkins, *The Selfish Gene* (New York: Oxford University Press, 1976).
21. Frank, "Does Studying Economics Inhibit Cooperation?"
22. Stephan Meier and Bruno S. Frey, "Do Business Students Make Good Citizens?" *International Journal of the Economics of Business* 11 (2004): 141–63; Donald M. McCabe et al., "Academic Dishonesty in Graduate School Business Programs: Prevalence, Causes, and Proposed Action," *Academy of Management Learning and Education* 5 (September 2006): 294–306.
23. Larissa MacFarquhar, "The Bench Burner: How Did a Judge with Such Subversive Ideas Become a Leading Influence on American Legal Opinion?" *New Yorker*, December 10, 2001.
24. David W. Barnes and Lynn A. Stout, *Law and Economics* (St. Paul, MN: West Publishing, 1992).

CHAPTER 4: GAMES PEOPLE PLAY

1. See, for example, David Hirshleifer, "Investor Psychology and Asset Pricing," *Journal of Finance* 56, no. 4 (August 2001): 1533–97.
2. Amos Tversky and Daniel Kahneman, "Availability: A Heuristic for Judging Frequency and Probability," *Cognitive Psychology* 5 (1973): 207–32.
3. See, for example, Jon D. Hanson and Douglas A. Kysar, "Taking Behavioralism Seriously: The Problem of Market Manipulation," *New York*

University Law Review 74 (June 1999): 630–93; Christine Jolls, Cass R. Sunstein, and Richard Thaler, "A Behavioral Approach to Law and Economics," *Stanford Law Review* 50 (1998): 1471–1550; Cass R. Sunstein, "Behavioral Analysis of Law," *University of Chicago Law Review* 64 (1997): 1175–95.

4. Although Kahneman and Tversky studied irrationality in their professional lives, their private lives provided considerable anecdotal evidence of unselfishness. While accepting the 2002 Nobel Prize, Kahneman offered a eulogy for Tversky in his own autobiographical statement. Daniel Kahneman, "Autobiography," Nobel Foundation, http://nobelprize.org/nobel_prizes/economics/laureates/2002/kahneman-autobio.html (accessed November 26, 2008). Tversky's life provides even more dramatic evidence of unselfishness. As a lieutenant in the Israeli Army, Tversky saved the life of another soldier who had lit an explosive charge and then frozen in panic. Tversky tackled the soldier, knocking him down, and was himself seriously wounded by the explosion.

5. Russell Korobkin, "Bounded Rationality, Standard Form Contracts, and Unconscionability," *University of Chicago Law Review* 70, no. 4 (Fall 2003): 1203–95.

6. Howard Latin, "'Good' Warnings, Bad Products, and Cognitive Limitations," *UCLA Law Review* 41 (June 1994): 1193–1295; Hanson and Kysar, "Taking Behavioralism Seriously," 630–93.

7. Jolls, Sunstein, and Thaler, "A Behavioral Approach to Law and Economics," 1539–40.

8. Jeffrey J. Rachlinski and Forest Jourden, "Remedies and the Psychology of Ownership," *Vanderbilt Law Review* 51 (November 1998): 1541–82.

9. Cass R. Sunstein, Daniel Kahneman, and David Schkade, "Assessing Punitive Damages (With Notes on Cognition and Valuation in Law)," *Yale Law Journal* 107 (May 1998): 2071–2153.

10. Chris Guthrie, Jeffrey J. Rachlinski, and Andrew J. Wistrich, "Inside the Judicial Mind," *Cornell Law Review* 86, no. 4 (May 2001): 777–830.

11. However, if players only cooperate in repeat prisoner's dilemmas out of fear of retaliation, we would see zero cooperation in repeat games where players know how many times they will play. This is because if both players know they will play ten rounds, neither will cooperate in the tenth round because there is no possibility of reciprocal cooperation thereafter. Knowing there is no possibility of cooperation in the tenth round, neither will cooperate in the ninth round, and so on in backwards induction to no cooperation in the first round. Fear of retaliation can only support cooperation in repeated prisoners' dilemmas when the players do not know how many rounds they will

play. It is unclear whether the RAND subjects were told how many rounds they would be playing.

12. Alvin E. Roth et al., "Bargaining and Market Behavior in Jerusalem, Ljubljiana, Pittsburgh, and Tokyo: An Experimental Study," *American Economic Review* 81, no. 5 (December 1991): 1068–95; Robert L. Slonim and Alvin E. Roth, "Learning in High-Stakes Ultimatum Games: An Experiment in the Slovak Republic," *Econometrica* 66 (1998): 569–96.

13. Joseph Henrich et al., "In Search of Homo Economicus: Behavioral Experiments in 15 Small-Scale Societies," *American Economic Review* 91, no. 2 (May 2001): 73–79.

14. Joseph Henrich et al., *Foundations of Human Sociality: Ethnography and Experiments in 15 Small-Scale Societies* (Oxford and New York: Oxford University Press, 2004), 10.

15. David Sally, "Conversation and Cooperation in Social Dilemmas: A Meta-Analysis of Experiments from 1958 to 1992," *Rationality and Society* 7, no.1 (January 1995): 58–92. Similarly, raising the stakes has only modest effects on behavior in dictator and ultimatum games. Lisa A. Cameron, "Raising the Stakes in the Ultimatum Game: Experimental Evidence from Indonesia, *Economic Inquiry* 37 (January 1999): 47–59; Jeffrey Carpenter et al., "The Effect of Stakes in Distribution Experiments," *Economics Letters* 86 (2005): 393–98.

16. Henrich et al., "In Search of Homo Economicus."

17. Sally, "Conversation and Cooperation in Social Dilemmas," 62.

18. Robyn M. Dawes and Richard H. Thaler, "Anomalies: Cooperation," *Journal of Economic Perspectives* 2, no. 3 (Summer 1988): 187–97.

19. Colin Camerer and Richard H. Thaler, "Anomalies: Ultimatums, Dictators and Manners," *Journal of Economic Perspectives* 9, no. 2 (Spring 1995): 209–19; Martin A. Nowak, Karen M. Page, and Karl Sigmund, "Fairness Versus Reason in the Ultimatum Game," *Science* 289 (September 8, 2000): 1773–75.

20. Nowak, Page, and Sigmund, "Fairness Versus Reason in the Ultimatum Game," 1773.

21. Henrich et al., *Foundations of Human Sociality*, 13.

22. Ibid., 12.

23. In addition to altruism and spite, there is at least one other way people behave as if they care about what happens to other people: people pay attention to others' circumstances to *compare with their own*. Economist Robert Frank has written extensively on such "relative preferences." Robert H. Frank, *Luxury Fever: Money and Happiness in an Era of Excess* (New York: Free Press, 1999).

24. Henrich et al., *Foundations of Human Sociality*, 27.

25. Ibid.

26. Camerer and Thaler, Anomalies: Ultimatums, Dictators and Manners," 216; see also Henrich et al., "In Search of Homo Economicus," 74–75.

27. Several legal scholars have leveled this critique at standard behavioral economics. As Jennifer Arlen has put it, "although behavioral economic analysis of law presents a powerful challenge to conventional economics . . . behavioral economic analysis of law is not yet—and may never be—in a position to supplant conventional law and economics . . . because it does not yet have a coherent, robust, tractable model of human behavior which can serve as a basis for such recommendations." Jennifer Arlen, "Comment: The Future of Behavioral Economic Analysis of Law," *Vanderbilt Law Review* 51, no. 6 (November 1998): 1765–88.

CHAPTER 5: THE JEKYLL/HYDE SYNDROME

1. Robert Louis Stevenson, *Strange Case of Dr. Jekyll and Mr. Hyde*, ed. Katherine Linehan (1886; New York: W.W. Norton, 2003).

2. Ibid., 53.

3. Ibid., 48.

4. Kevin A. McCabe et al., "A Functional Imaging Study of Cooperation in Two-Person Reciprocal Exchange," *Proceedings of the National Academy of Sciences* 98 (2001): 1662–73; James K. Rilling et al., "A Neural Basis for Social Cooperation," *Neuron* 35 (July 18, 2002): 395–405; Jean Decety et al., "The Neural Bases of Cognition and Competition: An fMRI Investigation," *NeuroImage* 23, no. 2 (October 2004): 744–51.

5. David Sally, "Conversation and Cooperation in Social Dilemmas: A Meta-Analysis of Experiments from 1958 to 1992," *Rationality and Society* 7, no.1 (January 1955): 62.

6. Ernst Fehr and Klaus M. Schmidt, "The Economics of Fairness, Reciprocity and Altruism—Experimental Evidence and New Theories," in *Handbook of the Economics of Giving, Altruism, and Reciprocity*, vol. 1, *Foundations*, ed. Serge-Christophe Kolm and Jean Mercier Ythier, 659 (Amsterdam and Oxford: North-Holland/Elsevier, 2006); James C. Cox, "How to Identify Trust and Reciprocity," *Games and Economic Behavior* 46, no. 2 (2004): 260–81.

7. John A. List and Todd L. Cherry, "Examining the Role of Fairness in High Stakes Allocation Decisions," *Journal of Economic Behavior and Organization* 65, no. 1 (January 2008): 1.

8. Rachel Croson and Nancy Buchan, "Gender and Culture: International Experimental Evidence from Trust Games," *Gender and Economic Transactions* 89, no. 2 (May 1999): 386–91; James Andreoni and Lise Vesterlund, "Which Is the Fair Sex?': Gender Differences in

Altruism," *Quarterly Journal of Economics* 116, no. 1 (February 2001): 293–312.

9. Tom W. Smith, "Altruism and Empathy in America: Trends and Correlates" (National Opinion Research Center, February 9, 2006).

10. Elizabeth Hoffman, Kevin McCabe, and Vernon L. Smith, "Social Distance and Other-Regarding Behavior in Dictator Games," *American Economic Review* 86 (June 1996): 653–54.

11. Sally, "Conversation and Cooperation in Social Dilemmas," 76, 78, 83; Bruno S. Frey and Iris Bohnet, "Identification in Democratic Society," *Journal of Socio-Economics* 26 (1997): 33.

12. Gary Charness and Matthew Rabin, "Understanding Social Preferences with Simple Tests," *Quarterly Journal of Economics* 117 (2002): 817–69.

13. Sally, "Conversation and Cooperation in Social Dilemmas," 58–92.

14. Colin Camerer and Richard H. Thaler, "Anomalies: Ultimatums, Dictators and Manners," *Journal of Economic Perspectives* 9, no. 2 (Spring 1995): 209–19; Robyn M. Dawes, "Social Dilemmas," *Annual Review of Psychology* 31 (1980): 169–93; Robyn M. Dawes, Alphons J. C. van de Kragt, and John Orbell, "Cooperation for the Benefit of Us—Not Me, or My Conscience," in *Beyond Self-Interest*, ed. Jane J. Mansbridge, 99–101 (Chicago: University of Chicago Press, 1990); Robyn M. Dawes and Richard H. Thaler, "Anomalies: Cooperation," *Journal of Economic Perspectives* 2, no. 3 (Summer 1988): 187–97; Joseph Henrich et al., "In Search of Homo Economicus: Behavioral Experiments in 15 Small-Scale Societies," *American Economic Review* 91, no. 2 (May 2001): 73–79; S. S. Komorita, C. D. Parks, and L. G. Hulbert, "Reciprocity and the Induction of Cooperation in Social Dilemmas," *Journal of Personality and Social Psychology* 62, no. 4 (1992): 607–17; Martin A. Nowak, Karen M. Page, and Karl Sigmund, "Fairness Versus Reason in the Ultimatum Game," *Science* 289 (September 8, 2000): 1773–75; Fehr and Schmidt, "The Economics of Fairness, Reciprocity and Altruism."

15. For more discussion of Milgram's famous experiments, see, for example, Stanley Milgram, "Behavioral Study of Obedience," *Journal of Abnormal and Social Psychology* 67 (1963): 371–378; Stanley Milgram, *Obedience to Authority: An Experimental View* (New York: Harper & Row, 1974); Thomas Blass, *The Man Who Shocked the World: The Life and Legacy of Stanley Milgram* (New York: Basic Books, 2004).

16. Blass, *The Man Who Shocked the World.*

17. Thomas Blass, "The Milgram Paradigm After 35 Years: Some Things We Now Know About Obedience to Authority," *Journal of Applied Social Psychology* 25 (1999): 955–78.

18. See, for example, David G. Myers, *Social Psychology*, 8th ed. (New York: McGraw Hill, 2005), 215–227; Shelley E. Taylor, Letitia Anne

Peplau, and David O. Sears, *Social Psychology*, 12th ed. (Upper Saddle River, NJ: Pearson Prentice Hall, 2006), 225–29.

19. Sally, "Conversation and Cooperation in Social Dilemmas," 75, 78.

20. Lee D. Ross and Andrew Ward, "Naïve Realism in Everyday Life: Implications for Social Conflict and Misunderstanding," in *Values and Knowledge*, ed. Edward Reed, Elliot Turiel, and Terrance Brown, 103, 106–7 (Mahwah, NJ: Lawrence Erlbaum Associates, 1996).

21. Camerer and Thaler, "Anomalies: Ultimatums, Dictators and Manners," 213.

22. Bibb Latané and John M. Darley, "Group Inhibition of Bystander Intervention in Emergencies," *Journal of Personality and Social Psychology* 10, no. 3 (1968): 215–21.

23. Allison and Kerr noted that "[n]umerous studies have reported that individuals are more likely to cooperate when they expect other group members to cooperate than when they expect others to defect." Scott T. Allison and Norbert L. Kerr, "Group Correspondence Biases and the Provision of Public Goods," *Journal of Personality and Social Psychology* 66 (1994): 688. Likewise, Yamagishi concluded that "'expectations about other members' behavior is one of the most important individual factors affecting members' decisions in social dilemmas." Toshio Yamagishi, "The Structural Goal/Expectations Theory of Cooperation in Social Dilemmas," *Advances in Group Processes* 3 (1986): 51, 64–65.

24. Sally, "Conversation and Cooperation in Social Dilemmas," 78.

25. Joyce Berg, John Dickhaut, and Kevin McCabe, "Trust, Reciprocity, and Social History," *Games and Economic Behavior* 10 (1995): 122–42.

26. Ibid.; Gary Charness and Martin Dufwenberg, "Promises and Partnership," *Econometrica* 74, no. 6 (November 2006): 1579–1601.

27. See, e.g., Thomas Gautschi, "History Effects in Social Dilemma Situations," *Rationality & Society* 12, no. 2 (2000): 131–62.

28. Armin Falk, Urs Fischbacher, and Simon Gächter, "Living in two Neighborhoods—Social Interactions in the Lab" (Working Paper 150, Institute for Empirical Research in Economics, November 2004).

29. Erin Krupka and Roberto Weber, "The Focusing and Informational Effects of Norms on Pro-Social Behavior," http://ftp.iza.org/dp3169.pdf (discussion paper, Institute for the Study of Labor, IZA DP 3169, August 2005).

30. Social inference may be relevant to the extent that test subjects look to others' behavior to decode what authority dictates is the proper course of conduct in that situation. In other words, while the experimental game is not an ambiguous situation from an economic perspective, it may be ambiguous from a social perspective.

31. Robert Axelrod and William D. Hamilton, "The Evolution of Cooperation," *Science* 211 (1981): 1390–96.

32. Herbert Gintis et al., "Explaining Altruistic Behavior in Humans," *Evolution and Human Behavior* 24, no. 3 (May 2003): 153–72; Ernst Fehr and Joseph Henrich, "Is Strong Reciprocity a Maladaptation?: On the Evolutionary Foundations of Human Altruism," in *Genetic and Cultural Evolution of Cooperation*, ed. Peter Hammerstein, 55–82 (Cambridge, MA: MIT Press, 2003).

33. Dawes, van de Kragt, and Orbell, "Cooperation for the Benefit of Us," 100–101.

34. For example, see Ernst Fehr and Herbert Gintis, "Human Motivation and Social Cooperation: Experimental and Analytical Foundations," *Annual Review of Sociology* 33 (August 2007): 45.

35. Robert D. Putnam, *Bowling Alone: The Collapse and Revival of American Community* (New York: Simon & Schuster, 2000), 135.

36. A second problem arises from the fact that both the dictator game in its entirety, and the second stage of the ultimatum game, are zero-sum transactions. (It is impossible for a dictator to share more with her partner without decreasing her own payoffs by the same amount, or for a responder in an ultimatum game to give more to the proposer without increasing her own sacrifice in direct proportion.) As a result two important factors—size of benefit to others and size of cost to oneself—are inextricably conflated in these games.

37. To quote from Sally's meta-analysis, "the size of the loss to the group if strictly self-interested choices are made instead of altruistic ones . . . is important and positive" in explaining cooperation rates. Sally, "Conversation and Cooperation in Social Dilemmas," 79.

38. James Andreoni and John Miller, "Giving According to GARP: An Experimental Test of the Consistency of Preferences for Altruism," *Econometrica* 70, no. 2 (March 2002): 737–53; see also Andreoni and Vesterlund, "Which Is the Fair Sex?" 2–3.

39. Tania Singer and Chris Frith, "The Painful Side of Empathy," *Nature Neuroscience* 8, no. 7 (2005): 845–46.

40. Eugene Linden, *The Parrot's Lament: and Other True Tales of Animal Intrigue, Intelligence, and Ingenuity* (New York: Plume, 1999), 19–20.

41. Russell M. Church, "Emotional Reactions of Rats to the Pain of Others," *Journal of Comparative and Physiological Psychology* 52 (1959): 132–34.

42. In another experiment, George Rice and Priscilla Gainer allowed rats to "rescue" another rat that had been strapped in a harness and hoisted off the floor by pressing a lever that lowered the victim to the floor. The "rescuers" acted more quickly when the victim struggled and squealed, than when the victim hung quietly. George E. Rice and Priscilla Gainer, "'Altruism' in the Albino Rat," *Journal of Comparative and Physiological Psychology* 55, no. 1 (1962): 123–25.

43. Sally, "Conversation and Cooperation in Social Dilemmas," 75.
44. Shaila Dewan, "Georgia Schools Inquiry Finds Signs of Cheating," *New York Times*, February 12, 2010.
45. "Hugh Thompson Jr., 62; 'One of the Good Guys' Saved Civilians at My Lai," obituary, *Los Angeles Times*, January 7, 2006, B15.
46. Warren Buffett, "How Buffett Views Risk," *Fortune*, April 4, 1994, 33.

CHAPTER 6: ORIGINS

1. Robert J. Sternberg, *Psychology* (Belmont, CA: Thompson/Wadsworth, 2004), 538–39.
2. Ibid., 373.
3. Ibid., 417. Older children use what Kolhberg called "conventional morality," meaning that they define right and wrong in terms of prevailing social convention and think of "morality" as obeying social rules without regard to whether the rules are good ones. At the third and highest stage of moral judgment, which Kolberg labeled "post-conventional morality," behavior is regulated not by self-interest or social code but an internalized set of abstract ethical principles. Kohlberg concluded from his studies that few individuals reach the highest stage of moral development before adulthood, and many never get there at all, getting stuck instead in the "conventional morality" stage. Ibid., 419.
4. Colin Camerer and Richard H. Thaler, "Anomalies: Ultimatums, Dictators and Manners," *Journal of Economic Perspectives* 9 (Spring 1995): 217.
5. William T. Harbaugh, Kate Krause, and Steven G. Liday, Jr., "Bargaining By Children," (working paper, Economics Department, University of Oregon, 2003): 2, 9.
6. Robert H. Frank, Thomas Gilovich, and Dennis T. Regan, "Does Studying Economics Inhibit Cooperation?" *Journal of Economic Perspectives* 7 (1993): 167–68.
7. Matthias Sutter and Martin G. Kocher, "Age and the Development of Trust and Reciprocity," (SSRN Working Paper Series, 2003): 21.
8. John A. List, "Young, Selfish and Male: Field Evidence of Social Preferences," *Economic Journal* 114 (January 2004): 122.
9. Ibid., 133–34.
10. Linda Mealey, "The Sociobiology of Sociopathy: An Integrated Evolutionary Model," *Behavioral and Brain Sciences* 18 (1995): 524, 526.
11. Lionel Dahmer, *A Father's Story* (New York: William Morrow, 1994), 46, 75–80, 98.
12. Mealey, "The Sociobiology of Sociopathy," 530. "Brethren" is appropriate as sociopaths are estimated to comprise 3–4% of the male

population but only 1% of the female population, although it is possible that men are diagnosed as sociopaths more often than women because men are more likely to aggressively act out asocial impulses. Ibid., 523.

13. Hanna Damasio et al., "The Return of Phineas Gage: Clues About the Brain from the Skull of a Famous Patient," *Science*, New Series 264 (May 1994): 1102; Raymond J. Dolan, "On the Neurology of Morals," Nature *Neuroscience* 2 (November 1999): 927.

14. Steven W. Anderson et al., "Impairment of Social and Moral Behavior Related to Early Damage in Human Prefrontal Cortex," *Nature Neuroscience* 2 (November 1999): 1033.

15. Charles Darwin, *The Descent of Man* 1871 in *Great Books of the Western World*, vol. 49, *Darwin*, edited by Robert Maynard Hutchins (London: Encyclopedia Britannica, Inc., 1952), 321–22.

16. William D. Hamilton, "The Genetical Evolution of Social Behavior I and II," *Journal of Theoretical Biology* 7 (1964): 1–16, 17–52.

17. Richard Dawkins, *The Selfish Gene* (New York: Oxford University Press, 1976).

18. Dr. Roger Lewin, "Accidental Career," *New Scientist* 61 (August 8, 1974): 325.

19. A somewhat loose relationship between altruism and genetic relatedness might arise in populations of related individuals living in groups with little out-migration. In such a case, it would make sense even from the perspective of a selfish gene to show some degree of altruism toward every member of the group, on the theory that every member likely shares some significant degree of genetic relatedness. Steven I. Rothstein, "Reciprocal Altruism and Kin Selection Are Not Clearly Separable Phenomena," *Journal of Theoretical Biology* 87 (1980): 255–61. This makes particular sense in the case of *homo sapiens,* as humans (unlike most mammals) show a marked propensity for mating in secret, leading to a certain amount of uncertainty about who in the group is exactly related to whom, and how.

20. David A. Hyman, "Rescue Without Law: An Empirical Perspective on the Duty to Rescue," *Texas Law Review* 84 (2006): 656, 668.

21. Robert L. Trivers, "The Evolution of Reciprocal Altruism," *Quarterly Journal of Biology* 46 (1971): 35.

22. Gerald S. Wilkinson, "Food Sharing in Vampire Bats," *Scientific American* (February 1990): 76–82.

23. See Ernst Fehr and Joseph Henrich, "Is Strong Reciprocity a Maladaptation? On the Evolutionary Foundations of Human Altruism," in *Genetic and Cultural Evolution of Cooperation* , ed. Peter Hammerstein (Cambridge, MA: MIT Press / Dahlem University Press, 2003), 56, for a description of the "maladaptation" thesis.

24. Sara Kiesler, Keith Waters, and Lee Sproull, "A Prisoner's Dilemma Experiment on Cooperation with People and Human-Like Computers," *Journal of Personality and Social Pyschology* 70 (1996). It may similarly explain why many people seem inclined toward altruism not only toward their own species but toward members of other species as well, including dogs, cats, dolphins, and so forth.

25. Ibid.

26. Hamilton, "The Genetical Evolution of Social Behavior I and II," 1–16, 17–52.

27. Dawkins, *The Selfish Gene*, 89.

28. Robert H. Frank, "If *Homo Economicus* Could Choose His Own Utility Function, Would He Want One with a Conscience?" *American Economic Review* 77 (September 1987): 593–95.

29. Yudhijit Bhattacharjee, "Friendly Faces and Unusual Minds," *Science* 310 (November 4, 2005): 804.

30. Ralph Adolphs, Daniel Tranel, and Antonio R. Damasio, "The Human Amygdala in Social Judgment," *Nature* 393 (June 4, 1998): 470–71.

31. Darwin, *The Descent of Man*, 322–23.

32. John Maynard Smith, "Group Selection and Kin Selection," *Nature* 201 (March 14, 1964): 1145.

33. Elliot Sober and David Sloan Wilson, *Unto Others: The Evolution of Unselfish Behavior* (Cambridge, MA: Harvard University Press, 1998).

34. Geoffrey Miller, "Norm Enforcement in the Public Sphere: The Case of Handicapped Parking," *George Washington Law Review* 71 (2003): 895.

35. See, for example, Ernst Fehr and Simon Gächter, "Altruistic Punishment in Humans," *Nature* 415 (January 10, 2002): 137; Ernst Fehr and Urs Fischbacher, "Third-Party Punishment and Social Norms," *Evolution and Human Behavior* 25 (2004): 63–87.

36. Joseph Henrich and Robert Boyd, "Why People Punish Defectors: Weak Conformist Strategy Can Stabilize Costly Enforcement of Norms in Cooperative Dilemmas," *Journal of Theoretical Biology* 208 (2001): 79–89; see also Robert Boyd et al., "The Evolution of Altruistic Punishment," *Proceedings of the National Academy of Sciences of the United States of America* 100 (March 18, 2003): 3531–35.

37. Robert Boyd and Peter J. Richerson, "Cultural Transmission and the Evolution of Cooperative Behavior," *Human Ecology* 10 (1982): 325; Herbert Gintis, "The Hitchhiker's Guide to Altruism: Gene-Culture Coevolution and the Internalization of Norms," *Journal of Theoretical Biology* 220 (2003): 407; Peter J. Richerson and Robert Boyd, *Not By Genes Alone: How Culture Transformed Human Evolution* (Chicago: University of Chicago Press, 2005).

38. Özgür Gürerk, Bernd Irlenbusch, and Bettina Rockenbach, "The Competitive Advantage of Sanctioning Institutions," *Science* 312 (April 2006): 108.

39. Amot Zahavi, "Mate Selection: A Selection for a Handicap," *Journal of Theoretical Biology* 53 (1975): 205.

40. Eric Alden Smith, "Why Do Good Hunters Have Higher Reproductive Success?" *Human Nature* 15 (2004): 343.

41. See also Herbert Gintis, Eric Alden Smith, and Samuel Bowles, "Costly Signaling and Cooperation," *Journal of Theoretical Biology* 213 (2001): 103.

42. Daniel C. Dennet, *Darwin's Dangerous Idea: Evolution and the Meanings of Life* (New York: Simon & Schuster, 1995), 86.

43. Paul J. Zak, Robert Kurzban, and William T. Matzner, "The Neurobiology of Trust," *Annals of the New York Academy of Sciences* 1032 (2004): 224–26.

44. Ernst Fehr and Bettina Rockenbach, "Human Altruism: Economic, Neural, and Evolutionary Perspectives," *Current Opinion in Neurobiology* 14 (2004): 788.

45. Golnaz Tabibnia, Ajay B. Satpute, and Matthew W. Lieberman, "The Sunny Side of Fairness: Preference for Fairness Activates Reward Circuitry (and Disregarding Unfairness Activates Self-Control Circuitry)," *Psychological Science* 19 (2008): 341.

46. Marilynn B. Brewer, "In-Group Bias in the Minimal Intergroup Situation: A Cognitive-Motivational Analysis," *Psychological Bulletin* 86 (1979): 307.

47. Darwin, *The Descent of Man*, 314.

CHAPTER 7: MY BROTHER'S KEEPER

1. *In Re Dale*, 199 B.R. 1014, 1017 (1995).

2. Ibid.

3. See generally David W. Barnes and Lynn A. Stout, *Law and Economics* (St. Paul, MN: West Publishing, 1992), 23–25.

4. See generally Gary T. Schwartz, "Mixed Theories of Tort Law: Affirming Both Deterrence and Corrective Justice," *Texas Law Review* 75 (1997): 1802–3.

5. Ibid.

6. Richard A. Posner, "A Theory of Negligence," *Journal of Legal Studies* 1 (1972): 31.

7. *U.S. v. Carroll Towing Co.*, 159 F.2d 169 (2d. Cir. 1947).

8. Ibid., 170–71.

9. Ibid., 173.

10. Stephen G. Gilles, "The Invisible Hand Formula," *Virginia Law Review* 80, no. 5 (August 1994): 115–16 and 116 note 4.

11. Barnes and Stout, *Law and Economics*, 165–166.
12. Harvard Medical Practice Study, *Patients, Doctors, and Lawyers: Medical Injury, Malpractice Litigation, and Patient Compensation in New York, a report of the Harvard Medical Practice Study to the State of New York* (Cambridge, MA: The President and Fellows of Harvard College, 1990).
13. Deborah R. Hensler et al., *Compensation for Accidental Injuries in the United States* (Santa Monica, CA: RAND, 1991), 175.
14. Barnes and Stout, *Law and Economics*, 106–15.
15. *West's Annotated California Civil Code*, sec. 3333.2 (West 2008).
16. Amanda Edwards, "Medical Malpractice Non-Economic Damages Caps," *Harvard Journal on Legislation* 43 (Winter 2006): 217–19.
17. *In Re Dale*, 199 B.R. 1014, 1018 (1995). In 1984, the United States Bankruptcy Code was amended to deny discharge of legal judgments against drunk drivers (Bankruptcy Amendments and Federal Judgeship Act of 1984, Pub. L. No. 98-353, sec. 371, codified at 11 U.S.C. sec. 523(a)(9)). As a result, Dale's bankruptcy petition was eventually denied. This does not mean, of course, that he ever succeeded in paying the judgment entered against him.
18. Gary T. Schwarz, "Reality in the Economic Analysis of Tort Law: Does Tort Law Really Deter?" *UCLA Law Review* 42, no. 2 (December 1994): 420, 434.
19. Barnes and Stout, *Law and Economics*, 175–79; Marc Galanter and David Luban, "Poetic Justice: Punitive Damages and Legal Pluralism," *American University Law Review* 42 (1993): 1404–8; Gary T. Schwarz, "Deterrence and Punishment in the Common Law of Punitive Damages: A Comment," *Southern California Law Review* 56 (1982): 141.
20. Andrea Gerlin, "A Matter of Degree," *Wall Street Journal*, September 1, 1994, A1.
21. Law and economics scholars tend to view punitive damages as justified only in situations where an injurer appears to be taking advantage of tort system's tendency to undercompensate. See, e.g., Robert D. Cooter, "Economic Analysis of Punitive Damages," *Southern California Law Review* 56 (1982): 79; A. Mitchell Polinsky and Steven Shavell, "Punitive Damages: An Economic Analysis," *Harvard Law Review* 111, no. 4 (February 1998): 874. For example, Mitchell Polinsky and Steve Shavell suggest that punitive damages should be calculated by a method roughly equivalent to taking the amount of harm actually suffered by the victim who sues and multiplying it by the number of likely victims who chose not to sue, thus ensuring the injurer pays for the full amount of the harm it causes. Polinsky and Shavell, "Punitive Damages," 874–75.

This approach to explaining punitive damages does not account for two important observations. First, virtually every potential injurer should assume there is a significant probability that he will not be sued successfully for his negligence. Thus, virtually every injury that prompts a suit should be a candidate for punitive damages. Second, punitive damages require a legal finding that the defendant acted with "utter indifference" to others' welfare. Requiring this finding makes no sense if, as in the *homo economicus* model, indifference toward others is the only state of mind a rational person would have.

22. See, for example, W. Kip Viscusi, "Why There Is No Defense of Punitive Damages," *Georgetown Law Journal* 87 (1998): 381–95.
23. Anthony J. Sebok, "Punitive Damages: From Myth to Theory," *Iowa Law Review* 92 (March 2007): 959.
24. *Exxon Shipping Co. v. Baker*, 128 S. Ct. 2605, 2626, 2633 (2008).
25. Barnes and Stout, *Law and Economics*, 122–23.
26. Schwartz, "Mixed Theories of Tort Law," 1809.
27. Gilles, "The Invisible Hand Formula," 134.
28. Ibid., 134–35.
29. Schwartz, "Mixed Theories of Tort Law," 1820.
30. It may also explain the significance of apology, which allows an injurer to express regret for selfishly ranking others' welfare below her own. Legal experts have begun to explore the value of apology in discouraging tort litigation. See, for example, Erin Ann O'Hara and Douglas Yarn, "On Apology and Consilience," *Washington Law Review* 77 (October 2002): 1121–1192; Jennifer K. Robbennolt, "Apologies and Legal Settlement," *Michigan Law Review* 102 (December 2003): 460–516. Remorse and apology also play roles in criminal law.
31. Joel Bakan, *The Corporation: The Pathological Pursuit of Profit and Power* (New York: Free Press, 2004).
32. Ibid., 60.
33. Einer Elhauge, "Sacrificing Corporate Profits in the Public Interest," *New York University Law Review* 80 (June 2005): 738–47.
34. Bakan, *The Corporation*, 40–50.
35. For an exception, see Jennifer Arlen and Reiner Kraakman, "Controlling Corporate Misconduct: An Analysis of Corporate Liability Regimes," *New York University Law Review* 72 (October 1997): 752–53.
36. *Sherman Antitrust Act*, 15 U.S.C. § 15 et seq. (2006).
37. *Racketeer Influenced and Corrupt Organizations Act*, 18 U.S.C. § 1964 et seq. (2006).

CHAPTER 8: PICKING PROSOCIAL PARTNERS

1. *Joy v. Hay Group, Inc.*, 403 F.3d 875, 876 (7th Cir. 2005).
2. Ibid.

3. Eric A. Posner, "Economic Analysis of Contract Law After Three Decades: Success or Failure?" *Yale Law Journal* 112 (2003): 829–80.
4. Adam Smith, *An Inquiry into the Nature and Causes of the Wealth of Nations* (1776; Chicago: Encyclopedia Britannica, 1952), 194.
5. Thomas Hobbes, *Leviathan*, ed. C. B. MacPherson (1651; Harmondsworth, UK: Penguin Books, 1968), 223.
6. Melvin Aron Eisenberg, "The Limits of Cognition and the Limits of Contract," *Stanford Law Review* 47 (January 1995): 213.
7. Steven Shavell, *Economic Analysis of Law* (New York: Foundation Press, 2004), 63.
8. Robert E. Scott, "A Theory of Self-Enforcing Indefinite Agreements," *Columbia Law Review* 103 (2003): 1641.
9. See generally Ian R. Macneil, "Relational Contract Theory: Challenges and Queries," *Northwestern University Law Review* 94 (Spring 2000): 894.
10. *Joy*, 403 F.3d at 877–78.
11. Ibid.
12. Stewart J. Schwab and Randall S. Thomas, "An Empirical Analysis of CEO Employment Contracts: What Do Top Executives Bargain For?" *Washington and Lee Law Review* 63 (Winter 2006): 240–41.
13. Scott, "A Theory of Self-Enforcing Indefinite Agreements," 1642.
14. Contract scholars often argue that when a contract is silent on how to resolve a dispute that arises during performance, the parties can take the matter to court and ask the judge to fill in the contract "gap" by deciding the issue in the fashion the judge believes the parties *would* have agreed to, if only they had bothered to explicitly address the problem in their contract. Judges imply "default terms" into contracts that resolve questions the contracting parties failed to explicitly address themselves. In this fashion, contract law can perform a second useful economic function, in addition to enforcing exchange: reducing the costs of drafting contracts. Parties who can rely on a court's implicit terms don't need to spend time and money drafting their own explicit ones.

Yet, while contract law's ability to provide implicit terms reduces negotiating and drafting costs, this still does not solve the problem of enforcing relational exchanges. To understand this point, it is important to recognize that contracting parties often leave relational contracts incomplete because many aspects of their proposed exchange are so uncertain, complex, or unobservable, *they have no choice*. A judge can resolve disputes arising from such unavoidable contract gaps, but there is no reason to think the judge can resolve the disputes *well*. The problems of uncertainty, complexity, and unobservability prevent courts from being able to figure out how parties would have resolved the disputed issue, just as they prevented the parties from contracting over the issue in the first place.

15. Eric A. Posner, "A Theory of Contract Law Under Conditions of Radical Judicial Error," *Northwestern University Law Review* 94, no. 3 (Spring 2000): 754.

16. Ibid. (emphasis in original).

17. Sir Walter Scott, *Ivanhoe* (1819; New York: Signet Classic, 2001).

18. Ibid., 451–56.

19. Oliver Williamson, *The Mechanisms of Governance* (New York: Oxford University Press, 1996), 116.

20. Ibid.

21. Macneil, "Relational Contract Theory: Challenges and Queries," 897.

22. Richard A. Epstein, "Contract and Trust in Corporate Law: The Case of Corporate Opportunity," *Delaware Journal of Corporate Law* 21, no. 1 (1996): 11.

23. Margaret M. Blair and Lynn A. Stout, "Trust, Trustworthiness, and the Behavioral Foundations of Corporate Law," *University of Pennsylvania Law Review* 149 (2001): 1803.

24. Barbara Hetzer, "A Binding Agreement Before You Tie the Knot?" *Business Week*, March 3, 1997, 114–15.

25. See, e.g., Bruno S. Frey and Reto Jegen, "Motivation Crowding Theory: A Survey of Empirical Evidence," *Journal of Economic Surveys* 15, no. 5 (December 2001): 589–621; Bruno S. Frey and Felix Oberholzer-Gee, "The Cost of Price Incentives: An Empirical Analysis of Motivation Crowding-Out," *American Economic Review* 87, no. 4 (September 1997): 746–55.

26. Uri Gneezy and Aldo Rustichini, "A Fine Is a Price," *Journal of Legal Studies* 29 (January 2000): 3.

27. See, e.g., Cass R. Sunstein, "On the Expressive Function of Law," *University of Pennsylvania Law Review* 144 (May 1996): 2021–53; Erin Ann O'Hara, "Trustworthiness and Contract," in *Moral Markets: The Critical Role of Values in the Economy*, ed. Paul J. Zak (Princeton, NJ: Princeton University Press, 2008), 173–203; but see Matthew D. Adler, "Expressive Theories of Law: A Skeptical Overview," *University of Pennsylvania Law Review* 148 (2000): 1363–1501.

28. O'Hara, "Trustworthiness and Contract," 186.

29. Ibid.

30. *Meinhard v. Salmon*, 164 N.E. 545, 548 (N.Y. App. 1928).

31. Blair and Stout, "Trust, Trustworthiness, and the Behavioral Foundations of Corporate Law," 1789–99.

32. Edward B. Rock, "Saints and Sinners: How Does Delaware Corporate Law Work?" *UCLA Law Review* 44 (1997): 1106.

33. Posner, "A Theory of Contract Law Under Conditions of Radical Judicial Error," 759.

34. Robert H. Frank, *Passions Within Reason* (New York: Norton, 1988), 5.
35. Oliver Wendell Holmes, Jr., "The Path of the Law," *Harvard Law Review* 10, no. 8 (March 25, 1897): 462.

CHAPTER 9: CRIME, PUNISHMENT, AND COMMUNITY

1. Sentencing Memorandum of Defendant at 2–3, People v. DiBlasi, No. KA042858 (Super. Ct. Aug. 10, 1999).
2. Steven D. Levitt and Stephen J. Dubner, *Freakonomics: A Rogue Economist Explores the Hidden Side of Everything* (New York: William Morrow/HarperCollins, 2005), 105.
3. Gary S. Becker, "Crime and Punishment: An Economic Approach," *Journal of Political Economy* 76, no. 2 (1968): 195.
4. Joe Domanick, *Cruel Justice: Three Strikes and the Politics of Crime in America's Golden State* (Berkeley and Los Angeles: University of California Press, 2004), 3.
5. Sentencing Memorandum, 1; Families to Amend California's Three Strikes, "The FACTS 150: Story # 112—Robert DiBlasi," http://www.facts1.com/ThreeStrikes/Stories/900112 (accessed January 28, 2009).
6. John Braithwaite, *Restorative Justice and Responsive Regulation* (Oxford and New York: Oxford University Press, 2002), 124.
7. DeeDee Correll, "Sentence: An Evening with Manilow," *Los Angeles Times*, January 21, 2009.
8. James J. Stephan, *State Prison Expenditures, 2001*, Bureau of Justice Statistics Special Report NCJ 202949 (U.S. Department of Justice, Office of Justice Programs, June 2003), 3, available at http://www.ojp.usdoj.gov/bjs/pub/pdf/spe01.pdf.
9. Becker, "Crime and Punishment," 193, 196; Richard A. Posner, "An Economic Theory of the Criminal Law," *Columbia Law Review* 85, no. 6 (October 1985): 1201–1205; George J. Stigler, "The Optimum Enforcement of Laws," *Journal of Political Economy* 78, no. 3 (1970): 526–36.
10. Posner, "An Economic Theory of the Criminal Law," 1204; see also Steven Shavell, "Criminal Law and the Optimal Use of Nonmonetary Sanctions as a Deterrent," *Columbia Law Review* 85, no. 6 (October 1985): 1236.
11. For an example, see Stigler, "The Optimum Enforcement of Laws," 527.
12. Posner, "An Economic Theory of the Criminal Law," 1221.
13. Robert Cooter, "Prices and Sanctions," *Columbia Law Review* 84 (1984): 1523–24, 1537, 1552; Posner, "An Economic Theory of the Criminal Law," 1215.
14. Posner, "An Economic Theory of the Criminal Law," 1205, 1215.
15. Ibid., 1221.
16. Stigler, "The Optimum Enforcement of Laws," 534.

17. See generally Richard J. Bonnie, Anne M. Coughlin, John C. Jeffries, Jr., and Peter W. Low, *Criminal Law* (New York: Foundation Press, 2004), 2–33; Joshua Dressler, *Criminal Law* (St. Paul, MN: West Publishing, 2003), 30–48; Sanford H. Kadish, Stephen J. Schulhofer, and Carol Se. Steiker, *Criminal Law and Its Processes* (New York: Aspen Publishers, 2007), 73–104; Wayne R. LaFave, *Criminal Law* (St. Paul, MN: West Publishing, 2000), 26–31.

18. Becker, "Crime and Punishment," 176.

19. Robert Louis Stevenson, *Strange Case of Dr. Jekyll and Mr. Hyde*, ed. Katherine Linehan (1886; New York: W.W. Norton, 2003), 52.

20. Ibid., 51.

21. Ibid., 56.

22. Stuart Banner, *The Death Penalty: An American History* (Cambridge, MA and London: Harvard University Press, 2002), 76.

23. Tom R. Tyler, *Why People Obey the Law* (Princeton, NJ: Princeton University Press, 2006).

24. One of the most famous examples was a 1954 experiment conducted at a boys' summer camp at Robber's Cave State Park in Oklahoma. Researchers divided the boys in the camp, who were strangers to each other, into two groups. The researchers easily manipulated each of the two groups into first competing aggressively against, and then cooperating with, the other group. Robert J. Sternberg, *Psychology* (Belmont, CA: Thompson/Wadsworth, 2004) 521.

25. Stephanos Bibos and Richard A. Bierschbach, "Integrating Remorse and Apology into Criminal Procedure," *Yale Law Journal* 114 (2004): 93–94.

26. *United States v. Beserra*, 967 F.2d 255, 256 (7th Cir. 1992).

27. Interestingly, tort law also pays more attention to intent and less to consequences in punitive damages cases where a defendant's conduct suggests "conscious indifference towards others." In other words, as many legal scholars have noted, punitive damages are a civil analog to criminal liability.

28. See generally Peter J. Richerson and Robert Boyd, *Not By Genes Alone: How Culture Transformed Human Evolution* (Chicago: University of Chicago Press, 2005); Joseph Henrich and Robert Boyd, "On Modeling Culture and Cognition: Why Cultural Evolution Does Not Require Replication of Representatives," *Journal of Cognition and Culture* 2, no. 2 (2002): 87–112.

29. Frans de Waal, *Our Inner Ape: A Leading Primatologist Explains Why We Are Who We Are* (New York: Riverhead Books/Penguin Group (USA), 2005), 77.

30. "The general object which all laws have, or ought to have, in common, is to augment the total happiness of the community; and there-

fore, in the first place, to exclude, as far as may be, everything that tends to subtract from that happiness: in other words, to exclude mischief. But all punishment is mischief: all punishment in itself is evil. Upon the principal of utility, if it ought to be at all admitted, it ought only to be admitted in as far as it promises to exclude some greater evil." Jeremy Bentham, *An Introduction to the Principles of Morals and Legislation*, ed. J. H. Burns and H.L.A. Hart (1789; London and New York: Methuen, 1982), 158.

31. Kevin M. Carlsmith, John M. Darley, and Paul H. Robinson, "Why Do We Punish?: Deterrence and Just Deserts as Motives for Punishment," *Journal of Personality and Social Psychology* 83, no. 2 (2002): 284–99.

32. Morris B. Hoffman and Timothy H. Goldsmith, "The Biological Roots of Punishment," *Ohio State Journal of Criminal Law* 1, no. 2 (Spring 2004): 630.

33. Cass R. Sunstein, "On the Expressive Function of Law," *University of Pennsylvania Law Review* 144 (May 1996): 2021–53; Kenneth G. Dau-Schmidt, "An Economic Analysis of the Criminal Law as a Preference-Shaping Policy," *Duke Law Journal* 1990, no. 1 (1990): 1–3, 37.

34. Dan M. Kahan, "Social Influence, Social Meaning, and Deterrence," *Virginia Law Review* 83 (1997): 363.

35. Ibid., 384.

36. Tracey L. Meares, "Norms, Legitimacy and Law Enforcement," *Oregon Law Review* 79 (2000): 403.

37. Kahan, "Social Influence, Social Meaning, and Deterrence," 353, 353 note 16.

38. James Q. Wilson and George L. Kelling, "Broken Windows: The Police and Neighborhood Safety," *Atlantic Monthly* 249, no. 3 (March 1982): 29–38.

39. Ibid., 5.

40. Bernard E. Harcourt and Jens Ludwig, "Broken Windows: New Evidence from New York City and a Five-City Social Experiment," *University of Chicago Law Review* 73 (2006): 276, 287.

41. Compare Kahan, "Social Influence, Social Meaning, and Deterrence," 368–69 with Harcourt and Ludwig, "Broken Windows," 283–87.

42. Kahan, "Social Influence, Social Meaning, and Deterrence," 356, 371; Harcourt and Ludwig, "Broken Windows," 300–310.

43. Kahan, "Social Influence, Social Meaning, and Deterrence," 379.

44. This idea is related to what criminologists call "general deterrence," the notion that punishing one person for a crime discourages other persons from committing crimes. From an economic perspective, it is difficult to see why general deterrence works: seeing someone else go to jail may educate others that crime carries a price, but surely

rational people already know crime can lead to punishment. Conformity helps explain the mechanism of general deterrence.

45. Jonathan M. Barnett, "The Rational Underenforcement of Vice Laws," *Rutgers Law Review* 54 (2002): 434, 475–76.

46. Ibid., 475.

47. Ibid., 478–80.

48. Marla Cone, "One Big Drug Test: Analyzing a City's Sewage Can Put a Number on Its Vices," *Los Angeles Times*, June 22, 2008.

49. Barnett, "The Rational Underenforcement of Vice Laws," 425.

50. Bryan Appleyard, "Church of the Child Brides," *Sunday New York Times*, June 22, 2008, 48.

51. Robert T. Garrett, "Texas Gov. Rick Perry Defends State's Seizure of Polygamist Sect's Kids," *Dallas Morning News*, June 6, 2008.

52. Michael Falcone, "Running Mates; On Tax Policy and Patriotism," *New York Times*, September 19, 2008.

53. Dau-Schmidt, "An Economic Analysis of the Criminal Law as a Preference-Shaping Policy," 2.

54. Ibid., 15.

CONCLUSION: CHARIOTS OF THE SUN

1. Lynnley Browning, "Ex-UBS Banker Pleads Guilty to Tax Evasion," *New York Times*, June 20, 2008.

2. Evan Perez, "Guilty Pleas by Ex-Banker Likely to Aid Probe of UBS," *Wall Street Journal*, June 20, 2008.

3. Samuel Bowles and Arjun Jayadev, "Garrison America," *The Economists' Voice* (March 2007): 1.

4. John Stuart Mill, "Principles of Political Economy," in *Essays on Some Unsettled Questions of Political Economy* (London: The London School of Economics and Political Science, 1948), 69.

5. Edward C. Banfield, *The Moral Basis of a Backward Society* (Glencoe, IL: Free Press, 1958).

6. For examples, see Francis Fukayama, *Trust: The Social Virtues and the Creation of Prosperity* (New York: Free Press, 1995); Robert D. Putnam, *Making Democracy Work: Civic Traditions in Modern Italy* (Princeton, NJ: Princeton University Press, 1993); Stephen Knack and Philip Keefer, "Does Social Capital Have an Economic Payoff? A Cross-Country Investigation," *Quarterly Journal of Economics* 112 (1997): 1251.

7. Paul J. Zak and Stephen Knack, "Trust and Growth," *Economic Journal* 111 (2001): 307.

8. Knack and Keefer, "Does Social Capital Have an Economic Payoff?" 1256–57.

9. Paul J. Zak, "Trust," *Capco Journal of Financial Transformation* 7 (2003): 24.
10. Luigi Guiso, Paolo Sapienza, and Luigi Zingales, "Cultural Biases in Economic Exchange" (working paper No. 11005, NBER Working Paper Series, 2004).
11. Thomas Hobbes, *Leviathan*, ed. C. B. MacPherson (Harmondsworth, UK: Penguin Books, 1968), 1651.
12. Peggy A. Thoits and Lyndi N. Hewitt, "Volunteer Work and Well-Being," *Journal of Health and Social Behavior* 42 (2001): 115–31.
13. Harvey S. James and Athanasios G. Chymis, "Are Happy People Ethical People? Evidence from Northern America and Europe" (working paper, No. AEWP 2004-8, University of Missouri Agricultural Economics, July 2004), available at http://ssrn.com/abstract=570181.
14. James K. Rilling et al., "A Neural Basis for Social Cooperation," *Neuron* 35 (July 2002): 397.
15. Mill, "Principles of Political Economy."
16. Robert D. Putnam, *Bowling Alone: The Collapse and Revival of American Community* (New York: Simon & Schuster, 2000) 39, 123, 131.
17. Ibid., 272–73.
18. Donald L. McCabe and Linda K. Trevino, "What We Know About Cheating in College: Longitudinal Trends and Recent Developments," *Change* 28 (January/February 1996): 31.
19. David Callahan, *The Cheating Culture: Why More Americans Are Doing Wrong to Get Ahead* (Orlando, FL: Harcourt, 2004), 220.
20. Putnam, *Bowling Alone*, 142.
21. Knack and Keefer, Does Social Capital Have an Economic Payoff? 1267.
22. For an example, śee Callahan, *The Cheating Culture*, 63–69.
23. Zak and Knack, "Trust and Growth," 312.
24. Putnam, *Bowling Alone*, 184.
25. Putnam, *Making Democracy Work*.
26. Zak, "Trust," 18, figure 1.
27. Putnam, *Bowling Alone*, 77–78, 126.
28. Ibid., 131–33, 247–76.
29. Steven D. Levitt and Stephen J. Dubner, *Freakonomics: A Rogue Economist Explores the Hidden Side of Everything* (New York: William Morrow/HarperCollins, 2005), 13 (emphasis deleted).
30. Ibid., 13 (emphasis in original).
31. Lucy Kellaway, "Strange Kind of Capitalism that Celebrates Self-Denial," *Financial Times*, July 21, 2008.
32. P. J. O'Rourke, "Fairness, Idealism, and Other Atrocities; Commencement Advice You're Unlikely to Hear Elsewhere," *Los Angeles Times*, May 4, 2008.

33. Robert H. Frank, Thomas Gilovich, and Dennis T. Regan, "Does Studying Economics Inhibit Cooperation?" *Journal of Economic Perspectives* 7 (1993): 159–71.

34. "By pursuing his own interest he frequently promotes that of the society more effectually than when he really intends to promote it." Adam Smith, *An Inquiry into the Nature and Causes of the Wealth of Nations* (1776; repr., Chicago: Encyclopedia Britannica, 1952), 194.

35. *Wilkow v. Forbes, Inc.*, 241 F.3d 552, 557 (7th Cir. 2001).

36. Gerald Marwell and Ruth Ames, "Economists Free Ride, Does Anyone Else? Experiments in the Provision of Public Goods, IV," *Journal of Public Economics* 15 (June 1981): 295–310.

37. Frank et al., "Does Studying Economics Inhibit Cooperation?" 171.

38. Zak and Knack, "Trust and Growth," 311.

39. Oliver Wendell Holmes, Jr., "The Path of the Law," *Harvard Law Review* 10 (March 1987): 459.

40. Alpheus Thomas Mason, *Brandeis and the Modern State* (Washington, DC: National Home Library Foundation, 1933), 221.

WORKS CITED

Adler, Matthew D. "Expressive Theories of Law: A Skeptical Overview." *University of Pennsylvania Law Review* 148 (2000): 1363–1501.

Adolphs, Ralph, Daniel Tranel, and Antonio R. Damasio. "The Human Amygdala in Social Judgment." *Nature* 393 (June 4, 1998): 470–74.

Allison, Scott T., and Norbert L. Kerr. "Group Correspondence Biases and the Provision of Public Goods." *Journal of Personality and Social Psychology* 66 (1994): 688–98.

American Psychiatric Association. *Diagnostic and Statistical Manual of Mental Disorders*, 4th ed. Washington, DC: American Psychiatric Association, 2000.

Anderson, Steven W., Antoine Bechara, Hanna Damasio, Daniel Tranel, and Antonio R. Damasio. "Impairment of Social and Moral Behavior Related to Early Damage in Human Prefrontal Cortex." *Nature Neuroscience* 2 (November 1999): 1032–37.

Andreoni, James, and John Miller. "Giving According to GARP: An Experimental Test of the Consistency of Preferences for Altruism." *Econometrica* 70, no. 2 (March 2002): 737–53.

Andreoni, James, and Lise Vesterlund. "Which Is the Fair Sex?: Gender Differences in Altruism." *Quarterly Journal of Economics* 116, no. 1 (February 2001): 293–312.

Appleyard, Bryan. "Church of the Child Brides." *Sunday New York Times*, June 22, 2008.

Arlen, Jennifer. "Comment: The Future of Behavioral Economic Analysis of Law." *Vanderbilt Law Review* 51, no. 6 (November 1998): 1765–88.

Arlen, Jennifer, and Reiner Kraakman. "Controlling Corporate Misconduct: An Analysis of Corporate Liability Regimes." *New York University Law Review* 72 (October 1997): 752–53.

Axelrod, Robert, and William D. Hamilton. "The Evolution of Cooperation." *Science* 211 (1981): 1390–96.

Backhaus, Jürgen G. *The Elgar Companion to Law and Economics*. 2nd ed. Cheltenham, UK and Northampton, MA: Edward Elgar, 2005.

Bakan, Joel. *The Corporation: The Pathological Pursuit of Profit and Power*. New York: Free Press, 2004.

Ballou, Dale. "Pay for Performance in Public and Private Schools." *Economics of Education Review* 20 (2000): 51–61.

Banfield, Edward C. *The Moral Basis of a Backward Society*. Glencoe, IL: Free Press, 1958.

Banner, Stuart. *The Death Penalty: An American History*. Cambridge, MA and London: Harvard University Press, 2002.

Barnes, David W., and Lynn A. Stout. *Law and Economics*. St. Paul, MN: West Publishing, 1992.

Barnett, Jonathan M. "The Rational Underenforcement of Vice Laws." *Rutgers Law Review* 54 (2002): 423–86.

Bauman, Jeffrey D. Alan R. Palmiter, and Frank Partnoy. *Corporations Law and Policy: Materials and Problems*. 6th ed. St. Paul, MN: Thomson West, 2007.

Bebchuk, Lucian, and Jesse Fried. *Pay Without Performance: The Unfulfilled Promise of Executive Compensation*. Cambridge, MA: Harvard University Press, 2004.

Becerra, Hector. "Ballad of the Poor Samaritan." *Los Angeles Times*. August 2, 2002.

———. "Honest Dishwasher: A Hero or an Idiot? Illegal Immigrant Returned $203,000." *Los Angeles Times*, August 25, 2002, A1.

Becker, Gary S. "Nobel Lecture: The Economic Way of Looking at Behavior." *Journal of Political Economy* 101, no. 3 (June 1993): 385–409.

———. "Crime and Punishment: An Economic Approach." *Journal of Political Economy* 76, no. 2 (1968): 169–217.

Bentham, Jeremy. *An Introduction to the Principles of Morals and Legislation*. 1789. Edited by J. H. Burns and H.L.A. Hart. London and New York: Methuen, 1982.

Berg, Joyce, John Dickhaut, and Kevin McCabe. "Trust, Reciprocity, and Social History." *Games and Economic Behavior* 10 (1995): 122–42.

Bhattacharjee, Yudhijit. "Friendly Faces and Unusual Minds." *Science* 310 (November 4, 2005): 802–4.

Bibos, Stephanos, and Richard A. Bierschbach. "Integrating Remorse and Apology into Criminal Procedure." *Yale Law Journal* 114 (2004): 85–137.

Blair, Margaret M., and Lynn A. Stout. "Trust, Trustworthiness, and the Behavioral Foundations of Corporate Law." *University of Pennsylvania Law Review* 149 (2001): 1735–1810.

Blass, Thomas. *The Man Who Shocked the World: The Life and Legacy of Stanley Milgram*. New York: Basic Books, 2004.

———. "The Milgram Paradigm After 35 Years: Some Things We Now Know About Obedience to Authority." *Journal of Applied Social Psychology* 25 (1999): 955–78.

Bonnie, Richard J., Anne M. Coughlin, John C. Jeffries, Jr., and Peter W. Low. *Criminal Law*. New York: Foundation Press, 2004.

Bowles, Samuel, and Arjun Jayadev. "Garrison America." *The Economists' Voice* (March 2007): 1.

Boyd, Robert, Herbert Gintis, Samuel Bowles, and Peter J. Richerson. "The Evolution of Altruistic Punishment." *Proceedings of the National Academy of Sciences of the United States of America* 100 (March 18, 2003): 3531–35.

Boyd, Robert, and Peter J. Richerson. "Cultural Transmission and the Evolution of Cooperative Behavior." *Human Ecology* 10 (1982): 325–51.

Braithwaite, John. *Restorative Justice and Responsive Regulation.* Oxford and New York: Oxford University Press, 2002.

Brewer, Marilynn B. "In-Group Bias in the Minimal Intergroup Situation: A Cognitive-Motivational Analysis." *Psychological Bulletin* 86 (1979): 307–24.

Brown, Donald E. *Human Universals.* Philadelphia: Temple University Press, 1991.

Browning, Lynnley. "Ex-UBS Banker Pleads Guilty to Tax Evasion." *New York Times,* June 20, 2008.

Buffett, Warren. "How Buffett Views Risk." *Fortune,* April 4, 1994, 33.

Burton, Steven J., ed. *"The Path of the Law" and Its Influence: The Legacy of Oliver Wendell Holmes, Jr.* Cambridge, UK and New York: Cambridge University Press, 2000.

Calabresi, Guido. *The Cost of Accidents: A Legal and Economic Analysis.* New Haven: Yale University Press, 1970.

Calabresi, Guido, and Douglas Melamed. "Property Rules, Liability Rules, and Inalienability: One View of the Cathedral." *Harvard Law Review* 85 (1972): 1089–1128.

Callahan, David. *The Cheating Culture: Why More Americans Are Doing Wrong to Get Ahead.* Orlando, FL: Harcourt, 2004.

Camerer, Colin, and Richard H. Thaler. "Anomalies: Ultimatums, Dictators and Manners." *Journal of Economic Perspectives* 9, no. 2 (Spring 1995): 209–19.

Cameron, Lisa A. "Raising the Stakes in the Ultimatum Game: Experimental Evidence from Indonesia." *Economic Inquiry* 37 (January 1999): 47–59.

Campbell, Noel D., and Edward J. López. "Paying Teachers for Advanced Degrees: Evidence on Student Performance from Georgia." Available at http://ssrn.com/abstract=1147162 (forthcoming in *Journal of Private Enterprise*).

Carlsmith, Kevin M., John M. Darley, and Paul H. Robinson. "Why Do We Punish?: Deterrence and Just Deserts as Motives for Punishment." *Journal of Personality and Social Psychology* 83, no. 2 (2002): 284–99.

Carpenter, Jeffrey, Eric Verhoogen, and Stephen Burks. "The Effect of Stakes in Distribution Experiments." *Economics Letters* 86 (2005): 393–98.

Charness, Gary, and Martin Dufwenberg. "Promises and Partnership." *Econometrica* 74, no. 6 (November 2006): 1579–1601.

Charness, Gary, and Matthew Rabin. "Understanding Social Preferences with Simple Tests." *Quarterly Journal of Economics* 117 (2002): 817–69.

Chartrand, Tanya L., and John A. Bargh. "The Chameleon Effect: The Perception-Behavior Link and Social Interaction." *Journal of Personality and Social Psychology* 76 (1999): 893–910.

Church, Russell M. "Emotional Reactions of Rats to the Pain of Others." *Journal of Comparative and Physiological Psychology* 52 (1959): 132–34.

Coase, Ronald H. "The Problem of Social Cost." *Journal of Law & Economics* 3 (1960): 1–44.

Cole, Daniel H., and Peter Z. Grossman. *Principles of Law and Economics.* Upper Saddle River, NJ: Pearson Prentice Hall, 2005.

Cone, Marla. "One Big Drug Test: Analyzing a City's Sewage Can Put a Number on Its Vices." *Los Angeles Times,* June 22, 2008.

Cooter, Robert. "Models of Morality in Law and Economics: Self-Control and Self-Improvement for the 'Bad Man' of Holmes." *Boston University Law Review* 78 (1998): 903–30.

———. "Expressive Law and Economics." *Journal of Legal Studies* 27 (June 1998): 585–608.

———. "Punitive Damages for Deterrence: When and How Much." *Alabama Law Review* 40, no. 3 (1989): 1143–96.

———. "Prices and Sanctions." *Columbia Law Review* 84 (1984): 1523–60.

———. "Economic Analysis of Punitive Damages." *Southern California Law Review* 56 (1982): 79.

Cooter, Robert, and Thomas Ulen. *Law and Economics,* 4th ed. Boston: Pearson Addison Wesley, 2004.

Correll, DeeDee. "Sentence: An Evening with Manilow." *Los Angeles Times.* January 21, 2009.

Cosmides, Leda. "The Logic of Social Exchange: Has Natural Selection Shaped How Humans Reason? Studies with the Watson Selection Task." *Cognition* 31 (1989): 187–276.

Cosmides, Leda, and John Toobey. "Cognitive Adaptations for Social Exchange." In *The Adapted Mind: Evolutionary Psychology and the Generation of Culture,* edited by Jerome H. Barkow, Leda Cosmides, and John Toobey, 163–228. New York: Oxford University Press, 1992.

Cowan, Tyler. *Discover Your Inner Economist: Use Incentives to Fall in Love, Survive Your Next Meeting, and Motivate Your Dentist.* New York: Dutton/Penguin Group USA, 2007.

Cox, James C. "How to Identify Trust and Reciprocity." *Games and Economic Behavior* 46, no. 2 (2004): 260–81.

Croson, Rachel, and Nancy Buchan. "Gender and Culture: International Experimental Evidence from Trust Games." *Gender and Economic Transactions* 89, no. 2 (May 1999): 386–91.

Dahmer, Lionel. *A Father's Story*. New York: William Morrow & Company, 1994.

Damasio, Hanna, Thomas Grabowski, Randall Frank, Albert M. Galaburda, and Antonio Damasio. "The Return of Phineas Gage: Clues About the Brain from the Skull of a Famous Patient." *Science*, New Series 264 (May 1994): 1102–5.

Darwin, Charles. *The Descent of Man*. 1871. In *Great Books of the Western World*, vol. 49, *Darwin*, edited by Robert Maynard Hutchins, 253–611. London: Encyclopedia Britannica, Inc., 1952.

Dau-Schmidt, Kenneth G. "Economics and Sociology: The Prospects for an Interdisciplinary Discourse on Law." *Wisconsin Law Review* 1997 (1997): 389–419.

————. "An Economic Analysis of the Criminal Law as a Preference-Shaping Policy." *Duke Law Journal* 1990, no. 1 (1990): 1–38.

Dawes, Robyn M. "Social Dilemmas." *Annual Review of Psychology* 31 (1980): 169–93.

Dawes, Robyn M., and Richard H. Thaler. "Anomalies: Cooperation." *Journal of Economic Perspectives* 2, no. 3 (Summer 1988): 187–97.

Dawes, Robyn M., Alphons J. C. van de Kragt, and John Orbell. "Cooperation for the Benefit of Us—Not Me, or My Conscience." In *Beyond Self-Interest*, edited by Jane J. Mansbridge, 97–110. Chicago: University of Chicago Press, 1990.

Dawkins, Richard. *The Selfish Gene*. New York: Oxford University Press, 1976.

Decety, Jean, Philip L. Jackson, Jessica A. Sommerville, Thierry Chaminade, and Andrew N. Meltzoff. "The Neural Bases of Cognition and Competition: An fMRI Investigation." *NeuroImage* 23, no. 2 (October 2004): 744–51.

Demsetz, Harold. "Rationality, Evolution, and Acquisitiveness." *Economic Inquiry* 34 (July 1999): 484–95.

Dennet, Daniel C. *Darwin's Dangerous Idea: Evolution and the Meanings of Life*. New York: Simon & Schuster, 1995.

De Waal, Frans. *Our Inner Ape: A Leading Primatologist Explains Why We Are Who We Are*. New York: Riverhead Books/Penguin Group (USA), 2005.

Dewan, Shaila. "Georgia Schools Inquiry Finds Signs of Cheating." *New York Times*, February 12, 2010, A16.

Dolan, Raymond J. "On the Neurology of Morals." Nature *Neuroscience* 2 (November 1999): 927–29.

Domanick, Joe. *Cruel Justice: Three Strikes and the Politics of Crime in America's Golden State*. Berkeley and Los Angeles: University of California Press, 2004.

Dressler, Joshua. *Criminal Law*. St. Paul, MN: West Publishing, 2003.

Edwards, Amanda. "Medical Malpractice Non-Economic Damages Caps." *Harvard Journal on Legislation* 43 (Winter 2006): 213–30.

Eisenberg, Melvin Aron. "The Limits of Cognition and the Limits of Contract." *Stanford Law Review* 47 (January 1995): 211–59.

Elhauge, Einer. "Sacrificing Corporate Profits in the Public Interest." *New York University Law Review* 80 (June 2005): 733–869.

Ellickson, Robert C. *Order Without Law: How Neighbors Settle Disputes*. Cambridge, MA: Harvard University Press, 1991.

Epstein, Richard A. "Contract and Trust in Corporate Law: The Case of Corporate Opportunity." *Delaware Journal of Corporate Law* 21, no. 1 (1996): 1–25.

Exxon Shipping Co. v. Baker. 128 S. Ct. 2605 (2008).

Falcone, Michael. "Running Mates; On Tax Policy and Patriotism." *New York Times*, September 19, 2008.

Falk, Armin, Urs Fischbacher, and Simon Gächter. "Living in Two Neighborhoods—Social Interactions in the Lab." Working Paper 150, Institute for Empirical Research in Economics, November 2004.

Families to Amend California's Three Strikes."The FACTS 150: Story # 112—Robert DiBlasi." http://www.facts1.com/ThreeStrikes/Stories/ 900112 (accessed January 28, 2009).

Fehr, Ernst, and Urs Fischbacher. "Third-Party Punishment and Social Norms." *Evolution and Human Behavior* 25 (2004): 63–87.

Fehr, Ernst, and Simon Gächter. "Altruistic Punishment in Humans." *Nature* 415 (January 10, 2002): 137–40.

Fehr, Ernst, and Herbert Gintis. "Human Motivation and Social Cooperation: Experimental and Analytical Foundations." *Annual Review of Sociology* 33 (August 2007): 43–64.

Fehr, Ernst, and Joseph Henrich. "Is Strong Reciprocity a Maladaptation? On the Evolutionary Foundations of Human Altruism." In *Genetic and Cultural Evolution of Cooperation*, edited by Peter Hammerstein. Cambridge, MA: MIT Press / Dahlem University Press, 2003.

Fehr, Ernst, and Bettina Rockenbach. "Human Altruism: Economic, Neural, and Evolutionary Perspectives." *Current Opinion in Neurobiology* 14 (2004): 784–90.

Fehr, Ernst, and Klaus M. Schmidt. "The Economics of Fairness, Reciprocity and Altruism—Experimental Evidence and New Theories."

In *Handbook of the Economics of Giving, Altruism, and Reciprocity*, vol. 1, *Foundations*, edited by Serge-Christophe Kolm and Jean Mercier Ythier, 615–91. Amsterdam and Oxford: North-Holland/Elsevier, 2006.

Figlio, David N., and Lawrence Kenny. "Individual Teacher Incentives and Student Performance." NBER Working Paper Series no. 12627, National Bureau of Economic Research, Cambridge, MA, October 2006.

Frank, Robert H. *Luxury Fever: Money and Happiness in an Era of Excess.* New York: Free Press, 1999.

———. *Passions Within Reason.* New York: Norton, 1988.

———. "If *Homo Economicus* Could Choose His Own Utility Function, Would He Want One with a Conscience?" *American Economic Review* 77 (September 1987): 593–604.

Frank, Robert H., Thomas Gilovich, and Dennis T. Regan. "Does Studying Economics Inhibit Cooperation?" *Journal of Economic Perspectives* 7 (1993): 159–71.

Freund, Paul A. *Oliver Wendell Holmes.* Vol. 3, *The Justices of the United States Supreme Court 1789–1969: Their Lives and Major Opinions.* Edited by L. Friedman and F. Israel. New York: R. R. Bowker Company, 1969.

Frey, Bruno S., and Iris Bohnet. "Identification in Democratic Society." *Journal of Socio-Economics* 26 (1997): 25–38.

Frey, Bruno S., and Reto Jegen. "Motivation Crowding Theory: A Survey of Empirical Evidence." *Journal of Economic Surveys* 15, no. 5 (December 2001): 589–621.

Frey, Bruno S., and Felix Oberholzer-Gee. "The Cost of Price Incentives: An Empirical Analysis of Motivation Crowding-Out." *American Economic Review* 87, no. 4 (September 1997): 746–55.

Friedman, David D. *Hidden Order: The Economics of Everyday Life.* New York: HarperBusiness, 1996.

Friedman, Milton. "The Social Responsibility of Business Is to Increase Its Profits." *New York Times*, September 13, 1979.

Fukayama, Francis. *Trust: The Social Virtues and the Creation of Prosperity.* New York: Free Press, 1995.

Galanter, Marc, and David Luban. "Poetic Justice: Punitive Damages and Legal Pluralism." *American University Law Review* 42 (1993): 1393–1463.

Garrett, Robert T. "Texas Gov. Rick Perry Defends State's Seizure of Polygamist Sect's Kids." *Dallas Morning News.* June 6, 2008.

Gautschi, Thomas. "History Effects in Social Dilemma Situations." *Rationality & Society* 12, no. 2 (2000): 131–62.

Gerlin, Andrea. "A Matter of Degree." *Wall Street Journal*, September 1, 1994, A1.

Gilles, Stephen G. "The Invisible Hand Formula." *Virginia Law Review* 80, no. 5 (August 1994): 115–54.

Gintis, Herbert. "The Hitchhiker's Guide to Altruism: Gene-Culture Coevolution and the Internalization of Norms." *Journal of Theoretical Biology* 220 (2003): 407–18.

Gintis, Herbert, Samuel Bowles, Robert Boyd, and Ernst Fehr. "Explaining Altruistic Behavior in Humans." *Evolution and Human Behavior* 24 (2003): 153–72.

Gintis, Herbert, Eric Alden Smith, and Samuel Bowles. "Costly Signaling and Cooperation." *Journal of Theoretical Biology* 213 (2001): 103–19.

Gneezy, Uri, and Aldo Rustichini. "A Fine Is a Price." *Journal of Legal Studies* 29 (January 2000): 1–17.

Goldhaber, Dan. "Teacher Quality and Teacher Pay Structure: What Do We Know, and What Are the Options?" *Georgetown Public Policy Review* 7 (Spring 2002): 81–92.

Greenfield, Kent, and Peter C. Konstant. "An Experimental Test of Fairness Under Agency and Profit-Maximization Constraints (With Notes on Implications for Corporate Governance)." *George Washington University Law Review* 71 (2003): 983–1023.

Guiso, Luigi, Paolo Sapienza, and Luigi Zingales. "Cultural Biases in Economic Exchange." Working paper No. 11005, NBER Working Paper Series, 2004.

Gürerk, Özgür, Bernd Irlenbusch, and Bettina Rockenbach. "The Competitive Advantage of Sanctioning Institutions." *Science* 312 (April 2006): 108–11.

Guthrie, Chris, Jeffrey J. Rachlinski, and Andrew J. Wistrich. "Inside the Judicial Mind." *Cornell Law Review* 86, no. 4 (May 2001): 777–830.

Hamilton, William D. "The Genetical Evolution of Social Behavior I and II." *Journal of Theoretical Biology* 7 (1964): 1–16, 17–52.

Hanson, Jon D., and Douglas A. Kysar. "Taking Behavioralism Seriously: The Problem of Market Manipulation." *New York University Law Review* 74 (June 1999): 630–749.

Harbaugh, William T., Kate Krause, and Steven G. Liday, Jr. "Bargaining By Children." Working paper, Economics Department, University of Oregon, 2003.

Harcourt, Bernard E., and Jens Ludwig. "Broken Windows: New Evidence from New York City and a Five-City Social Experiment." *University of Chicago Law Review* 73 (2006): 271–320.

Harford, Tim. *The Undercover Economist: Exposing Why the Rich Are Rich, The Poor Are Poor—and Why You Can Never Buy a Decent Used Car.* New York: Oxford University Press, 2005.

Harrison, Jeffrey L. *Law and Economics: Cases, Materials, and Behavioral Perspectives.* St. Paul, MN: Thomson/West, 2002.

Harrison, Jeffrey L., and McCabe G. Harrison. *Law and Economics in a Nutshell.* 3rd ed. St. Paul, MN: Thomson/West, 2003.

Harvard Medical Practice Study. *Patients, Doctors, and Lawyers: Medical Injury, Malpractice Litigation, and Patient Compensation in New York, a Report of the Harvard Medical Practice Study to the State of New York.* Cambridge, MA: The President and Fellows of Harvard College, 1990.

Henrich, Joseph. "Does Culture Matter in Economic Behavior? Ultimatum Game Bargaining Among the Machiguenga of the Peruvian Amazon." *American Economic Review* 90, no. 4 (September 2000): 973–79.

Henrich, Joseph, and Robert Boyd. "On Modeling Culture and Cognition: Why Cultural Evolution Does Not Require Replication of Representatives." *Journal of Cognition and Culture* 2, no. 2 (2002): 87–112.

———. "Why People Punish Defectors: Weak Conformist Strategy Can Stabilize Costly Enforcement of Norms in Cooperative Dilemmas." *Journal of Theoretical Biology* 208 (2001): 79–89.

Henrich, Joseph, Robert Boyd, Samuel Bowles, Colin Camerer, Ernst Fehr, and Herbert Gintis. *Foundations of Human Sociality: Ethnography and Experiments in 15 Small-Scale Societies.* Oxford and New York: Oxford University Press, 2004.

Henrich, Joseph, Robert Boyd, Samuel Bowles, Colin Camerer, Ernst Fehr, Herbert Gintis, and Richard McElreath. "In Search of Homo Economicus: Behavioral Experiments in 15 Small-Scale Societies." *American Economic Review* 91, no. 2 (May 2001): 73–79.

Hensler, Deborah R., Susan M. Marquis, Allan Abrahamse, Sandra H. Berry, Patricia A. Ebener, Elizabeth Lewis, Edgar Lind, Robert Mac-Coun, Willard G. Manning, Jeannette Rogowski, and Mary E. Vaiana. *Compensation for Accidental Injuries in the United States.* Santa Monica, CA: RAND, 1991.

Hetzer, Barbara. "A Binding Agreement Before You Tie the Knot?" *Business Week,* March 3, 1997, 114–15.

Hirshleifer, David. "Investor Psychology and Asset Pricing." *Journal of Finance* 56, no. 4 (August 2001): 1533–97.

———. "The Expanding Domain of Economics." *American Economic Review* 75, no. 6 (December 1985): 53–68.

Hobbes, Thomas. *Leviathan.* 1651. Edited by C. B. MacPherson. Harmondsworth, UK: Penguin Books, 1968.

Hoffman, Elizabeth, Kevin McCabe, and Vernon L. Smith. "Social Distance and Other-Regarding Behavior in Dictator Games." *American Economic Review* 86 (June 1996): 653–54.

Hoffman, Morris B., and Timothy H. Goldsmith. "The Biological Roots of Punishment." *Ohio State Journal of Criminal Law* 1, no. 2 (Spring 2004): 627–41.

Holmes, Oliver Wendell, Jr. "The Path of the Law." *Harvard Law Review* 10, no. 8 (March 25, 1897): 457–78.

Hyman, David A. "Rescue Without Law: An Empirical Perspective on the Duty to Rescue." *Texas Law Review* 84 (2006): 653–737.

James, Harvey S., and Athanasios G. Chymis. "Are Happy People Ethical People? Evidence from Northern America and Europe." Working paper, no. AEWP 2004-8, University of Missouri Agricultural Economics, July 2004. Available at http://ssrn.com/abstract=570181.

Jensen, Michael C., and William H. Meckling. "Theory of the Firm: Managerial Behavior, Agency Costs and Ownership Structure." *Journal of Financial Economics* 3, no. 4 (October 1976): 305–60.

Jensen, Michael C., Kevin J. Murphy, and Eric G. Wruck. "Remuneration: Where We've Been, How We Got to Here, What Are the Problems, and How to Fix Them." Harvard NOM Working Paper no. 04-28; ECGI-Finance Working Paper no. 44/2004. Available at http://ssrn.com/abstract=561305.

Jolls, Christine, Cass R. Sunstein, and Richard Thaler. "A Behavioral Approach to Law and Economics." *Stanford Law Review* 50 (1998): 1471–1550.

Joy v. Hay Group, Inc. 403 F.3d 875, 876 (7th Cir. 2005).

Kadish, Sanford H., Stephen J. Schulhofer, and Carol Se. Steiker. *Criminal Law and Its Processes.* New York: Aspen Publishers, 2007.

Kahan, Dan M. "Social Influence, Social Meaning, and Deterrence." *Virginia Law Review* 83 (1997): 349–95.

Kahn, Gabriel. "Top Cop in Los Angeles Says Cutting Crime Pays." *Wall Street Journal*, November 29–30, 2008.

Kahneman, Daniel. "Autobiography." Nobel Foundation. http://nobelprize.org/nobel_prizes/economics/laureates/2002/kahneman-autobio.html.

Kellaway, Lucy. "Strange Kind of Capitalism that Celebrates Self-Denial." *Financial Times*, July 21, 2008.

Kiesler, Sara, Keith Waters, and Lee Sproull. "A Prisoner's Dilemma Experiment on Cooperation with People and Human-Like Computers." *Journal of Personality and Social Psychology* 70 (1996): 47–65.

Knack, Stephen, and Philip Keefer. "Does Social Capital Have an Economic Payoff? A Cross-Country Investigation." *Quarterly Journal of Economics* 112 (1997): 1251–88.

Komorita, S. S., C. D. Parks, and L. G. Hulbert. "Reciprocity and the Induction of Cooperation in Social Dilemmas." *Journal of Personality and Social Psychology* 62, no. 4 (1992): 607–17.

Korobkin, Russell. "Bounded Rationality, Standard Form Contracts, and Unconscionability." *University of Chicago Law Review* 70, no. 4 (Fall 2003): 1203–95.

Korobkin, Russell, and Thomas S. Ulen. "Law and Behavioral Science: Removing the Rationality Assumption from Law and Economics." *California Law Review* 88, no. 4 (July 2000): 1051–1144.

Kosfeld, Michael, Markus Heinrichs, Paul J. Zak, Urs Fischbacher, and Ernst Fehr. "Oxytocin Increases Trust in Humans." *Nature* 435 (2005): 673–76.

Krupka, Erin, and Roberto Weber. "The Focusing and Informational Effects of Norms on Pro-Social Behavior." Institute for the Study of Labor Discussion Paper, IZA DP 3169, August 2005. Available at http://ftp.iza.org/dp3169.pdf.

LaFave, Wayne R. *Criminal Law*. St. Paul, MN: West Publishing, 2000.

Landsburg, Steven E. *The Armchair Economist: Economics and Everyday Life*. New York: Free Press, 1993.

Latané, Bibb, and John M. Darley. "Group Inhibition of Bystander Intervention in Emergencies." *Journal of Personality and Social Psychology* 10, no. 3 (1968): 215–21.

Latin, Howard. "'Good' Warnings, Bad Products, and Cognitive Limitations." *UCLA Law Review* 41 (June 1994): 1193–1295.

Levitt, Steven D., and Stephen J. Dubner. *Freakonomics: A Rogue Economist Explores the Hidden Side of Everything*. New York: William Morrow/HarperCollins, 2005.

Lewin, Dr. Roger. "Accidental Career." *New Scientist* 61 (August 8, 1974): 322–25.

Lewit, Eugene M., Douglas Coate, and Michael Grossman. "The Effects of Government Regulation on Teenage Smoking." *Journal of Law and Economics* 24 (December 1981): 545–69.

Linden, Eugene. *The Parrot's Lament: and Other True Tales of Animal Intrigue, Intelligence, and Ingenuity*. New York: Plume, 1999.

List, John A. "Young, Selfish and Male: Field Evidence of Social Preferences." *Economic Journal* 114 (January 2004): 121–49.

List, John A., and Todd L. Cherry. "Examining the Role of Fairness in High Stakes Allocation Decisions." *Journal of Economic Behavior and Organization* 65, no. 1 (January 2008): 1–8.

Los Angeles Police Department, Information Technology Division, Management Report Unit. "Statistical Digest: 2006." http://www.lapdonline.org/assets/pdf/2006Digest.pdf.

Lykken, David Thoreson. *The Antisocial Personalities*. Hillsdale, NJ: Lawrence Erlbaum Associates, 1995.

MacFarquhar, Larissa. "The Bench Burner: How Did a Judge with Such Subversive Ideas Become a Leading Influence on American Legal Opinion?" *New Yorker*, December 10, 2001.

Macneil, Ian R. "Relational Contract Theory: Challenges and Queries." *Northwestern University Law Review* 94 (Spring 2000): 877–907.

Mansbridge, Jane J., ed. *Beyond Self-Interest*. Chicago: University of Chicago Press, 1990.

Marwell, Gerald, and Ruth Ames. "Economists Free Ride, Does Anyone Else? Experiments in the Provision of Public Goods, IV." *Journal of Public Economics* 15 (June 1981): 295–310.

Mason, Alpheus Thomas. *Brandeis and the Modern State*. Washington, DC: National Home Library Foundation, 1933.

McAdams, Richard H. "The Origin, Development, and Regulation of Norms." *Michigan Law Review* 96 (1997): 338–433.

McCabe, Donald L., Kenneth D. Butterfield, and Linda K. Trevino. "Academic Dishonesty in Graduate School Business Programs: Prevalence, Causes, and Proposed Action." *Academy of Management Learning and Education* 5 (September 2006): 294–306.

McCabe, Kevin A., Daniel House, Lee Ryan, Vernon Smith, and Ted Trouard. "A Functional Imaging Study of Cooperation in Two-Person Reciprocal Exchange." *Proceedings of the National Academy of Sciences* 98 (2001): 1662–73.

McCabe, Donald L., and Linda K. Trevino. "What We Know About Cheating in College: Longitudinal Trends and Recent Developments." *Change* 28 (January/February 1996): 31.

Mealey, Linda. "The Sociobiology of Sociopathy: An Integrated Evolutionary Model." *Behavioral and Brain Sciences* 18 (1995): 523–99.

Meares, Tracey L. "Norms, Legitimacy and Law Enforcement." *Oregon Law Review* 79 (2000): 391–415.

Meier, Stephan, and Bruno S. Frey. "Do Business Students Make Good Citizens?" *International Journal of the Economics of Business* 11 (2004): 141–63.

Milgram, Stanley. *Obedience to Authority: An Experimental View*. New York: Harper & Row, 1974.

———. "Behavioral Study of Obedience." *Journal of Abnormal and Social Psychology* 67 (1963): 371–78.

Milgrom, Paul, and John Roberts. *Economics, Organization and Management*. Englewood Cliffs, NJ: Prentice Hall, 1992.

Mill, John Stuart. "On the Definition of Political Economy." In *Essays on Some Unsettled Questions of Political Economy*, chap. V. London: The London School of Economics and Political Science, 1948.

Miller, Geoffrey P. "Norm Enforcement in the Public Sphere: The Case of Handicapped Parking." *George Washington Law Review* 71 (2003): 895–933.

Mitchell, Lawrence E. "Understanding Norms." *University of Toronto Law Journal* 49 (Spring 1999): 177–248.

Myers, David G. *Social Psychology*. 8th ed. New York: McGraw Hill, 2005.

Nasar, Syvlia. *A Beautiful Mind: A Biography of John Forbes Nash, Jr., Winner of the Nobel Prize in Economics, 1994.* New York: Simon & Schuster, 1998.

Newman, Catherine. "I Do. Not: Why I Won't Marry." In *The Bitch in the House: 26 Women Tell the Truth About Sex, Solitude, Work, Motherhood, and Marriage,* edited by Cathi Hanauer and Ellen Gilchrist, 65–72. New York: Harper Collins, 2002.

Nowak, Martin A., Karen M. Page, and Karl Sigmund. "Fairness Versus Reason in the Ultimatum Game." *Science* 289 (September 8, 2000): 1773–75.

O'Hara, Erin Ann. "Trustworthiness and Contract." In *Moral Markets: The Critical Role of Values in the Economy,* edited by Paul J. Zak, 173–203. Princeton, NJ: Princeton University Press, 2008.

O'Hara, Erin Ann, and Douglas Yarn. "On Apology and Consilience." *Washington Law Review* 77 (October 2002): 1121–92.

O'Rourke, P. J. "Fairness, Idealism, and Other Atrocities; Commencement Advice You're Unlikely to Hear Elsewhere." *Los Angeles Times,* May 4, 2008.

Osterloh, Margit, and Bruno S. Frey. "Corporate Governance for Crooks? The Case for Corporate Virtue." ZEW Working Paper no. 164. Available at http://ssrn.com/abstract=430062.

Parisi, Francesco, and Charles Kershaw Rowley. *The Origins of Law and Economics: Essays by the Founding Fathers.* Cheltenham, UK and Northampton, MA: Edward Elgar, 2005.

Perez, Evan. "Guilty Pleas by Ex-Banker Likely to Aid Probe of UBS." *Wall Street Journal,* June 20, 2008.

Pinker, Steven. *The Blank Slate: The Modern Denial of Human Nature.* New York: Viking, 2002.

Polinksy, A. Mitchell. *An Introduction to Law and Economics.* 3rd ed. New York: Aspen Publishers, 2003.

Polinsky, A. Mitchell, and Steven Shavell. "Punitive Damages: An Economic Analysis." *Harvard Law Review* 111, no. 4 (February 1998): 869–962.

Posner, Eric A. "Economic Analysis of Contract Law After Three Decades: Success or Failure?" *Yale Law Journal* 112 (2003): 829–80.

———. *Law and Social Norms.* Cambridge, MA: Harvard University Press, 2000.

———. "A Theory of Contract Law Under Conditions of Radical Judicial Error." *Northwestern University Law Review* 94, no. 3 (Spring 2000): 749–74.

———. "Efficient Norms." In *The New Palgrave Dictionary of Economics and the Law,* edited by Peter Newman, 2:20. New York: Stockton Press, 1998.

Posner, Richard A. *Economic Analysis of Law.* 5th ed. New York: Aspen Law & Business, 1998.

—— "An Economic Theory of the Criminal Law." *Columbia Law Review* 85, no. 6 (October 1985): 1193–1231.

——. "Optimal Sentences for White-Collar Criminals." *American Criminal Law Review* 17 (1980): 409–18.

——. "A Theory of Negligence." *Journal of Legal Studies* 1 (1972): 29–96.

Pringle, Paul, and Hemmy So. "An Unlikely Friendship that Finally Unraveled." *Los Angeles Times,* August 19, 2006.

Putnam, Robert D. *Bowling Alone: The Collapse and Revival of American Community.* New York: Simon & Schuster, 2000.

——. *Making Democracy Work: Civic Traditions in Modern Italy.* Princeton, NJ: Princeton University Press, 1993.

Rachlinski, Jeffrey J., and Forest Jourden. "Remedies and the Psychology of Ownership." *Vanderbilt Law Review* 51 (November 1998): 1541–82.

Racketeer Influenced and Corrupt Organizations Act. 18 U.S.C. § 1964 et seq. (2006).

Rice, George E., and Priscilla Gainer. "'Altruism' in the Albino Rat." *Journal of Comparative and Physiological Psychology* 55, no. 1 (1962): 123–25.

Richerson, Peter J., and Robert Boyd. *Not By Genes Alone: How Culture Transformed Human Evolution.* Chicago: University of Chicago Press, 2005.

Ridley, Matt. The *Origins of Virtue: Human Instincts and the Evolution of Cooperation.* New York: Penguin Books, 1996.

Rilling, James K., David A. Gutman, Thorsten R. Zeh, Guiseppe Pagnoni, Gregory S. Berns, and Clinton D. Kilts. "A Neural Basis for Social Cooperation." *Neuron* 35 (July 2002): 395–405.

Robbennolt, Jennifer K. "Apologies and Legal Settlement." *Michigan Law Review* 102 (December 2003): 460–516.

Rock, Edward B. "Saints and Sinners: How Does Delaware Corporate Law Work?" *UCLA Law Review* 44 (1997): 1009–1107.

Ross, Lee D., and Andrew Ward. "Naïve Realism in Everyday Life: Implications for Social Conflict and Misunderstanding." In *Values and Knowledge,* edited by Edward Reed, Elliot Turiel, and Terrance Brown, 103–35. Mahwah, NJ: Lawrence Erlbaum Associates, 1996.

——. "Psychological Barriers to Dispute Resolution." *Advances in Experimental Social Psychology* 27 (1995): 255–304.

Roth, Alvin E., Vesna Prasnikar, Masahiro Okuno-Fujiwara, and Shmuel Zamir. "Bargaining and Market Behavior in Jerusalem, Ljubljiana, Pittsburgh, and Tokyo: An Experimental Study." *American Economic Review* 81, no. 5 (December 1991): 1068–95.

Rothstein, Steven I. "Reciprocal Altruism and Kin Selection Are Not Clearly Separable Phenomena." *Journal of Theoretical Biology* 87 (1980): 255–61.

Ryan, James E. "The Perverse Incentives of the No Child Left Behind Act." *New York University Law School* 79 (June 2004): 932–89.

Sally, David. "Conversation and Cooperation in Social Dilemmas: A Meta-Analysis of Experiments from 1958 to 1992." *Rationality and Society* 7 (1995): 58–92.

Samuelson, Judith, and Lynn A. Stout. "Are Executives Paid Too Much?" *Wall Street Journal*, February 25, 2009.

Schwab, Stewart J., and Randall S. Thomas. "An Empirical Analysis of CEO Employment Contracts: What Do Top Executives Bargain For?" *Washington and Lee Law Review* 63 (Winter 2006): 240–41.

Schwarz, Gary T. "Mixed Theories of Tort Law: Affirming Both Deterrence and Corrective Justice." *Texas Law Review* 75 (1997): 1801–34.

———. "Reality in the Economic Analysis of Tort Law: Does Tort Law Really Deter?" *UCLA Law Review* 42, no. 2 (December 1994): 377–444.

———. "Deterrence and Punishment in the Common Law of Punitive Damages: A Comment." *Southern California Law Review* 56 (1982): 133–53.

Scott, Robert E. "A Theory of Self-Enforcing Indefinite Agreements." *Columbia Law Review* 103 (2003): 1641–99.

Scott, Sir Walter. *Ivanhoe*. 1819. New York: Signet Classic, 2001.

Sebok, Anthony J. "Punitive Damages: From Myth to Theory." *Iowa Law Review* 92 (March 2007): 957–1036.

Seipp, David J. "Holmes's Path." *Boston University Law Review* 77 (June 1997): 515–58.

Sentencing Memorandum of Defendant. People v. DiBlasi Docket No. KA042858. California Superior Court. August 10, 1999.

Shavell, Steven. *Economic Analysis of Law*. New York: Foundation Press, 2004.

———. "Criminal Law and the Optimal Use of Nonmonetary Sanctions as a Deterrent." *Columbia Law Review* 85, no. 6 (October 1985): 1232–62.

Shelley, Percy Bysshe. *A Defense of Poetry*. 1840. Edited by Albert S. Cook. Boston: Ginn and Company, 1890.

Sherman Antitrust Act. 15 U.S.C. § 15 et seq. (2006).

Singer, Tania, and Chris Frith. "The Painful Side of Empathy." *Nature Neuroscience* 8, no. 7 (2005): 845–46.

Slonim, Robert L., and Alvin E. Roth. "Learning in High-Stakes Ultimatum Games: An Experiment in the Slovak Republic." *Econometrica* 66 (1998): 569–96.

Smith, Adam. *An Inquiry into the Nature and Causes of the Wealth of Nations.* 1776. Chicago: Encyclopedia Britannica, 1952.

Smith, Eric Alden. "Why Do Good Hunters Have Higher Reproductive Success?" *Human Nature* 15 (2004): 343–64.

Smith, John Maynard. "Group Selection and Kin Selection." *Nature* 201 (March 14, 1964): 1145–47.

Smith, Tom W. "Altruism and Empathy in America: Trends and Correlates." National Opinion Research Center, February 9, 2006.

Sober, Elliot, and David Sloan Wilson. *Unto Others: The Evolution and Psychology of Unselfish Behavior.* Cambridge, MA: Harvard University Press, 1998.

Stephan, James J. *State Prison Expenditures, 2001.* Bureau of Justice Statistics Special Report NCJ 202949. Washington, DC: U.S. Department of Justice, Office of Justice Programs, June 2003. Available at http://www.ojp.usdoj.gov/bjs/pub/pdf/spe01.pdf.

Sternberg, Robert J. *Psychology.* Belmont, CA: Thompson/Wadsworth, 2004.

Stevenson, Robert Louis. *Strange Case of Dr. Jekyll and Mr. Hyde.* 1886. Edited by Katherine Linehan. New York: W.W. Norton, 2003.

Stigler, George J. "The Optimum Enforcement of Laws." *Journal of Political Economy* 78, no. 3 (1970): 526–36.

Sunstein, Cass R. "Behavioral Analysis of Law." *University of Chicago Law Review* 64 (1997): 1175–95.

———. Cass R. "On the Expressive Function of Law." *University of Pennsylvania Law Review* 144 (May 1996): 2021–53.

Sunstein, Cass R., Daniel Kahneman, and David Schkade. "Assessing Punitive Damages (With Notes on Cognition and Valuation in Law)." *Yale Law Journal* 107 (May 1998): 2071–2153.

Sutter, Matthias, and Martin G. Kocher. "Age and the Development of Trust and Reciprocity." SSRN Working Paper Series, 2003.

Tabibnia, Golnaz, Ajay B. Satpute, and Matthew W. Lieberman. "The Sunny Side of Fairness: Preference for Fairness Activates Reward Circuitry (and Disregarding Unfairness Activates Self-Control Circuitry)." *Psychological Science* 19 (2008): 339–47.

Taylor, Shelley E., Letitia Anne Peplau, and David O. Sears. *Social Psychology.* 12th ed. Upper Saddle River, NJ: Pearson Prentice Hall, 2006.

Teles, Steven M. *The Rise of the Conservative Legal Movement: The Battle for Control of the Law.* Princeton, NJ and Oxford: Princeton University Press, 2008.

Thoits, Peggy A., and Lyndi N. Hewitt. "Volunteer Work and Well-Being." *Journal of Health and Social Behavior* 42 (2001): 115–31.

Trexler, Phil. "Masked Man Waits in Line; Robs Stow Bank." *The Beacon Journal*, January 8, 2009. http://www.ohio.com/.

Trivers, Robert L. "The Evolution of Reciprocal Altruism." *Quarterly Review of Biology* 46 (1971): 35–57.

Tversky, Amos, and Daniel Kahneman. "Availability: A Heuristic for Judging Frequency and Probability." *Cognitive Psychology* 5 (1973): 207–32.

Tyler, Tom R. *Why People Obey the Law*. Princeton, NJ: Princeton University Press, 2006.

United States Bureau of the Census. "State & County QuickFacts: Los Angeles (city), 2006." http://quickfacts.census.gov/qfd/states/06/0644000.html.

———. *2006 Statistical Abstract of the United States*. Washington, DC: United States Bureau of the Census, 2006.

U.S. Department of Education. "Overview: No Child Left Behind Act Is Working." Available at http://www.ed.gov/nclb/overview/importance/nclbworking.html (accessed November 10, 2008).

U.S. v. Beserra. 967 F.2d 255, 256 (7th Cir. 1992).

U.S. v. Birkenfeld. Case No. 08-Cr-60099, U.S. District Court, S.D. Fla., Transcript of May 13, 2008 Initial Appearance and Bond Hearing.

U.S. v. Carroll Towing Co. 159 F.2d 169 (2d. Cir. 1947).

Viscusi, W. Kip. "Why There Is No Defense of Punitive Damages." *Georgetown Law Journal* 87 (1998): 381–95.

Wilkinson, Gerald S. "Food Sharing in Vampire Bats." *Scientific American* (February 1990): 76–82.

Wilkow v. Forbes, Inc. 241 F.3d 552, 557 (7th Cir. 2001).

Williamson, Oliver. *The Mechanisms of Governance*. New York: Oxford University Press, 1996.

Wilson, James Q., and George L. Kelling. "Broken Windows: The Police and Neighborhood Safety." *Atlantic Monthly* 249, no. 3 (March 1982): 29–38.

Wolman, Benjamin. *The Sociopathic Personality*. New York: Brunner/Mazel, 1987.

Wright, Robert. *The Moral Animal: Evolutionary Psychology and Everyday Life*. New York: Vintage Books, 1994.

Yamagishi, Toshio. "The Structural Goal/Expectations Theory of Cooperation in Social Dilemmas." *Advances in Group Processes* 3 (1986): 51–87.

Zahavi, Amot. "Mate Selection: A Selection for a Handicap." *Journal of Theoretical Biology* 53 (1975): 205–14.

Zak, Paul J. "Trust." *Capco Journal of Financial Transformation* 7 (2003): 17–24.

Zak, Paul J., and Stephen Knack. "Trust and Growth." *Economic Journal* 111 (2001): 295–321.

Zak, Paul J., Robert Kurzban, and William T. Matzner. "The Neurobiology of Trust." *Annals of the New York Academy of Sciences* 1032 (2004): 224–27.

INDEX